Roxio® Easy Media Creat... For Dummies®

KU-660-072

Roxio Easy Media Creator 8 Home

Home is the starting point for all the digital media projects you create with the Roxio Easy Media Creator 8 Suite. From Home, you can launch any Roxio Creator application or tool and edit any media project that you've created recently.

Project list pane   Project window

Roxio Easy Media Creator 8 Home enables you to launch components and edit recently-created projects.

Roxio® Easy Media Creator™ 8 For Dummies®

Cheat Sheet

Selecting the Right Roxio Creator 8 Component to Use

Use	To Do This	Chapter Reference
Roxio Disc Copier	To make duplicate copies of CD or DVD discs	3 & 8
Creator Classic	Compile and burn data disc	8
	Compile and burn multimedia disc	8
Music Disc Creator	Rip tracks from audio CD	7
	Compile and burn MP3/WMA disc	7
	Compile and burn DVD Music Disc	7
Roxio Backup	Schedule regular data backups	3
CD Extra Disc Creator	Create Enhanced data and audio CD	7
	Create Mixed-Mode data and audio CD	7
Drag-to-Disc	Compile and burn data backup CD or DVD disc	3
Label Creator	Design and print CD and DVD disc labels and case inserts	8
Import Media	Acquire digital audio, photos, and video from connected analog and digital devices	9
Easy Audio Capture	Record audio with sound card either using internal or external input devices	5
Sound Editor	Edit audio mixes from audio clips saved on disk	5
	Convert from one audio file format to another	5
Media Manager	Collect and organize all types of digital media files	4
	Tag and annotate digital media file for search	4
	Search folders and collections for specific media	4
PhotoSuite 8	Fix and edit digital photos	6
Photo Projects Assistant	Create collages, calendars, and the like with photos	6
Panorama Assistant	Create panoramas from individual panned shots	6
VideoWave 8	Design video productions and output them as movies for playback on various devices	10
CineMagic Assistant	Arrange digital video and photos into video productions with background music	10
SlideShow Assistant	Arrange photo collections into slideshows with background audio	10
MyDVD 8	Design DVD projects and burn them to CD or DVD disc	11
Plug & Burn	Burn videotape direct to CD or DVD disc	11

For Dummies: Bestselling Book Series for Beginners

Roxio® Easy Media Creator™ 8

FOR

DUMMIES®

Roxio® Easy Media Creator™ 8

FOR DUMMIES®

by Greg Harvey, Ph.D.

WILEY

Wiley Publishing, Inc.

Roxio® Easy Media Creator™ 8 For Dummies®

Published by
Wiley Publishing, Inc.
111 River Street
Hoboken, NJ 07030-5774
www.wiley.com

WILEY

About the Author

Greg Harvey Ph.D. has authored tons of computer books, the most recent being *Excel 2003 For Dummies* and *Adobe Acrobat 6 PDF For Dummies*. He started out training business users on how to use IBM personal computers and their attendant computer software in the rough and tumble days of DOS, WordStar, and Lotus 1-2-3 in the mid-80s of the last century. After working for a number of independent training firms, he went on to teach semester-long courses in spreadsheet and database management software at Golden Gate University in San Francisco.

His love of teaching has translated into an equal love of writing. *For Dummies* books are, of course, his all-time favorites to write because they enable him to write to his favorite audience, the beginner. They also enable him to use humor (a key element to success in the training room) and, most delightful of all, to express an opinion or two about the subject matter at hand.

Dedication

To Chris — my partner and helpmate in all aspects of my life and Shandy, the newest addition to our family

Author's Acknowledgments

I'm always very grateful to the many people who work so hard to bring my book projects into being, and this one is no exception. This time, preliminary thanks are in order to Andy Cummings and Bob Woerner for giving me this opportunity to write about Roxio's great new suite of media creation programs.

Next, I want to express great thanks to my project editor, Christine Berman (a better person to work with you'll never find), and to my partner in crime, Christopher Aiken (I really appreciate all your editing, additions, and comments on this one). Thanks also go to Trevor Kay for the great technical edit, Adrienne Martinez for coordinating its production, and everybody at Wiley Publishing, Colleen Totz Diamond for the outstanding proofreading, and Techbooks for the indexing.

Special thanks to Patrick Nugent, Product Lead at Roxio, Inc., for all his personal help and speedy responses to my few questions about this great version of their most versatile software.

Publisher's Acknowledgments

We're proud of this book; please send us your comments through our online registration form located at www.dummies.com/register/.

Some of the people who helped bring this book to market include the following:

Acquisitions, Editorial, and Media Development

Project Editor: Christine Berman

Acquisitions Editor: Bob Woerner

Copy Editor: Christine Berman

Technical Editor: Trevor Kay

Editorial Manager: Jodi Jensen

Media Development Supervisor: Richard Graves

Editorial Assistant: Amanda Foxworth

Cartoons: Rich Tennant (www.the5thwave.com)

Composition Services

Project Coordinator: Adrienne Martinez

Layout and Graphics: Andrea Dahl, Stephanie D. Jumper, Barbara Moore, Lynsey Osborn, Heather Ryan

Proofreaders: Leeann Harney, Joe Niesen

Indexer: TECHBOOKS Production Services

Publishing and Editorial for Technology Dummies

Richard Swadley, Vice President and Executive Group Publisher

Andy Cummings, Vice President and Publisher

Mary Bednarek, Executive Acquisitions Director

Mary C. Corder, Editorial Director

Publishing for Consumer Dummies

Diane Graves Steele, Vice President and Publisher

Joyce Pepple, Acquisitions Director

Composition Services

Gerry Fahey, Vice President of Production Services

Debbie Stailey, Director of Composition Services

Contents at a Glance

Table of Contents

Part III: Creating Audio CDs and Photo Projects 135

Chapter 5: Editing Audio with Sound Editor 137

Chapter 6: Managing Digital Photos 163

Introduction

The good news is that programs included in Roxio Creator 8 are genuinely easy to use. The bad news, if there is any, is that because of its nature as a collection or suite of different applications and tools, you may initially find it a bit confusing as to which part to turn to get a particular job done. This is where *Roxio Creator 8 For Dummies* comes in. This book is designed to make you familiar with Roxio Creator's many capabilities and get you up and running and comfortable with its many features as quickly as possible.

If I had to choose just one word to characterize Roxio Creator 8, it would have to be versatility because this baby can do almost anything you might want to do Roxio Creator, you can go from capturing original digital media to editing it and then using it in a wide array of different projects that you can then output to disc in a very short time. Because the program's emphasis is always on making these processes as easy as can be, you don't have to worry if you don't have any background in working with digital media and have limited or even no experience with multimedia editing and design.

I just hope that you find using Roxio Creator 8 to design, build, and burn your own media projects half as much fun I found writing about them in this book. I want to congratulate the Roxio/Sonic engineers for providing all of us with a truly outstanding set of tools with which to transform the sounds and images of the world around us into memories that we can share with friends and family alike.

About This Book

Roxio Easy Media Creator 8 For Dummies is meant to be a simple reference to the major components and features offered in the Roxio Creator 8 Deluxe Suite (Creator 8 is also available in an Essentials and Standard version). If you did not choose to invest in this deluxe version of this suite, do not worry as you will still find you have access to all of the major applications and tools I cover in the text (just some of the fancier and more advanced options that are covered will be missing from your menus and dialog boxes).

I have, however, endeavored as much as possible to arrange this reference material according to the task you want to get done rather than according to the module that you use in performing it (as you sometimes use the same module to accomplish multiple tasks). This means that although the chapters in each part are laid in a logical order, each stands on its own, ready for you to dig into the information at any point.

Whenever I could, I have also tried to make the topics within each chapter stand on their own as well. When there's just no way around relying upon some information that's discussed elsewhere, I include a cross-reference that gives you the chapter and verse (actually the chapter and section) for where you can find that related information if you're of a mind to.

Use the Contents at a Glance along with the full Table of Contents and Index to look up the topic of the hour and find out exactly where it is in this compilation of Roxio Creator information. You'll find that although most topics are introduced in a conversational manner, I don't waste much time cutting to the chase by laying down the main principles at work (usually in bulleted form) followed by the hard reality of how you do the deed (as numbered steps).

Foolish Assumptions

I'm going to make only one foolish assumption about you and that is that you have the means to acquire some sort of digital media (be that audio, photos, or video) and you now want to be able to something with that media (be that burn the audio into CDs, use the photos in collages, or create video productions that you can view in your DVD player). I'm not assuming that you have any experience in creating any of the kinds of projects you'd like to create with your digital media, so you don't have to be concerned about your level of multimedia expertise (or the lack thereof).

As far as your computer hardware and software goes, I'm assuming only that you have a computer that is robust enough to meet the rather stringent memory and storage requirements for Roxio Creator 8 and that this machine is running Windows 2000 or XP and is equipped with a CD-recordable or, hopefully, a DVD-recordable drive. I am not, however, assuming that you have access to the other peripherals such as a digital still camera, camcorder, scanner, DVD recorder, and the like that I describe in the text. If you do have all these goodies, so much the better, as this enables you to use all of Roxio Creator's wonderful features. If not, you can still use the parts of the program that pertain to kind of system you have.

How This Book Is Organized

Roxio Easy Media Creator 8 For Dummies is divided into five parts. Each part is organized around a central topic (getting to know Easy Media Creator and digital media, making data backup discs, audio discs and photo projects, DVD projects, and the like). All the chapters in each part are then related to some aspect of performing the central task. In case you're the least bit curious, here's the lowdown on each of the six parts and their chapters and what you can expect to find there.

Part 1: A Bit About Easy Media Creator 8 and Digital Media

This part provides you with an orientation to Easy Media Creator 8's components and capabilities, along with an introduction to the sometimes confusing world of digital media.

Chapter 1 is your place to go to find out just what exactly is included in the Roxio Creator 8 suite. It also introduces you to the Roxio Creator 8 Home, the central bridge from which you can access all the other applications and tools in the suite.

Chapter 2 is not to be missed, even by those of you who do not consider yourselves beginners by any stretch of the imagination. This chapter covers the world of digital media, including the essential difference between analog and digital media, the many different types of CD and DVD media and media formats out there, as well as the different types of digital gear that Roxio Creator supports. The chapter ends with my advice on the proper treatment of CD and DVD discs.

Part II: Creating Data CDs

Part II focuses on the important tasks of backing up and organizing your media files. Chapter 3 takes up the call on how to use the Creator Classic and Drag-to-Disc modules to compile and burn data backup discs. This chapter also includes information on how to use the Roxio Backup program to schedule backups so that you're never at risk for losing invaluable data due to some computer malfunction.

Chapter 4 covers how to use the Media Manager module to organize, manage, and backup all the different types of media files (audio, still images, and video) that you use in your Roxio Creator media projects. It covers tagging and annotating media files for quick retrieval later using Media Manager's Search capability as well.

Part III: Creating Audio CDs and Photo Projects

This part takes an in-depth look at two of the most popular types of digital media out there: digital audio and photos. Chapter 5 covers mixing audio clips that you record and rip from the audio CDs and DVDs you own using Roxio Creator's now more powerful than ever Sound Editor.

Chapter 6 turns to the subject of digital photos and how you can use the PhotoSuite module not only to fix, edit, and enhance them but also to use them in all sorts of great photo projects including slideshows, photo collages, calendars, and the like. It concludes by giving you the lowdown on printing your digital photos as well as sharing them electronically with friends and family.

Chapters 7 and 8 gives you the blow-by-blow for compiling and burning audio CDs, MP3/WMA, and DVD Music Discs with the new Music Disc Creator and then using the Label Creator program to design and print labels for the discs and inserts for their jewel cases.

Part IV: Creating Projects for DVDs

Part IV is devoted to the subject of DVD projects. Chapter 9 concentrates on how to use the Roxio Media Import to acquire all the types of digital media (audio, photo, and video) that you need for your DVD projects.

Chapter 10 then covers the use of Roxio Creator's powerful VideoWave 8 application to design video productions to be used as titles for your DVD projects. Chapter 11 fills out the part by giving you the lowdown on using the MyDVD program to construct the titles for your DVD project complete with interactive menus and then burn the finished project to CD or DVD disc.

Part V: The Part of Tens

Part V contains two chapters that together make up the Part of Tens. Chapter 12 is the place to consult for a concise description of what each major application and tool in the Roxio Creator 8 suite can do for you. This chapter also gives cross references to the appropriate chapters in the book that give you in-depth information on the use of a particular module.

Chapter 13 highlights what I consider to be the top ten coolest features in the entire Roxio Creator 8 suite (and, of course, that's saying a lot when you have as many features to choose from as you do with this baby).

Icons Used in This Book

The following icons are strategically placed in the margins throughout all the chapters in this book. Their purpose is to get your attention and each has its own way of doing that.

This icon denotes some really cool information (in my humble opinion) that if you pay particular attention to will pay off by making your work just a lot more enjoyable or productive (or both).

This icon denotes a tidbit that you ought to pay extra attention to; otherwise, you may end up taking a detour that wastes valuable time.

This icon denotes a tidbit that you ought to pay extra attention to; otherwise, you'll be sorry.

This icon denotes a tidbit that makes free use of (oh no!) technical jargon. You may want to skip these sections (or, at least, read them when no one else is around).

Where to Go from Here

The question of where to go from here couldn't be simpler — why off to read the great Rich Tennant cartoons at the beginning of each of the four parts, of course. Which chapter you go to after that is a matter of personal interest and need. Just go for the gold and don't forget to have some fun while you're digging!

Part I

A Bit About Easy Media Creator 8 and Digital Media

The 5th Wave   By Rich Tennant

"I ran this Bob Dylan CD through our voice recognition system, and he really is just saying, 'Manaama-manaaabadhaabadha...'"

In this part . . .

Roxio Easy Media Creator 8, as you discover in this part, is not one single program but a collection or suite of several different application programs and tools that you can use to create a wide variety of audio, photo, and video projects. In Chapter 1 of this part, you get introduced to each of the programs and tools you'll be using and what they can do for you. Chapter 2 then presents essential information about the surplus of digital media and media file formats that you come in contact with as you create your various media projects. This chapter then concludes by giving you a rundown of the various pieces of cool digital gear you can use to play all the great projects you come up with in Roxio Creator 8, and guidelines on the proper care of CDs and DVDs.

Chapter 1

Getting Acquainted with Easy Media Creator 8

*F*irst things first: Before you can use your newly installed Roxio Easy Media Creator 8 suite to go off and create a copy of your favorite Coldplay audio CD or to burn a DVD of the family's most recent outing in the Adirondacks, you're going to need to know your way around the program. As you're about to discover, there's very little that Roxio Easy Media Creator 8 can't do when it comes to dealing with all the many types of digital media that are apt to come your way.

Better yet, not only is this baby versatile, but it's as good as its name. The Roxio Easy Media Creator 8 suite offers you consistently easy ways to complete all of your media projects — from ripping, arranging, and burning your own copies of your favorite CDs to finally organizing and tagging those gazillions of digital photos you've dumped into nondescript folders all over your computer's hard disk.

The only catch (oh, there's always a catch) is that in order for the Easy Media Creator 8 to be as multitalented as it is, the good engineers at Sonic Solutions had to carve the program up into dozens of different little specialized programs and utilities that taken in at once can be a bit overwhelming (to say the least). This is where Chapter 1 comes in: Here you not only get a much needed overview of the many individual and specialized components now at your fingertips but a good feel for the Roxio Media Creator Home that ties them all together. Once you get your bearings in this all important hub, you're ready to see what this program can really do by looking at each of the individual components.

Welcome to the Roxio Media Creator Home

When you install the Roxio Easy Media Creator 8 suite on your computer's hard disk, the Windows Installer automatically puts a Roxio Roxio Media Creator Home 8 shortcut on the Windows desktop. To open the Roxio Media Creator Home, you simply locate this shortcut icon (shown in the left margin of this paragraph) and double-click it.

Figure 1-1 shows the Welcome screen of the Roxio Media Creator Home window (also known as Easy Media Creator Central) that appears after you double-click this desktop shortcut. As you can see in this figure, the Welcome screen of the Home window that forms the hub of the Roxio Easy Media Creator 8 suite is divided into four distinct areas:

- **Menu bar:** Contains the four menus, File, Tools, View, and Help, which you can use to launch and save new media projects, access any of the Media Creator tools, change the size and appearance of the Home window, and get help on using Home

- **Project List:** Lists the categories of projects available in the Easy Media Creator 8 suite — to expand a category to display a list of all its particular projects, click the link attached to the category name or click the tab button to the right of the name (the one with downward-pointing triangle)

Figure 1-1:
The Roxio Media Creator Home offers a hub tying together the program's many components.

✔ **Project Window:** Displays a list of links for specific tasks or apps associated with the project you've selected in the Project List pane or, in some cases, lists the steps necessary to complete a particular task (such as to back up or copy a disc)

✔ **Control Panel:** This area is divided into three sections: the Media Information Display, which shows a visual representation of the disc or drive designated as the destination for your project; the Input Area, which displays a drop-down menu for selecting the recorder to use for your project, a display showing the recording progress of the project, or audio and video playback controls; and the Action Area, which displays an Options button for displaying a list of options associated with your project, or controls that enable you to start or stop the project.

Note that you can save space in the Roxio Media Creator Home by condensing the Project List pane so that it displays only icons. To do this, click the Hide Project Pane button or choose View⇨Hide Project Pane on the Roxio Media Creator Home Menu bar. To expand the Project List so that it again displays both icons and category labels, click the Show Project Pane button (or choose View⇨Show Project Pane).

Figure 1-2 shows the Easy Media Creator 8 Home window after condensing the Project List pane and selecting the Audio CD project. Note that Project Window now displays instructions on how to proceed in creating an audio CD for a typical CD player and that the Action Area now contains a Continue button that you click after selecting the recorder to use in the Input Area, inserting the blank CD disc, and adding the audio files to be burned onto the new CD.

If you have a great need for open space on the Windows desktop (as you might when dragging and dropping files from open folder windows that you want use in your current project) you can reduce the entire Easy Media Creator window to a bare bones minimum. To do this, click the Switch to Mini Mode button or choose View⇨Mini Mode on the window's menu bar.

Figure 1-3 shows the Roxio Media Creator Home window shown in Figure 1-2 after clicking the Switch to Mini Mode button. Note that even when the Home window is in mini mode, you can still go about the business of adding the audio files for the new CD, while at the same time keeping free most of the desktop for displaying the contents of other open windows.

To make it easy to open the Roxio Media Creator Home, you can add this Roxio Easy Media Creator 8 shortcut to the Windows Quick Launch toolbar by dragging its icon to this bar and dropping it at the place on this toolbar that immediately follows the Start button on the Windows taskbar.

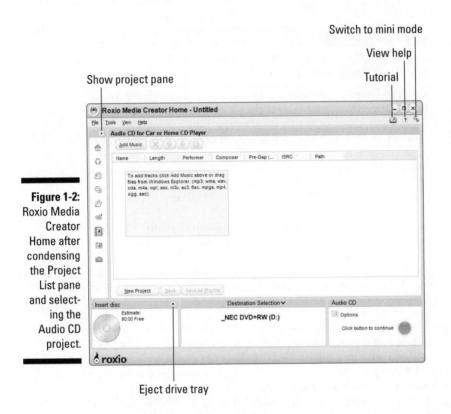

Figure 1-2:
Roxio Media
Creator
Home after
condensing
the Project
List pane
and select-
ing the
Audio CD
project.

If you're like me and are apt to become a really serious user of Easy Media
Creator, you may also want to fix the Roxio Media Creator Home option on
the Windows Start menu (provided that you don't run Windows in Classic
mode). To do this, you follow these steps:

1. **Double-click the Roxio Media Creator Home8 shortcut on the desktop.**

   If you don't have an Roxio Media Creator Home8 shortcut on your desktop,
   you can click the Start button on the Windows taskbar, mouse over the All
   Programs option on the Start menu, the Roxio Easy Media Creator 8 option
   on the All Programs menu, and then click the Roxio Media Creator Home
   option on the Roxio Easy Media Creator 8 submenu.

   The Welcome screen of the Roxio Easy Media Creator Home window
   shown in Figure 1-1 then opens.

2. **Click the Start button on the Windows taskbar to open the Start menu.**

   The Roxio Media Creator Home option sporting the famous Roxio logo
   (a disc with what appears to be a shark fin coming out the top of it) now
   appears on the left side of the Windows Start menu.

3. **Right-click the Roxio Media Creator Home option to open its shortcut
   menu and then click the Pin to Start Menu option on this menu.**

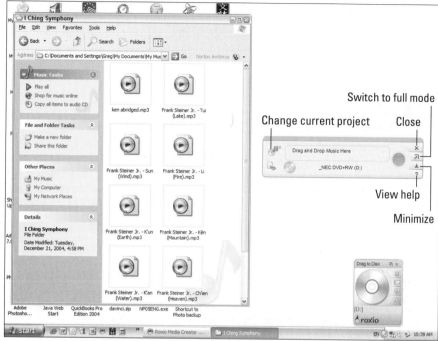

Figure 1-3:
Desktop
showing the
Roxio Media
Creator
Home in
mini mode.

As soon as you click the Pin to Start Menu option, Windows moves the Roxio Media Creator Home option to the upper area of the left side of the Start menu (under such Start menu stalwarts as the Internet Explorer and Outlook Express). If you later decide that you don't need this option to be a permanent part of the Start menu, you can remove it by right-clicking the option and then clicking the Unpin from Start Menu option on its shortcut menu.

Attending to the Tasks at Hand

The Most Frequent Tasks links on the right side of the Welcome screen in the Roxio Media Creator Home window (refer to Figure 1-1) give you immediate access to many of the most common tasks, such as creating audio CDs, copying and erasing discs, creating DVDs, and performing file backups. Clicking the link associated with a particular task temporarily opens the appropriate application in the Project Window of the Roxio Creator 8 Home window. The beauty of the More Frequent Tasks section in the Welcome screen of the Home window is that you don't have to give a second thought as to which Easy Media Creator application to use in order to get done the project you have in mind.

The only problem is that the tasks listed in the Most Frequent Tasks section represent only the most common disc-related things that you can do with

Roxio Easy Media Creator 8. Although you can rely on this section for most of your media backup and data disc projects, be aware that there's much more to the Easy Media Creator 8 suite than still pictures. Therefore, you will also definitely want to become well-acquainted with the additional tasks and tools offered on the other tabs in the Project List pane.

So Many Apps, So Little Time

As soon as you click the Applications link located immediately beneath Welcome on the Home tab of the Project List pane in the Roxio Media Creator Home window, the Project Window name changes to Applications. The Applications Project Window gives a full listing of all the standalone applications included in the suite in a column on the left and a bunch of neat utilities in a column on the right (see Figure 1-4).

The following sections give you a brief introduction to each of the components that you can load by clicking its Applications or Utilities link in the Applications Project Window of the Roxio Media Creator Home. Use this information to get a quick overview of the capabilities and functions of each of Roxio Easy Media Creator 8 applications and utilities.

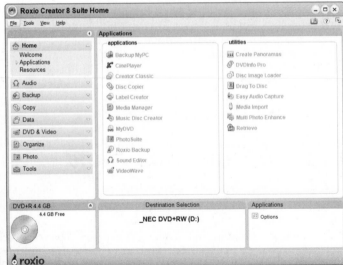

Figure 1-4: The Applications Project Window of the Roxio Media Creator Home showing all the available apps and utilities.

Would you please Backup MyPC

Backup MyPC is a super utility that enables you to make disc backups of all the files and folders on your computer. It also gives the ability to restore these files and folders in case their data becomes corrupted so that you're no longer able to open them.

In addition to creating these kinds of complete or partial backups of your data files, you can use Backup MyPC to create a set of disaster recovery discs that you can use in case of a hard disk failure or crash.

Figure 1-5 shows the Backup MyPC window as it first appears when you launch this program by clicking the Backup MyPC link in the Applications Project Window of the Roxio Media Creator Home.

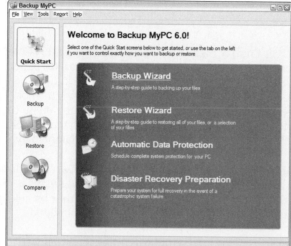

Figure 1-5: Backup MyPC enables you to create a complete disc backup of all the files on your computer.

Playing around with CinePlayer

CinePlayer is a full-fledged DVD player for your computer (one that you may well end up preferring to the Windows Media Player). You can use this program to play all the DVD movies that you create and burn to disc with the MyDVD program in the Creator 8 suite as well as professionally produced DVDs that you rent or purchase.

The heart of the CinePlayer is the Sonic CinePlayer Control Panel shown in Figure 1-6. Note that this panel often disappears behind the CinePlayer window where the DVD's video appears as soon you pop the disc you want to play into your computer's CD/DVD drive. To re-display CinePlayer Control Panel when the CinePlayer window is less than full screen, click the Sonic CinePlayer Control Panel button on the Windows taskbar. When the CinePlayer window is full-screen, press Alt+Tab until the CinePlayer Control Panel appears on top of the CinePlayer window.

Figure 1-6:
The
CinePlayer
Control
Panel man-
ages all
aspects of
playing your
own or
commercial
DVD discs.

When the CinePlayer Control Panel first opens, the side panel containing the cursor and numeric pad is not displayed. To display this side panel, which you then can use to select DVD menu items, you need to click the Expand/Collapse Panel button (the one on the right side with the double vertical bar). If you don't display this side panel, you can select items from the menu that is currently displayed in the CinePlayer window by clicking the item (something you certainly can't do when viewing the DVD on a standalone player).

The playback controls on the CinePlayer Control Panel are standard with the exception of the Jump To button, which when clicked displays a submenu that enables you go to a particular place in the DVD either by selecting its chapter (assuming that the DVD uses chapters) or its timecode.

To open a movie that you created with VideoWave (see Chapter 10) or a DVD project that you created with MyDVD (see Chapter 11), click the Open Disc or File button and then select either the Browse for File to find the movie file or the DVD project file on your computer's hard disk. To edit a DVD project that you created with MyDVD and burned to disc after viewing it in CinePlayer, you click the Edit OpenDVD disc (meaning one that to which you have full editing rights).

If you're viewing a commercially produced DVD that supports subtitles (either in English or another language such as Spanish), you can display them in the CinePlayer window. Click the Other DVD Options button, click the Choose Subpicture option on the pop-up menu, and then select the language, English (United States) or Spanish (Traditional Sort), on the Subpicture submenu.

Keep in mind that you can capture key frames (the ones that are clear and not part of a scene transition) in bitmap graphic files in CinePlayer. Simply click the Play/Pause button to pause the video at the frame you want to capture as a still image before you click the Capture Video Frame button. As soon as you click this button, CinePlayer captures the image in a bitmap file (indicated by the rather loud click). The first time you save an image from a DVD, a Browse for Folder dialog box appears, enabling you to designate the folder and drive where all movie stills are to be saved. This is followed by a Media Name dialog box in which you can enter a descriptive name (usually the name of the film you're watching). CinePlayer then creates the filename for the bitmap images you capture by appending the descriptive name to the frame's timecode.

The comforts of Creator Classic

Creator Classic is the application you use primarily to assemble and burn your audio and data CDs. The Creator Classic window is divided into four major areas:

- ✔ **Projects** where you choose between creating a Data Disc (one consisting only of data files), Multimedia Disc (one that combines data files and other media such as music or graphics files), or Bootable Disc (one that contains enough of the Windows operating system that you can use it to boot from one of your computer's drives)

- ✔ **Other Tasks** where you can launch programs to make other types of data discs (CD Extra Disc Creator or Backup Projects), burn a CD or DVD from an image of the disc stored on one of your computer's drives (Burn From Disc Image File), get information and check the status on your computer's recorder (Disc and Device Utility), or start the Express Labeler (Make a Disc Label) to create a label for your CD or DVD

- ✔ **Select Source** where you locate and select the files you want to copy to data or audio CD

- ✔ **Data Disc Project** which displays the name of your disc as well as all the files you've added for burning onto the CD

Whereas you can use Disc Copier (discussed in the section immediately following) to make a copy of an existing audio or data CD or DVD, you use Creator Classic to actually put together and burn your data CDs or DVDs. You use Creator Classic when you want to make backups or archive data files on your disk. See Chapters 3, 5, and 6 for specific information and examples on using Creator Classic to assemble and burn audio and data CDs.

Copying discs with Disc Copier

As the name says, Disc Copier is the application you use when you need to make a copy of an unprotected CD or DVD. When you click the Disc Copier link in the Applications Projects Window in the Roxio Media Creator Home, the program opens the window shown in Figure 1-7. Or, I should say, this window opens after you dismiss an alert dialog box reminding you that you should use the Disc Copier component only to make copies of digital media for which you have the clear legal right to make copies. Knowing that none of you would ever do anything like that, you can click the Don't Show Me This Again check box before you click OK to close this alert dialog box (for once and all).

Figure 1-7:
Disc Copier
makes it
easy to copy
audio or
data CDs
and DVDs.

You can use Disc Copier to copy an audio or data CD or DVD (usually one that you've created with Roxio's MyDVD, since almost every single commercial movie on DVD that you rent or purchase is copy-protected and can't be copied with Disc Copier). You can also use it to create a compilation of different movies from different sources. As you can see in Figure 1-1, all you need to do to copy one of these discs is to specify the source and destination drive. The great thing is, if your situation is like mine and you have only one CD or DVD drive on your computer system, you can still use Disc Copier to copy your audio, data, or video discs (see Chapters 3 and 5 for steps with concrete examples of how you use Disc Copier to copy audio and data CDs).

Lauding the Label Creator

You use the Label Creator link in the Applications Project Window of the Roxio Media Creator Home to launch the Roxio Label Creator. This application enables you to design and print labels for the CD and DVD discs that you burn with the other Roxio Easy Media Creator applications. The Label Creator makes quick work of designing both disc labels and the inserts for their jewel cases. Figure 1-8 shows the Roxio Label Creator window as it first opens. Note that you open this window not only from Applications Project Window but also by clicking a Create Label button in the final dialog box when burning CD and DVD discs (see Chapters 5 and 12 for details).

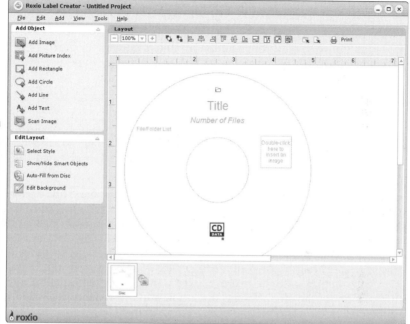

Figure 1-8:
Label
Creator
enables you
to design
and print
disc labels
and jewel
case inserts
for your CD
and DVD
projects.

The Label Creator window is divided into three panes:

- **Add Object** with the tools for adding or drawing images that you want to include in your label project

- **Edit Layout** with tools for selecting one of the ready-made label styles for your disc label or assigning it a new color or background image or to automatically add album information in the case of labels for copies of commercially produced audio CDs

- **Layout** pane for previewing the contents of your disc label or jewel case insert (the front and back printed cards that go inside the clear plastic case that holds the disc), while at the same time enabling you to edit these contents

For detailed information on using the Roxio Label Creator to design and print labels for any of your CD or DVD discs, see Chapter 9.

Media Manager at your service

You use the Media Manager to organize the many types of media files (video clips, still images, audio, and video projects) that you use in the CD and DVD projects you create. This handy-dandy little program enables you to keep tabs on particular media files through the use of *albums*, special Easy Media

Creator files that associate selected media files together regardless of where these files are actually physically located on your computer system. Because albums reference to the media files you want to associate as a group, you don't have to go through all the trouble of copying or moving the files into a single folder. You can also use the Media Manager to peruse your media files, tag them with keywords for easy searching, as well as backing these files up by burning them onto CD or DVD discs.

Figure 1-9 shows the Media Manager window that appears when you launch the program by clicking the Media Manager link on the Applications Project Window or the Organize link on the Organize tab of the Project List in the Roxio Media Creator Home.

Deceptively simple at first glance, this window is made up of only two panes. On the left, you see a pane named My Media, My Albums, Folders, or My MediaSpace (UpnP), depending on which type of media container you select. This pane enables you to select any drive or folder on your system. On the right, you find a pane with the name of the selected media type, album, drive or folder that displays all the folders and files within that particular type of container. You do the rest of the organizing magic with the buttons at both the top of the Media Manager window and these panes (see Chapter 4 for details).

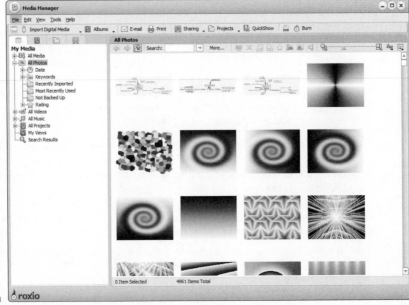

Figure 1-9: Use the Media Manager tool to organize, view, and search the many types of media files you use in your CD and DVD projects.

Audio discs that are music to your ears

You use the new Roxio Easy Media Creator 8 Music Disc Creator to build and burn audio CDs and DVDs. The music you include in your audio projects can come from tracks of commercial audio CDs that you've purchased as well as audio files that you've recorded yourself. Audio discs that you create with this nifty application can be saved in any of the popular audio file formats including the standard WMA and the ever popular MP3.

Figure 1-10 shows the Music Disc Creator program window that opens when you click the Music Disc Creator link in the Applications Project Window of the Roxio Media Creator Home window. The Music Disc Creator window is divided into the following panes:

- ✔ **Project Type** where you choose between creating a standard audio CD, MP3/WMA disc, and a DVD music disc

- ✔ **Add to Project** where you can add music files to your audio disc project, including tracks from pre-recorded audio CDs or imported from other audio CD or DVD discs, as well as record audio files for the project

- ✔ **Audio CD – Untitled Project** which shows the name of your audio project along with the tracks in the order in which they will be burned on the new CD or DVD disc

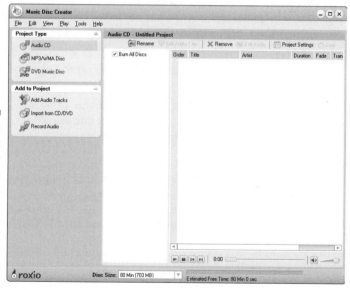

Figure 1-10: Use Music Disc Creator to burn music CDs and DVDs in popular formats including WMA and MP3.

Easy multimedia projects thanks to MyDVD

MyDVD is the application that you use to assemble and burn multimedia projects on DVD discs. Multimedia projects are those that can combine more than one type of media, including video clips, still photo images, text, and audio tracks. You can use MyDVD to quickly and easily convert your digital home movies into menu-driven productions that you can play on a computer DVD drive or a standalone DVD player attached to your TV. You can also use MyDVD to assemble your digital photo collections into slideshows that, when burned onto a DVD disc, can be played in the selfsame computer DVD drives or standalone DVD players.

Figure 1-11 shows the program window that first opens after you click the MyDVD link in the Applications Project Window launch or click the Create DVD link on the DVD & Video tab in the Project List pane of the Roxio Media Creator Home window. The MyDVD 8 window, as you can see in Figure 1-13, is divided into the following four panes:

- ✔ **Menu Tasks** where you add movies or slideshows you've already created in the Easy Media Creator 8 suite as menu items or capture and import video clips, music, or graphics for your DVD project

- ✔ **Edit** where you can edit a movie or split it into individual chapters as well as specify a visual theme for the project's menu screens (including layout and labeling of the menu buttons), select a photo or video to use as the background of all menu screens, or add music or sound effects to play whenever the project's menu screens are displayed on the screen

- ✔ **Project view** which visually represents the hierarchy and layout of your DVD project

- ✔ **Preview** which shows you the layout of the menu items and the background of the main menu of your DVD project and where you can edit any of the menu titles

MyDVD is possibly the most versatile application in the entire Easy Media Creator suite. Because you can combine all types of media (video, still images, text, and audio) as you want, this is the place where you can be really creative. In no time, you'll be creating personalized and professional-looking multimedia projects that you can share with all your friends and family who have access to either a DVD drive in their computers or a standalone DVD player. See Chapters 9, 10, and 11 for details on using the MyDVD to create your own DVD projects.

Figure 1-11:
Use MyDVD
to assemble
photo
slideshows,
video clips,
and the like
into multi-
media pre-
sentations
burned to a
DVD disc.

Picture it in PhotoSuite

Photo Suite is the application that you use to organize, edit, and share the digital photos that you take. You can use this component to enhance the photos, organize them into albums, use them in creating projects like greeting cards and calendars, as well as easily share them with friends and family. Figure 1-12 shows you the PhotoSuite window after launching this program by clicking the PhotoSuite link in the Applications Project Window or the Fix & Enhance link on the Photo tab in the Project List of the Roxio Media Creator Home and opening a photo to edit.

As you can see in this figure, the startup window for PhotoSuite is divided into three panes:

- ✔ A task pane along the left edge containing a **Common** tab and an **All** tab, both of which are subdivided into Open/Create, Fix, Tools, and Enhance panes that contain the common options for editing your digital photos and starting new photo projects

- ✔ **Canvas** pane on the upper right where the photo you're currently editing appears

- ✔ **Open File(s)** pane directly below it showing thumbnails of the all the photos you have open. The Common and All tabs are both.

Figure 1-12:
Use
PhotoSuite
to correct
and
enhance
digital
photos as
well as
share them
with family
and friends.

Note that the Canvas pane on the right side of the PhotoSuite window gives you general information about the digital photo you're currently editing, including its rotation, width, and height. It also contains controls for zooming in and out on the photo, changing its orientation, saving, printing, and e-mailing the edited photo. See Chapter 8 for detailed information on using all the PhotoSuite options.

Getting Secure with Roxio Backup

Roxio Backup enables you to create CD and DVD data file projects that back up certain folders and files on your computer system. This versatile little tool not only enables you to make one-time backups of important files but also to schedule regular backups for important files and to do incremental backups that include only files modified since your last backup.

Figure 1-13 shows the Roxio Backup window that appears when you first launch this applet either by clicking the Roxio Backup link in the Applications Project Window or the File Backup link on the Backup tab in the Project List pane of the Roxio Media Creator Home. The Roxio Backup window is divided into three panes:

- **Backup Tasks** to create a new backup project, refresh the list of files to be backed up, or to display a report showing the history of backups made using the current backup project

✔ **Other Tasks** to open the Disc and Device Utility where you can select the device to use in making the backup (usually your CD or DVD drive) and to launch Express Labeler, a special quick version of the Label Creator application

✔ **Backup Projects** that displays the name of the backup project as well as the files you want copied as part of the backup

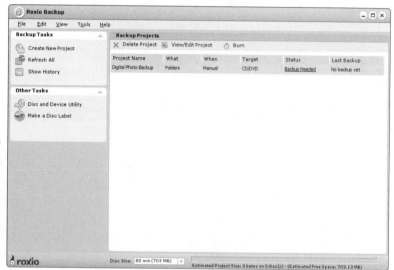

Figure 1-13: Use Backup to back up important files on CD or DVD data discs.

Saying hello to Sound Editor

You can use the Sound Editor tool to edit or enhance the audio recordings you make with such tools as Easy Audio Capture and the LP and Tape Assistant (covered later in this chapter) and convert them to any of the supported digital audio file formats, including MP3, WAV, OGG, and WMA (see Chapter 2 to find out what in the world all these acronyms stand for).

Figure 1-14 shows you the Sound Editor window that appears when you launch this utility by clicking the Sound Editor link in the Applications Project Window of the Roxio Media Creator Home and after opening an MP3 audio file for editing. As you can see in this figure, the Sound Editor interface represents the audio file graphically with a sort of waveform readout (reminiscent of a snapshot of an oscilloscope display). This waveform displays the relative amplitude of the sound for the left and right channels (marked L and R) of the audio file.

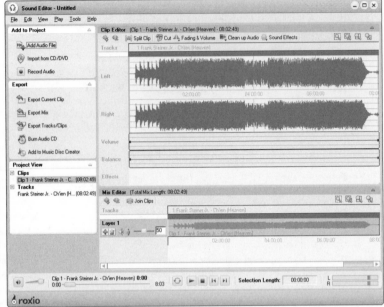

You can then use the controls at the bottom of the Sound Editor to play back all of or any part of the audio track. You can also use the zoom controls located immediately above the waveform display to magnify portions of the audio's waveform display or zoom out on it so that more of the entire track is shown in the Sound Editor. See Chapter 5 for details on using the Sound Editor to edit the audio files that you burn to CD or use in your DVD projects.

Riding the VideoWave

VideoWave is the application that you use to assemble and edit video projects (referred to in the Roxio documentation as *productions*) that can include video clips, still images, and audio. After assembling and editing a production in VideoWave, you can either add it to a DVD project that you're making in MyDVD or use MyDVD to burn it onto a DVD (see "Easy multimedia projects thanks to MyDVD" that precedes this section).

Figure 1-15 shows you the VideoWave 8 window that appears after launching the program by clicking the VideoWave link in the Applications Project Window of the Roxio Media Creator Home and opening an existing slideshow to edit (you must designate whether to create a new production or edit an existing one as part of the program startup). When you open the VideoWave 8 window to create a new production or edit an existing one, it is divided into the four major panes shown in this figure:

- ✔ **Add Content** where you add the photos or video clips you want included in the production as well as select among the various effects and transitions you want to use

- ✔ **Tools** which includes tools for selecting new media and to include in the production and effects to apply as well as to launch a CineMagic Production or New Slideshow built with the Slideshow Assistant (see description in the bullet list immediately following this one)

- ✔ **Preview** where you can preview how the your production will play as you create and edit it

- ✔ **Production Editor: Storyline** displaying a storyboard view of the video production, showing all the individual video clips and stills with any in-between transitions in the order in which they will play in the final production (this pane can also display the production in a Timeline view which shows the timing of each element in the production along with any audio or narration track that you've added)

Figure 1-15:
Use
VideoWave
to assemble
video clips,
still images,
and audio
into produc-
tions that
you incorpo-
rate into
DVD pro-
jects or burn
directly onto
DVD discs.

Personally, I find that VideoWave interface is one of the easiest and most straightforward for editing video that I've run across. I'm sure that with just a little experience using this beauty, you're going to *love* video editing. If, however, you're a complete newbie to video editing and are the least bit intimidated about producing your own videos, you'll be glad to know that VideoWave includes two new components designed to make video editing nearly foolproof:

- ✔ **CineMagic,** which automatically edits your video production by trimming your video clips and adjusting the tempo of the audio to fit the flow and transitions you use (perfect for making MTV-type videos)

- ✔ **Slideshow Assistant,** which uses a Wizard-type interface, providing step-by-step guidance through assembling the various elements in a new slideshow production including transitions and background music

Starting your video-editing career with CineMagic and the Slideshow Assistant is a perfect way to become familiar with the VideoWave interface and its capabilities. From there, you can quickly move on to video editing on your own right using the Storyline and Timeline views. See Chapter 11 for complete details on using all aspects of VideoWave.

Although you normally launch VideoWave from the Roxio Media Creator Home, you can also launch VideoWave directly from within the MyDVD application when you need to do some advanced editing on a video production created earlier with VideoWave that you've imported into the Video Project you're currently working on or to do similar editing to the contents of a new title that you added to DVD project. Suffice it to say that knowing how to use VideoWave goes a long way in mastering the video end of the Easy Media Creator suite.

Utilities Perfect for Particular Media Needs

In addition to all the nifty programs listed in its Applications list, the Applications Project Window of the Roxio Media Creator Home also inlcudes a Utilities list that provides the following useful tools:

- ✔ **Create Panoramas** to launch the Panorama Assistant that enables you to stitch together a sequence of photos into a single panoramic picture (see Chapter 6 for details)

✔ **DVDInfo Pro** to use Roxio DVDInfo Pro to get all sorts of information about the capacities of your computer's DVD drive as well as information on those of a DVD disc that you want to use in the burning of your Roxio media projects

✔ **Disc Image Loader** to create a virtual drive on your computer into which you can load disc image files containing audio or video data culled from different physical discs, thus enabling you to play or to back up the data without having to do any disc swapping (see Chapter 3 for details)

✔ **Drag To Disc** to copy data and media files onto the CD or DVD disc in your computer's CD/DVD drive by simply dragging them to the program's icon (see "Instant data copying thanks to Drag to Disc" in the section that follows immediately for details)

✔ **Easy Audio Capture** for recording audio with your computer's sound card either externally using some sort of microphone or internally using a program such as the Windows Media Player that plays audio on your computer (see Chapter 7 for details)

✔ **Media Import** to launch Roxio Media Import which enables you to capture photo, video, and audio clips for your Roxio media projects (see "The importance of Media Import" later in this chapter for details)

✔ **Multi Photo Enhance** for doing group editing on a bunch of digital photos that all require the same types of fixes and enhancements (see Chapter 6 for details)

✔ **Retrieve** for recovering data files from a multi-disc CD or DVD data project where the data from some files can be split across more than one disc (see Chapter 3 for details)

Instant data copying thanks to Drag to Disc

Drag to Disc is one of the neatest yet simplest applications in the Easy Media Creator suite. You can use this nifty program to make CD or DVD backups or archives of data files on your hard disk or network simply by dragging their folder or file icons on the Windows desktop and dropping them on the Drag to Disc icon (shown in Figure 1-16). The Drag-to-Disc application is great because it automatically does any formatting for the data CD or DVD as needed to accommodate the files that you add.

To display the Drag to Disc icon on your Windows desktop, click the Drag To Disc link in the Utilities column of the Applications Project area in the Roxio Media Creator Home window or click the Drag to Disc icon (shown in the left margin of this paragraph) that appears in the Systems Tray on the right side of the Windows taskbar immediately to the left of the clock. For details on making quick data backups and archives with Drag to Disc, see Chapter 3.

Figure 1-16:
Use the Drag to Disc icon on your Windows desktop to make quick, one-time backups of file data.

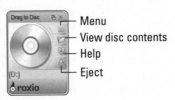

The importance of Media Import

As the name suggests, you use the Media Import to bring in media files from various devices such as a digital photo camera, video camera, scanner, and microphone that's connected to your computer system. You can also use Media Import to capture media files from CD or DVD discs (which aren't copy protected and to which you have the right to make copies) loaded into the CD or DVD drive built into your computer.

Figure 1-17 shows the Roxio Media Import window as it appears when I launch the program by clicking the Media Import link in the Utilities column of the Applications Project Window in the Roxio Media Creator Home window and then select the Video tab when my Sony digital video camera is connected to my PC. Your Capture window will undoubtedly differ depending on the actual devices you have connected to your computer. As you can see, this window contains the controls for capturing a video clip directly from the connected video camera on the left with a listing of the clips recently imported on the right. See Chapter 10 for details on using Media Import to capture various types of media files for your Roxio Easy Media Creator 8 projects.

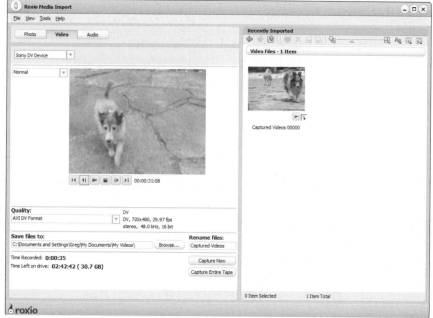

Figure 1-17:
Media
Import
enables you
to import
media files
from the
various
devices
connected
to your com-
puter.

Help Is on the Way!

The best place to go for online help on using any of the nifty applications and
utilities outlined so far in this chapter is the Help menu of the Roxio Media
Creator Home. The Help menu in this window contains the following options:

- **Help** to open the Roxio Help Center where you can get help on the Roxio
  Media Creator Home and doing media projects from it as well as on particular apps and utilities included in the suite

- **Tutorial** to open a local Web page in your Web browser with links to particular step-by-step tutorials on topics such as Start a New Project and
  Import Photos from Your Camera

- **Media Guide** to open a local Web page in your Web browser with information on the recommended media to use when undertaking a particular media project such as creating an audio CD, a backup data disc, or a
  video DVD

- **Gracenote – Your Source for Music Information** to connect to the
  Internet and open in your Web browser the Home page of the Gracenote
  Web site where you can search its enormous online music database

(consisting of almost 4 million CDs and more than 50 million songs) for all kinds of information about your favorite artist or track

✔ **Technical Support on the Web** to connect to the Internet and open in your Web browser a Sonic Web page from which you can get technical tips and seek direct help for any snafus you happen to run into when running the Roxio Easy Media Creator 8 suite

✔ **Sonic Store** to connect to the Internet and open in your Web browser a Sonic Web page from which you can purchase upgrades to any product from Sonic Solutions or disc labels to use in your Roxio media projects

✔ **Check for Updates** to connect to the Internet and open in your Web browser a Sonic Web page which checks for and downloads any updates to your version of the Roxio Easy Media Creator 8 suite

✔ **About This Software** to open a window with information about the specific version of the Roxio Easy Media Creator 8 suite installed on your computer

Using the Roxio Help Center

Figure 1-18 shows the Roxio Help Center window. As you can see from this figure, the Roxio Help Center presents its information in a standard Windows Help window with its Contents, Index, Search, and Favorites tabs in a pane on the left and the text of the currently selected help topic displayed on the right.

Figure 1-18: The Roxio Help Center is the place to go for help on Home or any of the suite's modules.

Note that you can quickly open the Help Center from the Roxio Media Creator Home window by clicking the Help button (the one with the question mark immediately beneath Maximize button in the upper-right corner of the Home window) or by simply pressing F1 when this window is active.

The easiest way to get to general help on the use of any of the suite's modules is from the Contents tab. This tab contains a list of Using topics that comprise all the suite's modules from Using Roxio Home all the way to Using Disc Image Loader (with all applications outlined earlier in this chapter in between). In addition, when you expand the Using Roxio Home topic at the top of the Contents tab (by clicking the plus-sign button to the immediate left of its book icon), you find project-specific help subtopics with loads of good information on making specific types of Audio, Copy, and Data projects.

Getting application-specific help

In addition to the help available in the Roxio Media Creator Home, each of the indvidual apps included in the suite such as Creator Classic, PhotoSuite, MyDVD, and the like offer their own application-specific help in two forms:

- **Help for this Window** (the first item on the particular program window's Help menu or opened by pressing F1) that acquaints you with the particular module's interface

- **Help Center** for the specific module you're using (the second item on the module's Help menu) that contains help topics on how to use the particular module's features

Figure 1-19 shows you the Help For the Sound Editor window that opens when you choose Help⇨Help for this Window on the Sound Editor menu bar or press F1 when the Sound Editor program window is active. As you can see, this particular help window contains callouts for the Sound Editor window that enable you to identify its major areas and controls.

Figure 1-20 shows you the Sound Editor Help Center window that opens when you choose Help⇨Sound Editor Help Center on the Sound Editor's menu bar. The left pane of this help center is arranged as a standard Windows help window with its Contents, Index, Search, and Favorites tabs. The right pane contains a list of links to get general information about Sound Editor and its basic functions as well as links to online resources.

To get information particular things that Sound Editor can do and specifically how specific features work, start by perusing the general topics on the Contents tab. When you find a general topic that might contain information of interest, click its name or closed-book icon to display a list of links to its subtopics in the pane on the right. Then, when you locate a subtopic of interest, click its individual link to replace the list in the right pane with a display of its specific help information.

Figure 1-19:
The Help for the Sound Editor window helps you quickly identify the parts of the Sound Editor window.

You can also expand any of the general help topics in the left pane of the General tab by clicking the plus-sign button right before the closed-book icon. When you do this, the closed-book icon becomes an open-book icon and a list of related subtopics appears under the name of the general one. To display the help information for any of these subtopics in the right pane of the Help center, you have only to click its name in the left pane.

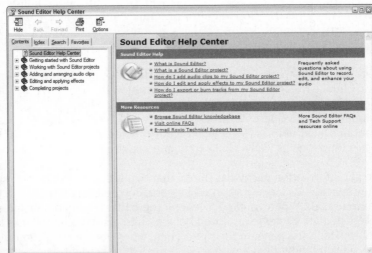

Figure 1-20:
The Sound Editor Help Center window gives you loads of information on how to use the Sound Editor's many features.

If you know the name of the feature with which you want help, click the Index tab and then type the first few letters of the feature's name. The index will immediately jump to the topics that start with those letters. To display information on a particular feature in the right pane of the Help center, click its feature name in the Index pane on the left.

If you know what you want to do in a particular application or tool but don't know the name of the feature that is used in accomplishing the task, you might find the Search tab to be of more help. After clicking the Search tab in the left pane of the Help Center window, type in the word or phrase that describes the task you want to accomplish and then press Enter or click the List Topics button to begin the search. The Help Center then displays all the topics that contain the word or phrase you just searched for. To display a particular help topic in the right pane of the Help Center window, double-click its name or click it and then click the Display button.

If in your searches you come across a particularly useful help topic to which you are likely to refer on more than one occasion, you can mark the topic as a favorite and then display its information again quickly by selecting it from the Favorites tab. To do this, after you've located the really useful topic on the Contents, Index, or Search and have displayed its information in the right pane of the Help Center window, click the Favorites tab and then click the Add button at the bottom of the left pane (this button appears right below the name of the displayed topic in the Current Topic text box).

After adding a topic to the Favorites tab, you can redisplay its help information by selecting the tab and then either double-clicking it name in the Topics list box or clicking its name followed by the Display button.

To print a copy of the help topic displayed in the right pane of the Help Center window, click the Print button on the very first toolbar displayed at the top of the Help Center window and then click OK in the Print dialog box. To copy the displayed help topic or step-by-step instructions into a document in another Windows program, drag through the text in the right pane of the Help Center window with the I-beam pointer to select all the text you want to copy. Then press Ctrl+C to copy the selected text to the Windows Clipboard, switch to the document in the other program, click the insertion point at the place where you want the help text copied, and then press Ctrl+V to insert the help text into the document at the insertion point.

Chapter 2

The Ins and Outs of Digital Media and Gear

In This Chapter

▶ Getting familiar with the wide range of digital media file formats

▶ Converting analog media to digital

▶ Selecting your digital camera and camcorder

▶ Selecting your DVD and MP3 player

▶ The proper care and handling of your CD and DVD discs

The many tools the Roxio Easy Media Creator 8 suite puts at your disposal certainly make it easy to create your own audio and video projects. This ease of use, however, is not quite matched when it comes to making heads or tails of the many and sundry media formats and equipment you can use in recording and saving these projects.

To help dispel potential confusion over your choices of media formats for the particular audio and video gear you're using, this chapter begins by examining the relationship of media formats to digital recording and playback equipment. It then goes on to introduce you to the essential difference between analog and digital media, why you want to get on the digital bandwagon, and some of the devices you can use to convert your analog media to digital for use with the Easy Media Creator.

Finally, this chapter looks at some of your options in terms of digital recording and playback paraphernalia, including digital still cameras, video cameras, and audio recorders, not to mention CD and DVD drives, and CD, MP3, and DVD players. It ends with a few important pointers on the care and feeding (I mean, handling) of the CD and DVD discs you use for saving and recording your Easy Media Creator projects.

Feeling at Home in the Digital Media Menagerie

Before I can clear up any perplexity that you may have about the different types of media that are available to you as you start working with the Easy Media Creator suite, you need to be clear about the relationship between the digital media formats and the kinds of recorders and playback gear you have.

The standard media formats for both CD and DVD discs come in several flavors (see the sidebar that follows for the essential difference between CD and DVD discs). As you see in Table 2-1, by and large these formats differ according to how much data they hold, their recording speed, and whether or not they enable you to record data on them only once or erase and rerecord data multiple times (referred to by the term *rewritable*).

Table 2-1	Digital Media and Data Capacity		
Media Types	*Maximum Capacity*	*Record Once*	*Rewritable*
CD-R	210 MB, 650 MB, or 700MB	✔	
CD-RW	210 MB, 650 MB, or 700MB		✔
DVD-R, DVD+R	4.7 GB	✔	
DVD-RW, DVD+RW	4.7 GB		✔
DVD-RAM	from 2.6 GB up to 9.4 GB		✔

When shopping for discs to use for your various Easy Media Creator projects, you need to match the capacities of your recording and playback hardware with the proper media. Be sure to check the boxes of media for the following pieces of information:

- ✔ CD or DVD indicating whether the discs are formatted for recording and playback of CDs or DVDs

- ✔ Maximum data capacity expressed in megabytes (MB) or gigabytes (GB)

- ✔ Recording speed, anywhere from 1x (times) up to about 8x for DVDs and anywhere up 52x for CDs

- ✔ R or RW indicating whether the discs can be recorded once or are rewritable

You may be scratching your head wondering about what's up with the DVD-R and DVD+R and the DVD-RW and DVD+RW formats listed in Table 2-1. Basically, the minus and plus indicate two slightly different single and multi-session DVD recording formats. The -R and -RW formats were the first DVD recording formats that were compatible with standalone DVD players (the ones you connect to your TV). The +R and +RW formats are newer and boast some improvements in recording (newer DVD-ROM computer drives tend to be DVD+RW compatible drives).

DVD-R and DVD+R are the non-rewritable formats that are compatible with almost all DVD players and DVD-ROM drives. DVD-RW and DVD+RW are the rewritable formats and are compatible with about 75 percent of the DVD players and almost all DVD-ROM drives.

Note that the DVD+RW format supports both a single-side 4.7 GB disc (known as DVD-5) and a double-side 9.2 GB disc (known as DVD-10). The DVD-RAM has the best recording features but it is not compatible with most DVD-ROM drives and standalone DVD-video players (you need to check to make sure that your recorder and player can deal with DVD-RAM discs).

In terms of selecting new hardware for your computer, keep in mind the following distinctions among drives:

- **CD-ROM** drives can only read CDs
- **DVD-ROM** drives can only read CDs and DVDs
- **CD-RW/DVD** combo drives can read and write CDs but only read DVDs
- **DVD-R and DVD+R** drives can read and write CDs but only read DVDs
- **DVD-RW and DVD+RW** drives can read and write both CDs and DVDs

 If you're in a position of selecting among the different types of drives for a new computer system, go with a DVD+RW drive if you can possibly afford it. By selecting a DVD+RW drive, you get the benefits of all the other three types of drives as well as the ability to back up data and video on your own DVDs. This means that you get to play your favorite music CDs and movies and videos on your computer while at same time being able to take full advantage of the Roxio Easy Media Creator software to create and burn your own CD and DVD creations (including data and audio CDs and data and multimedia DVDs).

Let's hear it for the Video and Super Video CD formats

In addition to the regular CD-R format used to record standard data and audio CDs, you need to be aware of two other CD formats, both of which can incorporate both audio and video like a DVD:

- ✔ **Video CD (VCD),** which can hold up to 74/80 minutes of video on a 650/700 MB CD and can be played in most of the new standalone DVD players

- ✔ **Super Video CD (SVCD)** which can hold up to 35-60 minutes of video on a 650/700 MB CD and can be played in many of the new standalone DVD players

Note that SVCD format supports higher quality video than your regular VCD but as you can see from the above descriptions is less compatible and holds less video. When creating a new multimedia project with Roxio's DVD Builder application, you can choose to create in either the VCD or SVCD format instead of the standard DVD format.

Ripping through those pesky audio formats

Audio file formats vary almost as much as CD and DVD formats. These formats, however, only contain information about the shape and duration of the audio's waveform. In addition, the format will specify the *sample rate* (the resolution of the audio that determines the sound quality), *bit-depth* (the number of bits, 0 and 1, used to describe the volume of the sample at any given point in the audio stream), and may include the type of compression used (assuming that the audio is compressed at all).

When an audio file uses an audio format without compression, it is naturally a larger file that requires more computer memory to play than files using different compression schemes. As a general rule, a second of uncompressed audio of the quality of your typical store-bought album on CD, which uses a sample rate of 44.1 kHz (kilohertz), a bit-depth of 16-bit, and is stereo, takes about 172 Kb to store on your computer (that's about 10 Mb per minute and 604 Mb per hour).

On computers running Windows, uncompressed audio is almost always stored in the so-called WAV audio format (pronounced *wave*). This format is also known as PCM (Pulse Code Modulation) and carries a .WAV file extension. WAV files store are standard CD quality (44.1 kHz, 16-bit, stereo), meaning that they are big files that hog up your disk space.

In terms of compressed audio, you'll run into a number of different schemes — each of which is technically known as a *codec* (short for compress/decompress) — for compressing and later decompressing the audio stream.

What separates the CDs from the DVDs

CD stands for Compact Disc and comes in two very familiar forms: audio CDs that play in all standard CD players and CD-ROMs that play in your computer's CD or DVD drive. DVD stands for Digital Versatile Disc (although some replace the *Versatile* with *Video*) and is most familiar in the form of movies on DVD that you rent or purchase.

Both CDs and DVDs rely on laser technology to decode their sequence of binary (0 and 1) data. The big difference between CDs and DVDs is their data capacity. Because DVDs use smaller tracks than CDs (0.74 microns wide as opposed

to 1.6 microns), they can store much more digital data on the same size disc (both CD and DVD are the same diameter and often the same thickness), about two hours of video or about 4.7 GB (gigabytes or one billion bytes!) of digital data compared to about 74 minutes of audio or about 700MB (megabytes or one million bytes) of digital data or less. Because DVDs use smaller tracks to fit more data on the same-size disc, they also require special computer drives for recording and playing their discs. Fortunately, DVD drives can also record and play back CDs (although CD drives cannot record and play back DVD discs).

The most popular audio codecs for computers running some flavor of Microsoft Windows are the ever-present MP3 (MPEG 3) and WMA (Windows Media Audio). The WMA format was developed by Microsoft for its Windows Media Player. This codec does not compress audio files as much as the much more popular, MP3 but it does tend to have slightly better sound quality. MP3 is, however, the most popular codec for storing and streaming music (thus the plethora of so-called MP3 players — see "I want my MP3" later in this chapter for details).

MPEG actually stands for Motion Picture Experts Group, the name of a highly prestigious committee that sets standards for the encoding of digital video and sound. MPEG 3 actually uses the so-called MPEG 1, a video codec for compressing video in digital cameras and camcorders and in the creation of VCDs (Video CDs supported by DVD Builder) with what's called the Audio Layer 3 codec, thus the name MPEG 3 or, as it's more commonly known, MP3.

In addition to MP3 and WMA compression, in the Roxio Easy Media Creator components, you may also run across the OGG codec. OGG refers to Ogg Vorbis, an open, patent-free codec for audio encoding and streaming that is gaining some popularity. Ogg is not, as far as I can tell, an acronym like WMA or MP3 (perhaps it refers to Ogg, the former gamekeeper before Hagrid takes over the post at Hogwarts in book four of *Harry Potter*?). Where the name Vorbis comes from is anyone's guess.

Codecs for more than just audio

Although this section deals solely with audio compression, codecs are by no means restricted to audio compression. Digital photos and video both use their own codecs in order to keep down the size of their visual media. The most popular codec for digital photos is JPEG (Joint Photographic Experts Group), which can vary in terms of its size/quality ratio. For digital video, the most popular codecs are MPEG 1, used primarily for video from digital cameras and camcorders, and MPEG 2, used primarily for commercially produced movies on DVD and in TiVo-type hard disk video recorders.

If you're a user of Apple's iTunes, you run into another compression scheme known popularly as AAC (Advanced Audio Coding). This scheme uses MPEG 4 compression codec, and Audio files saved in AAC are often smaller than MP3 files with better sound quality (unfortunately, Roxio's Easy Media Creator 7 sound applications do not support this audio file format).

Don't you hate those "lossy" codecs?

There's one more consideration when it comes to compression schemes. When considering a codec to select for your audio, you need to reflect on whether or not the codec is lossy or lossless. A lossy codec is one that actually loses content that is considered to be duplicated or not essential in listening to the audio. A lossless codec is just the opposite: in compressing audio, it does not remove any of the bits from the original audio file that it cannot restore when the audio stream is decompressed for playback.

As you might guess, lossy codecs make for smaller compressed audio files but with slightly lesser sound quality. Lossless codecs, on the other hand, make for larger compressed files but usually with great fidelity to the original. This is the reason that MP3 audio files are generally a little smaller than the same WMA audio files and that WMA audio files are generally considered of slightly higher quality than MP3 files because MP3 is the lossy codec of the two and WMA the lossless one.

When applying lossy codecs such as MP3, JPEG (for digital images), and MPEG1 (for digital camera and camcorder video) to your media files, the Easy Media Creator applications and tools normally allow you to adjust the amount of compression to apply by selecting the relative quality for the compressed file. Select the best quality when larger file sizes aren't an issue and lesser quality when the relative size of the file is most important.

Ripping and burning those audio files

Before leaving behind the fascinating subject of audio file formats, you should be aware of a couple more procedures, namely *ripping* and *burning* audio files (terms, I admit, that suggest a degree of violence that is totally absent in their actual processes). Ripping refers to the process of taking audio tracks from one source in one audio format and saving them to another in a second audio format. The most common example of ripping is when you take tracks from a commercially produced CD and save them in another compressed digital format on your hard disk such as MP3 or WMA with the Creator Classic application.

Burning refers to the process of then taking the audio files that you've ripped to a new audio format such as MP3 and WMA on your computer's hard disk and then transferring them to a blank CD disc for playback on other devices (like a CD or MP3 player). Note that although you hear the term ripping applied mostly to audio files, it can also be applied to video files saved on DVDs as well (although this requires special software besides Roxio Easy Media Creator, as most DVDs are highly copy-protected).

The term burning is, however, applied equally to the creation of both CDs and DVDs so that you find Burn buttons in both the Creator Classic and DVD Builder applications.

Make Mine Digital!

It's true that nowadays digital is king (and as the immortal Mel Brooks is so fond of telling us, "It's good to be king!"). Nowhere is this rush to digital seen more clearly than in the purchase of consumer electronics, which today are almost entirely digital in nature, as in digital cameras, camcorders, DVD players, and digital audio players. It seems like the only electronics gear that is still analog is tape recorders and even then you have the choice of going digital with DAT (Digital Audio Tape) recorders.

So what's this all about, this *analog* versus *digital* business? Well, let me start by giving you the textbook definition of each, followed by the classic example that hopefully makes their rather dry explanations all clear.

By definition, analog devices are apparatuses in which the data is represented by continuously variable physical quantities (you say what?). Digital devices, however, are machines in which the data is represented by discrete units, namely the binary number system which consists of just two measly numbers, 0 and 1.

Okay, now that that's clear as mud, take a look at the classic example of an apparatus that exists in both analog and digital forms, namely your wristwatch. If your watch happens to have a dial that shows the sequence of the twelve hours and represents the current time on this time with the placement of its hands (at least an hour and minute hand and perhaps even a hand to keep track of the passing seconds), then you're wearing an analog device. And this device represents its data (that is, the passing hours, minutes, and seconds on the twelve-hour dial) "by continuously variable physical quantities" (that's the moving watch hands to you and me).

If, however, you're wearing a wristwatch that has no hour dial and uses no hands but actually tells you the current time in Arabic numerals, as in 6:15:33 or 22:05:09, you are the proud owner of a digital device, one that represents its data (the same passing hours, minutes, and seconds) in discrete binary units (which the clock manufacturer has skillfully disguised as a readout showing the current time).

Now nice as the wristwatch example is, it doesn't help too much in terms of the kinds of devices you'll be using with your Easy Media Creator software. For examples closer to the work you'll be doing, I prefer the examples of the long-playing record versus the audio CD and the videocassette versus video on DVD. Records are prime examples of analog audio media just as videocassettes are great examples of analog video media. And you guessed it; audio CDs and video DVDs are excellent examples of their digital audio and video counterparts.

One way to keep analog mechanisms straight from digital ones is to remember that the word "analog" is related to the term "analogous," denoting something that is similar to something else so that most analog devices capture their data by acting like the sense organs with which we collect data. So, analog cameras have lenses that capture light in similar ways that the lens in the human eye and analog audio recorders have microphones that vibrate like the tympanic membrane in the ear. Even the classic analog clock with its dial and moving hands in some ways mimics a sundial in the way that the sun's shadow moves across its disk.

Why digital rules

And now I can tell you the main reasons that digital has been crowned king. The first reason is that devices that play back such analog media as LPs and videocassettes can only access their data (sound and music, in this case) sequentially. The ramification of this fact becomes abundantly clear in the case of a videocassette when you go to try to find and replay a favorite scene in a movie on tape. Instead of being able to jump right to the scene as you can do with the controller for your DVD player (assuming that the movie is also available on DVD, which nowadays is almost always true), you have to fast forward or reverse until you recognize the place in the movie you want to replay. The discrete rather than continuous nature of digital audio and video media is what makes this kind of *random access* of the data possible.

The second reason that digital is riding so high and mighty comes from the fact that copies of any type of digital media (including sound, photos, and video) are every bit (pun intended) as good as the original, since both the original and copy contain the exact same sequence of 0 and 1s. This is definitely not true of analog media. The quality of each copy of an analog master is slightly degraded and copies made from copies are even worse (just as a photocopy made from a photocopy of an original is fainter and lacks much of the original detail).

So too, the quality of most media that store analog data (with film being the most notorious) naturally degrades with time (you have only to thumb through an album filled with your baby pictures to know what I'm talking about). By and large, this is not true of most digital media (hard disks and DVD discs stored properly should last you a really long time) and, of course, in the cases where it is, you can always create a new master from any copy that is still intact (thus the singular importance of making backups and the beauty of the fact that a copy made from a copy of an original is equal in quality to that copy and, indeed, the original itself).

Converting analog media to digital

The best way to protect your precious analog data (usually stored in photos, home movies, audio tape recordings, videocassettes, and LPs) is to convert the analog data to digital data. In fact, this may well be your primary motivation for learning how to use the applications and tools in the Roxio Easy Media Creator suite and may turn out to be your primary use for the software.

Like me, you may have shoeboxes of family pictures in the attic, a closet full of Super 8 home movies, drawers full of videocassettes, and a basement full of the most incredible collection of records, both LPs and 45s (now virtually abandoned and utterly unplayed). Fortunately, you can take steps to preserve this very precious data and all the wonderful memories it contains by making digital copies of their media. The device you use to convert analog data to digital depends on the type of analog media you're converting. The next two sections look at two of the most common and most reasonably priced analog-to-digital conversion devices: the digital scanner that you can use to digitize photos and, in some cases, slides and the analog-to-DV (digital video) converters that enable you to convert video saved as home movies and videocassettes.

"Scotty, scan me up . . ."

A digital scanner is one of the most useful and cost-effective analog-to-digital conversion devices you can own. Scanners come in several flavors: film scanners designed specifically for scanning photos from film (including negatives) and 35mm slides and film, handheld scanners that you pass over the object or page you want digitized, sheetfed scanners where you feed the photo or page to scanned, and flatbed scanners designed for scanning any object that you can fit on its flatbed (especially printed text and images and photos developed from film).

For about a $100 or less, you can get a really decent flatbed scanner with which you can digitize all your family photos, news clippings, and favorite cards and letters and preserve them in digital form before they become too faded and stained to enjoy. If you want to be able to scan photo negatives, slides, and filmstrips as well, you'll have to pay more but you can still find a flatbed scanner that can scan these without having to resort to purchasing a special film scanner (which doesn't enable you to scan items like cards, letters, and pages of a book).

Note that almost any scanner that you buy today can connect to your computer through a USB (Universal Serial Bus) 2.0 cable (the type of cable connector typically used to connect a mouse to newer computers. Higher end (and more costly) scanners can also connect to your computer through the so-called FireWire (officially known by its much more boring designation, IEEE-1394) cable.) Although a FireWire connection between your scanner and computer is not necessary, keep in mind that FireWire connectivity is completely necessary when it comes to transferring digital video from a digital camera or camcorder to your computer (in such cases, USB 2.0 just isn't fast enough).

Analog-to-DV converters

Analog-to-DV converters are standalone devices that enable you to connect analog devices such as an 8mm video camera or VHS format VCR to them via Composite video or S-video and RCA audio cables. The converter then converts the analog signal from the movie or tape to digital and sends the resulting 0 and 1 bits to your computer's hard disk via a FireWire cable. And once you've got the video data converted to digital and saved on your hard disk, you can then use Easy Media Creator applications such as VideoWave and DVD Builder to arrange and enhance the content (see Chapters 11 and 12 for details).

The nice thing about analog-to-DV converters like the Pyro A/V Link is that the conversion is not limited to analog to digital. After you arrange and enhance your digital video data with the Easy Media Creator software, you can then use the converter to convert it back to analog and transfer it out to a connected analog device such as a VCR. That way, you can save your final digital video project on VHS tape and then share the resulting videocassette with those in your family who haven't yet crossed over the digital divide.

Sorting Out Your Digital Recording Gear

While it's great to be able to convert your analog data to digital for use in your Easy Media Creator projects, it's even better (and a heck of a lot easier) to capture the data in digital form in the first place. To be able to capture digital media for use in your Easy Media Creator projects, at the very minimum you'll want to have access to a digital still camera (sometimes abbreviated to digicam) and a digital video camera (commonly called a camcorder, a truncation of camera-recorder).

When selecting a digital camera or camcorder, the quality of the camera lens is critical in determining the quality of your photos as with their analog counterparts, but another unique factor comes into play, as well: the resolution of a sensor called a CCD (Charge Coupled Device), whose pixels actually register the photographed image on the camera's disk. It is the resolution of the camera's CCD that most affects the sharpness of the photographed image.

Both digital still and movie cameras are rated by the highest CCD resolution they support (measured in megapixels that are a factor of the product of the number of horizontal and vertical pixels used on the CCD sensor). With still cameras, you can select a resolution beneath the camera's highest megapixel rating, enabling you to store a greater number of lesser resolution photos on the camera's storage disk. With camcorders, you can't modify the CCD resolution so that your movies are always recorded at the camera's highest setting.

In addition to the megapixel rating of the camera's CCD sensor, when selecting a digital still camera, you'll want to pay attention to the following factors:

- Whether or not the camera has a zoom lens (usually a mechanical zoom lens is superior to the so-called digital zoom that doesn't actually move the lens forward and back)

- How much built-in memory the camera has and whether this memory is expandable through some kind of flash memory disk or memory stick (the amount of memory determines how many photos you can take before you have to transfer them onto your computer's hard disk)

- Whether or not the camera has an LCD screen which enables you to preview the photo right after you take it

- The kind of computer interface the camera has (most support USB 2.0 connectivity, although the higher-end cameras also support FireWire connectivity)

When selecting a digital camcorder, you apply many of the same criteria as when choosing a digital still camera (megapixel rating, zoom lens, LCD screen, and USB versus FireWire connectivity). Of course, the big difference between a digital still camera and camcorder is how they record their images.

Many camcorders still record their video on film, although a few of the smallest ones use flash memory cards and a few of the very newest ones can record their video directly on MiniDVD discs. Most camcorders, however, continue to record their video on Mini DV cassettes (which support the DV media format with CD quality sound). Mini DV cassettes are normally available in 30-, 60-, and 90-minute sizes.

Be aware that MiniDVD discs (3-inch diameter or about half the size of a standard DVD disc) do not play in all DVD players. Before you invest in a camcorder that uses MiniDVD discs, be sure that your DVD Player plays media this size. Otherwise, you'll end up always having to dump the video that you take with the camera onto your hard disk and then use one of the Easy Media Creator applications to burn it onto a standard-size DVD in order to play it in your machine.

When It's "Playback" Time

Getting your digital recording gear is truly only half the story, for what good is a digital camcorder if you have no way to play the movies you make with it outside of its tiny LCD screen or on your computer screen? The other half of the story has got to be what you are going to use to play all those great audio and video projects you create with the Roxio Easy Media Creator 8.

The next two sections give you an overview of the capabilities of today's crop of DVD and MP3 players. Both of these devices are surely among the hottest digital electronics on the market and ones that you want to consider investing in given the capabilities of your Roxio Easy Media Creator software.

Delving into the world of DVD players

DVD players have eclipsed videocassette players much faster than most people anticipated. This is probably not only due to their much superior video and sound quality but also to the dramatic decrease in their pricing: you can now get a decent player for anywhere between $100 and $200.

When choosing a DVD player, you have to consider what media formats (DVD and otherwise) that the player supports (see "Feeling at Home in the Digital Media Menagerie" earlier in this chapter for details). Some DVD players not only support a number of DVD media formats but audio DVD, CD, and MP3 as well. This feature enables you to play the audio DVD, CDs, and MP3 discs as well as the DVD video discs that you assemble and burn with your Easy Media Creator software.

If you still have a lot of videocassettes that you like to play (and you haven't yet bought into the idea of converting them all into digital DVD discs), you might want to consider purchasing a DVD/VCR player that can play both DVD video discs and your VHS cassettes.

If you're into recording your favorite television programs as well as being able to play your DVDs, you might consider investing in a DVD recorder (often abbreviated DVR). These beauties enable you to record your favorite programs onto DVD-R or DVD-RAM discs (remember that a DVD-RAM disc holds a whopping 9.4 GB of data and can be rewritten over 100,000 times). Some models are so fancy that they enable you to watch programs that have been recorded on a DVD-R or DVD-RAM disc while the recorder is in the process of recording another TV program on the same disc!

If you have a DVD recorder and you're like me and want to be able to record TV programs while you're away from home or watching another program, the TiVo service is the only to go. TiVo enables you to program your DVD recorder to save your favorite programs on a daily or weekly basis, any time of the day. In addition, TiVo offers a new Home Media Option that lets you program the recording of a TV program remotely through a computer, record a program on a DVR in one room of your house and then play it on another DVR in a different room, as well as use your MP3 playlists to play MP3s on MP3 discs and organize a slideshow for viewing digital photos saved on data CDs or DVDs.

I want my MP3!

Today's DVD players enable you to play the audio CDs and MP3 discs that you burn with the Roxio Easy Media Creator software with no problem. But what about the times when you're on the move (which is probably more often than not) and you want to take your tunes with you? For that you're going to need a portable digital audio player more commonly referred to as an MP3 player.

MP3 players, like those in Apple's amazing iPod series, are now available in an array of music capacities and price points. In general, they run the gamut from $69 all the way to just over $500 (ouch!). The primary determinant of the price of an MP3 is, by and large, the amount of built-in memory the device has (which translates directly into how many MP3 music tracks it can store and how many minutes/hours of audio listening you have available). For example, at the low end, the $69 Rio has only 64MB of memory which gives you about two hours of music. At the high end, the $470 Apple iPod has 40GB of memory which enables it to hold up to a whopping 10,000 tracks for more than 20 hours of back-to-back playback.

Technically speaking, the Apple iPod is not really just an MP3 player. It is, in fact, an MP4 player in that it's capable of not only playing MP3 audio but digital audio stored in the more advanced MPEG-4 audio codec with the so-called AAC (Advanced Audio Coding) compression. This type of compression not only makes for smaller files but ones that some people say are equal to their digital masters in sound quality. The only thing that you need to be aware of is that when you purchase an iPod, you're tied pretty heavily to the iTunes music store (which is great in its own right), while the Roxio Easy Media Creator software that you'll be using to rip and burn your MP3 tracks is tied heavily to the Napster music store.

The Care and Handling of CD and DVD Discs

Earlier in this chapter when I was extolling the virtues of digital and telling you why it's king, I went so far as to claim that if stored properly digital data should theoretically "last forever." Well, when it comes to the most popular forms of digital storage, CD and DVD discs, that statement is definitely an exaggeration bordering on a blatant untruth.

Although disc manufacturers claim a life expectancy of up to 100 years for their CD and DVD discs, you understand that this claim is not based on any real experience (as CD and DVD disc media haven't been around even half that long). Some skeptics even worry that instead of a century of good use, even CD and DVD discs stored under the most optimum conditions may not have a life expectancy much beyond 5 to 10 years (a bit on the short side of forever, I'd say).

With this lowball estimate comes a strong reminder to make multiple backup copies of your CD and DVD discs, especially those that contain data vital to your business. (And, of course, because Roxio's Disc Copier application is making this kind of disc backup so ridiculously easy that you now have no excuse for not doing it.) Of course, regardless of how long the actual life expectancy is for the CDs and DVDs that you create with the Easy Media Creator, improper handling of these discs can drastically reduce it to nothing at all (they're only made of pretty thin plastic after all).

When it comes to the proper care and handling of your CD and DVD discs, keep these important guidelines in mind:

- Always handle your discs by the outer edge or the center hole — avoid touching the shiny surface of the disc where the laser reads the data at all costs
- Keep dirt and dust and all other foreign material by storing your discs in their jewel cases

✔ Always store your discs upright (like books on a shelf) in their cases

✔ Store your discs in a cool, dry, dark environment (they don't take kindly to extremes of temperature and humidity)

✔ Remove any dirt, fingerprints, smudges, and liquids from the shiny bottom surface of your discs with a clean cotton cloth — always wipe in a straight line from the center toward the outer edge and never with a circular motion going around the disc

✔ Always use a non-solvent-based felt-tip permanent marker when marking the label side of your discs (and, of course, never, ever write on the shiny side which the laser reads)

✔ Remove stubborn dirt or gunk from the shiny, bottom surface of your discs with CD/DVD-cleaning fluid or isopropyl alcohol if no commercial cleaner is available

Most of you have the good sense to keep your hands off the shiny underside of a CD or DVD disc, knowing full well that if you mess up this surface, your disc is toast. Unfortunately, many of you don't realize that you can destroy your precious disc just as fast by messing with the topside of the disc where you put the label. The truth is that this upper dye layer of a CD or DVD disc is actually the most sensitive part of the disc so that if you inadvertently scratch or damage this layer, your data is cooked as good as if you'd taken a butcher knife to the shiny underside! For this reason, it is not recommended that you ever apply an adhesive label to your CD or DVD discs, as the adhesive disc labels degrade rather quickly and if the label starts to peel off, it could take part of the dye layer with it.

Despite the potential danger, I still cover using the Easy Media Creator's great Label Creator tool for making professional-looking CD and DVD disc labels in Chapter 9. Just be aware that you're better off labeling a disc that contains important data that you want to last as long as possible with a non-solvent felt-tip marking pen rather than applying a printed adhesive label.

Part II
Creating Data Discs

The 5th Wave   By Rich Tennant

DAD ADDS MULTIMEDIA SOUND AND GRAPHICS TO THE TRADITIONAL CAMPFIRE GHOST STORY.

In this part . . .

*O*ne of the primary tasks that you'll be doing in the Roxio Creator 8 suite is backing up the vast amounts of data and media files that you accumulate on your computer system. Chapter 3 of this part presents all the information you need to use Creator Classic to create and burn these backup discs. Chapter 4 gives you the low-down on using Easy Media Creator's very handy Media Manager tool to organize and manage these data files on your computer. Taken together, Creator Classic and Media Manager make it possible to finally get a handle on all that data you're sitting on and protect it from mishap.

Chapter 3

Backing Up and Copying Data Files

*T*hanks to the advent of CD and DVD discs and their great capacity for holding data (about 700MB for CD and an impressive 4.7GB for your average DVD), gone are any excuses for making disc backups of all your important data. The Roxio Easy Media Creator offers you two different applications for backing up the data you rely on all over your computer system. You can use the quick-and-easy Drag to Disc utility to make data backup discs on the fly or you can turn to Creator Classic when you want to create a data disc project that you can save and reuse to make copies of important folders and files. You can also use Roxio Backup to create backup disc projects that make scheduled backup copies of such files on a regular basis.

This chapter gives you all the information you need to use either application for backing up your data. It also gives you some recommendations for which type of CD or DVD disc you should use in different kinds of backup situations (refer to Chapter 2 if you need a refresher in the differences between CD-R, CD-RW, DVD-R, DVD-RW, and so on).

Drag-and-Drop Magic

Drag to Disc is the program to use when you need to make a onetime backup of certain files and folders on your computer system. For example, suppose you've used Easy Media Creator Media Import to capture a whole bunch of video clips for later use in a DVD project with MyDVD and want to back them up on disc so that you can free up the hard disk space. As you're not going to be backing up the video files on a regular basis, Drag to Disc is the perfect way to make the backup disc before deleting the video clips from your hard disk.

As good as its name, to make a data disc with Drag to Disc all you have to do is follow these easy steps:

1. **Insert a blank CD or DVD disc in your computer's CD or DVD drive.**

   Remember that you can't put a DVD disc into a CD drive but that you can put a CD disc into a DVD drive (see Chapter 2 for the reason).

2. **Double-click the My Documents, My Computer, or My Network Places icons to open the corresponding folder on your Windows desktop; then locate and select the folders or files in them that you want copied onto the disc.**

   Remember that you can select multiple folders and files by holding the Control key as you click their icons.

3. **Drag the selected folders and files over to the Drag to Disc program window (shown in Figure 3-1) and release the mouse button.**

That's all there is to it! If your CD or DVD disc needs formatting, the Drag to Disc program alerts to this fact (and takes care of necessary formatting). If your disc already has data on it (meaning you forgot to label it — shame on you), Drag to Disc alerts you to this fact and gives you an opportunity to replace it with a blank disc. If the disc is one of the rewritable types (see Chapter 2), you can choose to add the selected folders and files (assuming that they will all fit within the remaining free space) to the disc.

Note that if you drag a bunch of audio files rather than just plain old regular data files to the Drag to Disc program icon, an alert dialog box appears informing you that the files you are about to copy can be made into an audio disc by sending them to Music Disc Creator (so that they can be played back on other devices such as a standalone CD player or MP3 player as well as on the computer). To make a music CD using Music Disc Creator (see Chapter 7), click OK in this dialog box. To go ahead and have Drag to Disc perform a straight copy of the audio files (strictly for backup purposes and use on the computer), click the Send the Files to Drag to Disc to Make a Data Disc option on the Choose What You Want to Do With These Files drop-down list before you click OK. To abort the copy operation entirely, click the Cancel button.

Figure 3-1:
Just drag
the folders
and files and
drop them
on to this
Drag to Disc
program
icon to start
copying to
the blank CD
or DVD in
your drive.

When the Drag to Disc application finishes copying the selected folders and files to the target CD or DVD, the program automatically opens a window for the disc showing you its new contents. If there's additional space, you can then add folders and files to the disc by dragging their icons either to this open window or the Drag to Disc desktop icon.

When you finish, be sure to eject the CD or DVD from its drive by clicking the Eject button on the Drag to Disc desktop icon or by pressing Alt+J (for eJect) after making the Drag to Disc desktop icon active rather than pressing the eject button on your CD or DVD drive. That way, the Drag to Disc application has the chance to prepare the disc for use in other computer drives. It also saves you from having to reach around and physically press the drive's eject button.

Launching Drag to Disc on startup

Most of the time, you'll want keep the Drag to Disc program icon (shown in Figure 3-1) on your desktop so that it's ready and available to do its backup magic anytime you're ready to feed it some files. With the installation of the Roxio Easy Media Creator 8 suite, the setting to routinely launch the Drag to Disc application whenever Windows starts up is not automatically selected.

This means that you need to follow these steps if you want the Drag to Disc program icon to appear on your Windows desktop each time you boot your computer:

1. **If Drag to Disc is not yet running, double-click the Roxio Easy Media Creator 8 icon on the desktop to open the Roxio Media Creator Home, and then click the Applications link on the Home tab in the Project List pane on the left and click the Drag To Disc link in the Utilities column of the Applications Project window to the right.**

   After the Drag to Disc program icon appears, you can reduce the Home window to an icon on the Windows taskbar by clicking its Minimize button or close the Roxio Media Creator Home by clicking its Close button.

2. **If Drag to Disc is running but its program icon is currently hidden, click the Show Desktop icon in the Quick Launch toolbar to minimize all other open windows or click the Drag to Disc icon in the Systems Tray to bring the Drag to Disc desktop icon to the top.**

3. **Click the Menu button (the one right below the Close button with the menu icon) on the Drag to Disc program icon to open its pop-up menu or right-click the program icon.**

   The Drag to Disc pop-up menu appears.

4. **Click the Settings item on the Drag to Disc shortcut menu or press Alt+S.**

   The Drag to Disc Settings dialog box, shown in Figure 3-2, opens.

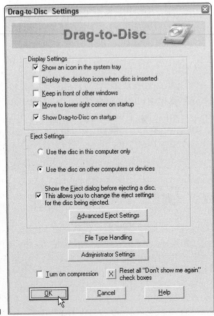

Figure 3-2:
Use the Drag-to-Disc Settings dialog box to change the Display and Eject settings for the Drag to Disc application.

5. **Click the Show Drag to Disc on Startup check box to put a check mark in its check box.**

   If you want to have the desktop icon always appear in the lower-right corner of the Windows desktop, also put a check mark in the Move to Lower Right Corner of Desktop check box.

6. **Click OK to close the Drag to Disc Settings dialog box and put your new settings into effect.**

If you don't want the Drag to Disc program icon on your desktop each time you start your computer, you can launch the program when needed by following these four steps:

1. **Click the Start button on the Windows taskbar.**

2. **Position the mouse pointer on the All Programs item on the Start menu to highlight it and open the All Programs submenu.**

3. **Position the mouse pointer on the Roxio Easy Media Creator 8 item on the All Programs menu to highlight it and open the Creator 8 submenu.**

4. **Position the mouse pointer on the Data item on the Creator 8 submenu and then click the DragToDisc item on the Data submenu.**

 If the Roxio Media Creator Home window is already open, you can forgo these steps involving the Start menu altogether and start the Drag to Disc application by clicking the Drag to Disc link in the Utilities column of the Applications Project Window (opened by clicking the Applications link on the Home tab of the Project List pane — see Chapter 1). So too, you can manually start Drag to Disc by clicking the Roxio Drag-to-Disc icon (the one with the blue disc) on the Systems Tray on the right side of the Windows taskbar.

 By clicking the Roxio Drag-to-Disc icon in the Systems Tray on the Windows taskbar when the Drag to Disc application is already running, you can display the desktop icon on top of whatever window is currently obscuring your view of it. Use this technique to redisplay the Drag to Disc desktop icon when it's hidden beneath a window holding the folders and files that you selected for copying to the CD or DVD disc. That way, you can drag the selected folders and files to the redisplayed Drag to Disc desktop icon without having to first resize or close their window. If you want to ensure that Drag to Disc is always on top of any other open windows, put a check mark in the Keep In Front of Other Windows check box in the Drag to Disc Settings dialog box (Alt+S).

You have to admit that compared to the other program icons on your Windows desktop, the Drag to Disc desktop icon (which is technically a program window and not an icon at all) is pretty large. You can, however, reduce this window to a more manageable size. To do this, click the Roxio Drag-to-Disc icon on the System tray to display the Drag to Disc desktop icon or click its title bar to make it active and then press Alt+I (as in Icon View). Note that you can also reduce the icon by clicking the Drag-to-Disc Icon View button — the one with the image of two windows, one in front of the other — on the title bar of the Drag to Disc icon, but pressing Alt+I is so much quicker and easier. Figure 3-3 shows you the Drag to Disc after reducing it this smaller size with its buttons displayed as a slide-out menu that appears to the button's right.

Figure 3-3:
The reduced
Drag to Disc
program icon
showing its
buttons on
a slide-out
menu to
the right.

After you reduce the size of the Drag to Disc desktop icon, you can still use it to copy selected folders and files to a CD or DVD disc. Simply drag your selected folders and files and then drop them onto this smaller version. If you decide that it's too much effort to drag stuff onto this smaller desktop icon, you can enlarge it before doing your drag-and-drop operation by pressing Alt+I a second time.

Ejecting a disc

After you finish copying your files to a CD or DVD disc with Drag to Disc, you need to use the program's Eject button to open the drive rather than manually ejecting the disc by pressing the CD or DVD recorder's eject button. By selecting the Drag to Disc Eject button, you give yourself the opportunity to select ejection options you want applied to the new disc in the Drag-to-Disc Eject Options dialog box that automatically appears as soon as you click it.

As you see in Figure 3-4, this options dialog box enables you to designate whether the CD or DVD disc will only be used on a computer like the one that created it that runs the Drag to Disc program (in which case, you select the This Disc Will Be Used on This Computer Only option button) or will be used on a computer or other disc-playing device that doesn't have the Drag to Disc program installed on it (in which case you leave the default option button, This Disc Will Be Used on Other Computers or Devices, selected).

Figure 3-4:
Selecting
the Drag-to-
Disc ejection
options to
apply after
copying files
to a CD or
DVD disc.

When using the default This Disc Will Be Used on Other Computers or Devices option, you can also protect the disc so that no one can record over its data by selecting the Protect Disc So That It Cannot Be Written to Again check box.

After selecting the ejection options you want applied to the disc you've just created, click the Eject button at the bottom of the Drag-to-Disc Eject Options dialog box to close it and have Drag to Disc pop open the drive tray after applying your desired settings to the disc. A dialog box showing you the progress in preparing the disc for ejection will appear until the time that the drive tray actually opens (this usually takes a couple of minutes).

If you always intend to apply the This Disc Will Be Used on Other Computers or Devices option to all the discs you make with Drag to Disc and don't anticipate having to choose between write-protecting some discs and not others, you can click the Always Show This Dialog When Ejecting a Disc check box to remove its check mark before clicking its Eject button. After that, Drag to Disc will always apply this setting to each new disc you create without bothering you with the display of the Drag-to-Disc Eject Options dialog box.

When ejecting a CD-R or DVD-R or DVD+R disc (as opposed to a CD-RW or DVD-RW or DVD+RW — see Chapter 2 to find out the difference) after selecting the This Disc Will Be Used on Other Computers or Devices option that is not full, an alert dialog box appears warning you that if you close the disc now, additional information will not be readable in standard CD- or DVD-ROM drive. If you want to be able to add more data to the disc, click the No button in this dialog box and then continue using Drag to Disc to copy more files to it. If you have all the files you need on the disc, go ahead and click the Yes button to have Drag to Disc to prepare the disc for ejection and open the drive tray.

Customizing other Drag to Disc settings

You may have noticed in Figure 3-2 that the Drag-to-Disc Settings dialog box controls more than just when and where the Drag to Disc desktop icon is displayed on your Windows desktop. In addition, this dialog box contains a bunch of Eject, File Type and Administrator settings that you can modify along with a check box that turns on disc compression and a button that resets all your "Don't Show Me Again" alert dialog boxes that sometimes pop up when using the Drag to Disc application.

Modifying the Eject Settings

Beneath the Display Settings in the Drag-to-Disc Settings dialog box, you find the following Eject Settings, which are not only very to the ones found in the Drag-to-Disc Eject Options dialog box (discussed in the section immediately preceding this one) but which can be used to change a disc's ejections options when you have deselected its Always Show This Dialog When Ejecting a Disc check box.

These Eject Settings include:

- **Use the Disc in this Computer Only**: Choose this option button only when you're sure that the backup CD or DVD will be used only in this computer's drive or a computer that uses the very same version of the Drag to Disc application.

- **Use the Disc on Other Computers or Devices**: Keep this option button selected whenever there's a chance that you'll use the backup CD or DVD in a computer using a different type of operating system (such as UNIX or LINUX) or one where Drag to Disc isn't installed.

- **Show the Eject Dialog before Ejecting a Disc**: Keep this check box selected to have the program display the Eject Dialog box whenever you physically attempt to eject the backup CD or DVD that enables you to choose between This Disc Will Be Used on This Computer Only option button and the default This Disc Will Be Used on Other Computers or Devices option button before physically ejecting the disc.

- **Advanced Eject Settings**: Choose this option to access the Advanced Eject Settings dialog box where you can individually modify the settings for non-rewritable and rewritable discs that determine which version of UDF (Universal Disk Format) is used (a standard designed to make optical media as compatible in various systems as possible) and whether or not ISO/Joliet setting is used (enabling Macintosh systems to recognize the long filenames from a Windows' disc — normally you won't have to fiddle around with these settings as the they're already set to make your discs as readable as possible by diverse computer systems).

Changing the File Type Handling Settings

In addition to the Display Settings and Eject Settings, the Drag-to-Disc Settings dialog box also enables you to change the File Type Handling Settings and the Administrator Settings. By default, all of the File Type Handling Settings prompt you only with the options for a particular file type (such as audio files saved as MP3, WAV, WMA, or OGG files or graphic images saved as BMP, JPG, or TIF files, and the like) when you add that type of file to the disc.

If you want to predetermine how Drag to Disc handles a particular type of file when you add that type of file to the disc, click the File Type Handling button in the Drag-to-Disc Settings dialog box. Drag to Disc then opens the Default File Type Handling dialog box (shown in Figure 3-5). Then, click the drop-down button for the particular type of file (Audio Files, MP3 Files, Photos or Images, and so on) and click the appropriate option on its drop-down menu.

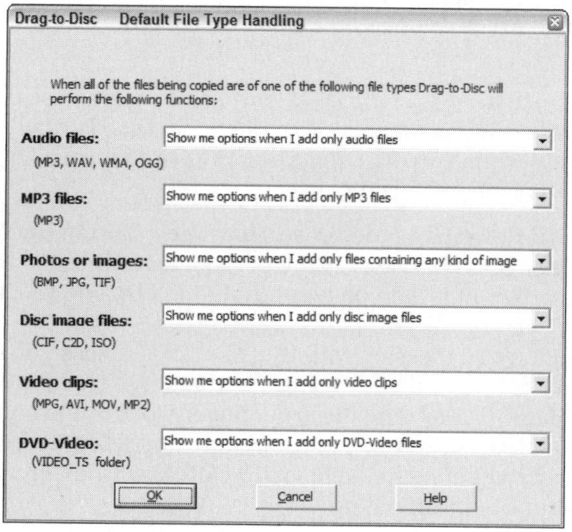

Figure 3-5:
Use the
Default
File Type
Handling
dialog box to
predeter-
mine what
Drag to Disc
does when
you add a
particular
type of file
to a disc.

For example, if you click the drop-down button to the right of Audio Files, you can choose between the following two handling options:

✔ Send the Files to Music Disc Creator to Make an Audio Disc

✔ Send the Files to Drag-to-Disc to Make a Data Disc

The handling options for the other file types listed in the Default File Type Handling dialog box are similar except that they target the Easy Media Creator 8 application designed to deal with that particular type of file in addition to sending the files to Drag to Disc to make a data disc (so that the Video Clips option enables you to send the files to DVD Builder to make a video disc).

Changing the Administrator Settings (if you dare)

When you click the Administrator Settings button in the Drag-to-Disc Settings dialog box, an Administrator Settings dialog box appears with the following four check box options:

- ✔ **Verify RW Media on Full Format** (checked by default) to have Drag to Disc double-check rewritable media (CD-RW, CD+RW, DVD-RW, and DVD+RW) for errors when fully formatting the disc

- ✔ **Verify Recording Using Read After Write** to have Drag to Disc verify the data it burns to disc by comparing it to the original data on your hard disc (selecting this option slows down the recording process but ensures greater data fidelity)

- ✔ **Enable EasyWrite (MRW) Support** (checked by default) to be able to perform a quick format of a rewritable disc on an EasyWrite recorder (also known as Mt.Rainier, this refers to types of CD and DVD recorders that use a standard developed by Philips for recording CD-RW and DVD+RW discs)

- ✔ **Use UDF 2.0 Instead of 1.5 (For DVD Only)** to burn the disc using an older, less compatible version of UDF (Universal Disc Format) — select this option only when you are using Drag to Disc to burn a DVD-R for playback in a consumer DVD recorder

- ✔ **Protect All Non-Rewritable Media So That They Cannot Be Written to After Ejecting** to prevent Classic Creator from attempting to reformat and then write over new data on non-rewritable CDs and DVDs

For heaven's sake, don't go messing with these settings unless you know what you're doing or you're told to make changes to them by someone who does (or who you can blame if your data discs no longer work in the company's computers). Changing these settings may not only degrade the performance of these discs to a crawl but make them incompatible with different computer systems used in your organization!

Turning on disc compression

The last option on the Drag-to-Disc Settings dialog box (besides the Reset All "Don't Show Me Again" Check Boxes button that enables you to reactivate the display of all those lovely alert dialog boxes) is the Turn On Compression check box. When you click this check box option to put a check mark in it, Drag to Disc automatically compresses all of the files that you drop on its desktop icon as it burns them to disc. This is great in that it reduces the size of each of the files you add, enabling you to add more files to a given disc.

Using compression does, however, mean that Windows computers which aren't running the latest copy of Drag to Disc won't be able to decompress and read the files unless the computer has a copy of the UDF (Universal Disc Format) reader installed on it. It also means that computers not running the Windows operating system (such as Macs and computers running under UNIX or LINUX) won't be able to decompress and read the files. Keep these limitations in mind when making discs for coworkers or clients who may not be so fortunate as to have the Roxio Easy Media Creator 8 suite or the UDF reader installed on their Windows systems or don't run Windows at all.

Also keep in mind that you can use the compression option when making a disc with an EasyWrite recorder.

Manually formatting a blank disc

Although Drag to Disc will automatically prompt you to format any blank disc as soon as you attempt to add folders or files to it, you can also manually format the disc before you start dragging-and-dropping your files. To do this, insert the blank CD or DVD disc in the appropriate computer drive, launch Drag to Disc if it is not already running, and then follow these steps:

1. **If the Drag to Disc desktop icon is hidden beneath other windows on the desktop, click the Roxio Drag-to-Disc icon on the taskbar's System Tray to display it.**

2. **Click the Menu button on the Drag to Disc program icon and then click the Format Disc item or press Alt+F.**

    The Drag-to-Disc Format Options dialog box shown in Figure 3-6 appears.

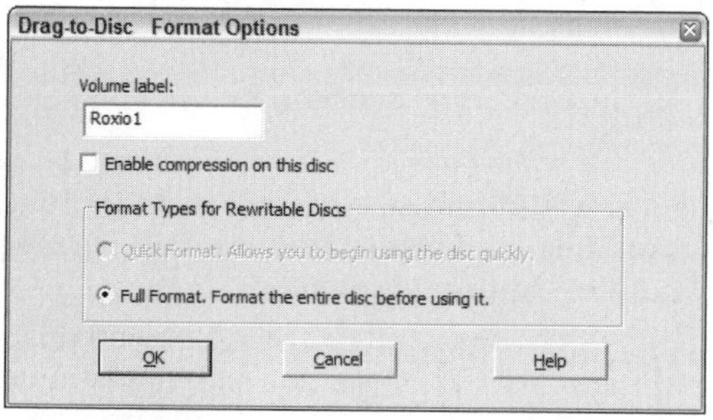

Figure 3-6:
The Drag-to-Disc Format Options dialog box appears whenever you manually format a blank disc.

Drag-to-Disc   Format Options

Volume label:

Roxio1

☐ Enable compression on this disc

Format Types for Rewritable Discs

○ Quick Format. Allows you to begin using the disc quickly.

⊙ Full Format. Format the entire disc before using it.

| OK | Cancel | Help |

3. **Click the Volume Label text box and enter a descriptive volume label for your new disc.**

   Volume labels appear at the bottom of the Drag to Disc desktop icon after the drive letter. When entering a volume label, keep in mind that they can be no longer than 11 characters total and can't contain spaces or any of the following characters:

   \(backslash

   / (forward slash)

   : (colon

   ; (semicolon)

   * (asterisk)

   ? (question mark)

   " (double quotes)

   < (less than)

   > (greater than)

   | (vertical bar)

   + (plus sign)

   = (equal sign)

   . (period)

   , (comma)

   [(open square brace)

   ] (close square brace)

4. **Click the Enable Compression on This Disc check box if you want to compress all the files you add to the formatted disc.**

   Keep in mind the limitations on using compression (listed under the Remember icon in the preceding section) before you select this option.

5. **If you're formatting a rewritable disc, you will want to do a full rather than a quick format on it, so make sure that the Full Format the Entire Disc Before Using It option button is selected.**

   Selecting this option button automatically deselects the default Quick Format Allows You to Begin Using the Disc Quickly option button.

6. **Click the OK button to begin formatting your blank disc.**

Instead of deleting the contents on a previously recorded disc that is rewritable (such as CD-RW, DVD-RW, DVD+RW, and DVD-RAM), you can completely get rid of all its files by manually formatting it using these same steps for manually formatting a blank disc. Just be sure that you don't want any of the files on the rewritable disc before you manually reformat it, as there's no way to retrieve files after a disc has been reformatted.

You can use the Drag to Disc program's Rename Disc command to change the volume label for your CD or DVD disc. Make the program's desktop icon active; click the Menu button and then click the Rename Disc command on its pop-up menu or press Alt+R. Then replace the existing volume label with a new name (following the guidelines pointed out following Step 3 in the preceding steps) in the Name for Disc text box in the Drag to Disc Rename Disc dialog box before you click OK.

Note that renaming a disc's volume label in this manner does not change the disc name that appears on the title bar of any window you open on the disc with the Windows Explorer; the original volume label which gives rise to the disc name continues to be associated with this disc according to Windows. The new volume label does appear, however, in the Label text box if you open a Properties dialog box for the disc.

Also, the new volume name that you give the disc does not appear at the bottom of the Drag to Disc desktop icon until the next time you insert the disc in the drive. This is because ejecting and re-inserting the disc in the drive is the only way to force the Drag to Disc application to read the new volume label and display it in the desktop icon (in other words, unlike your Web browser, the application does not have a refresh button).

Editing a data disc

After you copy files to a CD or DVD disc using Drag to Disc, you can use those files just as you would any files saved on your computer's hard disk or disks to which you have access on a network. The biggest question in editing a backup CD or DVD created with Drag to Disc is whether the disc is of the rewritable or nonrewritable type.

Although you can theoretically edit the contents of either type of disc, keep in mind that only rewritable discs actually update the disc contents to reflect your changes. Therefore, practically speaking, the editing of a rewritable can include reformatting the disc so that you can entirely replace its contents rather piecemeal editing of its folders and files.

Displaying the properties of a data disc

Before you start editing the contents of a data disc, especially before adding new files to it, you'll probably want to get the basic statistics on the disc, including whether the disc is rewritable or nonrewritable or how much disc space is used and how much is free. The easiest way to get this information is to follow these steps:

1. **Put the backup CD or DVD disc in the appropriate computer drive.**

2. **If the Drag to Disc desktop icon is hidden beneath other open windows on the desktop, click the Roxio Drag-to-Disc icon on the taskbar's System Tray to display on top.**

3. **Click the Menu button on the Drag to Disc desktop icon and then click Disc Properties on its pop-up menu or press Alt+O (for PrOperties).**

Drag to Disc opens a Disc Properties dialog box similar to the one shown in Figure 3-7. Note in this figure that in addition to getting basic stats on the disc (including its type, total capacity, and used and free space), you can also change its volume name in it Label text box.

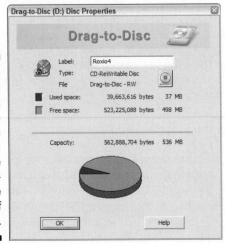

Figure 3-7:
Use the Disc Properties dialog box to ascertain the type of disc (rewritable or nonrewritable) and the amount of free space.

Displaying the contents of a data disc

The easiest way to perform routine editing operations on a data disc (such as adding, updating, or deleting files) is to open a window showing its contents and then manipulate the file icons in this window. To display the contents of a CD or DVD, make the Drag to Disc desktop icon active, click its Menu button, and click the View Disc Contents item on its pop-up menu or press Alt+V (for View).

Drag to Disc responds by opening a separate disc window showing all the folders and files that you've copied on it. Because this is a standard Windows Explorer window, you can manipulate its contents much as you would a window showing the contents of your computer's hard disk or any disk to which you have access on your network.

You can click the Details button at the bottom of the left panel of a window showing a data disc's contents to display the total capacity and free space on that disc instead of having to resort to using the Drag to Disc program's Disc Properties option to get this information.

Copying files from a data disc

After the folders and files on the data disc are displayed in its own window, you can then perform standard file operations on them such as cutting and copying their files to your computer's hard disk or disks that are available to you on your network.

To copy folders or particular files from the CD or DVD data disc to another disk on your computer system disk, open a window for its disk on your hard disk and then simply select and drag the icons for the folders or files you want to copy over to that window. To copy selected files into a particular folder on the computer disk, drop their files on the particular folder into which they're to be copied.

To cut files from the CD or DVD data disc that you can then copy onto one of your computer's disks, open a window with the data disc's files and then select their folder and file icons before you press Ctrl+X (you can also do this by selecting Edit⇔Cut on the disc window's menu bar). After cutting the files from the data disc, you can insert one of your computer's disks by making its window active and then selecting Edit⇔Paste on its menu or by pressing Ctrl+V.

If you cut folders or files from nonrewritable CD or DVD discs (see Chapter 2 for a list), their names are removed from the disc, but the space they take up on the disc is not recovered. When, however, you cut folders or files from a rewritable CD or DVD disc, the space they took up is recovered and you can reuse by copying new files in their place. After all is said and done, this ability to reuse the space from file you've cut or deleted from the disc is the essential difference between rewritable and nonrewritable CDs and DVDs.

Deleting files from a data disc

The story on deleting disc files or replacing them with newer, updated versions is pretty much the same as when cutting files from the disc. To delete files from a CD or DVD data disc, open its window, select the files' icons, and press the Delete key or choose Edit⇔Delete on the disc window's menu bar.

When you delete files from a rewritable disc, their filenames are not only removed from the disc, but the file space they occupied is recovered on the disc. When, however, you delete them from a nonrewritable disc, their filenames are removed from the disc (rendering them impossible to access) but their file space is not recovered for later reuse.

Files that you delete from a data CD or DVD are not placed in your computer's Recycle Bin. Therefore, when you press the Delete key or choose Delete on the window's Edit menu, the files are gone for good. This means that you need to be really careful to not select files that you really don't want to delete, especially if you don't have copies of the files saved elsewhere.

You can use the Drag to Disc program's Erase Disc option (Alt+E) to delete all the files on a data disc. However, keep in mind that erasing all the files does not actually remove their data from the disc. Instead, this option removes only the list of folder and filenames on it. This means that it is possible for someone to reconstruct the list and have access to some or all of the disc's contents. If the disc contains extremely sensitive data, you're much safer physically destroying the disc so that it can never be read again (you can do this most easily by peeling off the disc's label, rendering it completely unreadable).

If your goal is to reuse the disc for backing up files, you're better off reformatting the disc (see "Manually formatting a blank disc" earlier in this chapter for details) and before copying new files, provided that you're using a rewritable disc.

Replacing files on a data disc

You can replace files on a backup CD or DVD by dragging file icons with the same filenames and dropping them onto the Drag to Disc desktop icon or the CD or DVD's open window. When you do this, Microsoft Windows opens a Confirm File Replace dialog box that gives you the opportunity not to go ahead with overwriting a particular file with one of the same name by clicking the No instead of the Yes button. If do click the Yes button, Windows replaces the identically named disc file with the one you've dragged onto the Drag to Disc desktop icon or into the CD or DVD disc window.

When you replace a file on a rewritable disc, the original file is deleted and only the new replacement file takes its place. When dealing with a nonrewritable disc, however, only the name of the original file is removed from the disc so that both the data in the original and replacement file remains on the disc, taking up twice the space.

Repairing discs with ScanDisc

ScanDisc is a great little utility that's part of the Drag to Disc application. It enables you often to repair CD or DVD data discs whose files have become corrupted and somehow rendered unreadable. To start the ScanDisc utility to scan a CD or DVD data disc for errors and then, possibly try to fix them, click the Menu button on the Drag to Disc desktop program icon and then click Launch ScanDisc on its pop-up menu.

When you select the Launch ScanDisc option at the bottom of the Drag to Disc shortcut menu, the ScanDisc dialog box appears. Click the Scan button to have the program check your CD or DVD data disc for errors. The ScanDisc dialog box then changes to display its progress in checking the disc. When the utility finishes checking the entire contents of the data disc, a new dialog box showing files that have been pegged as damaged or lost (lost files are those that don't have filenames associated with them) may appear.

If you should be so lucky as to have a disc with no problems, no further dialog box appears (see Figure 3-8) and you can click the Done button to close the ScanDisc program and go on your merry way.

Figure 3-8: After scanning all the files on a CD or DVD, ScanDisc displays the status of its check as shown here.

If you do receive an indication of problems in the form of a File Recovery dialog box listing the damaged or lost files that are considered recoverable, you should take steps to copy these files to another destination on your hard disk before taking the final step of having ScanDisc try to repair the disc. That way, you'll have the data files intact even if ScanDisc can't repair the damaged disc.

To copy the recoverable or lost files (which are given sequential numerical filenames when they're copied that you can then later change), click the Yes button in the dialog box and then select the drive and folder that will serve as the place to which the damaged or lost files are copied in the Destination Drive drop-down list box.

When selecting the destination drive, you can select any local drive on your computer except for the one that contains the CD or DVD that you're scanning for errors. Also note that you're computer is part of a network; you can't copy the recoverable or lost files to any drive or folder on the network unless that drive or folder has previously been mapped as such, meaning that it's been assigned its own drive letter between A and Z (to do this, open the My Documents Window and then choose Tools⇨Map Network Drive and follow the prompts in Map Network Drive dialog box).

After designating the destination drive, you then designate the folder on that drive into which you want the recoverable files copied (do this by selecting the folder in the Destination Folder list or by clicking the New Folder button and creating a new folder). After indicating the drive and folder location, click the Copy button in the File Recovery dialog box to begin copying the files. When the copies are made, click the Done button.

After enabling you to copy and recover damaged and lost files to another location on your computer system, the ScanDisc utility prompts you to attempt to repair the damaged disc to make it usable again. Click the Yes button when the program asks you if you want to repair the disc; then click the Done button when the ScanDisc program finishes this operation (including checking the integrity of the files).

ScanDisc is not able to repair all damaged discs. You may find that even after attempting to repair a data disc, the disc is still unreadable in your computer's drive. You may also find that after repairing a disc, both Drag to Disc and Windows can no longer access the files on it. For this reason, be sure that your data disc is essentially a disc which backs up data that you also have elsewhere and from which you can generate a new backup CD or DVD.

Turning to Creator Classic for Regular Backups

Creator Classic is the application you want to turn to when you need to make CD or DVD data discs on a regular basis from particular sets of data files or when you want to make a multimedia CD or DVD disc that mixes audio, graphics (usually photos), and video files. To start Creator Classic from the Roxio

Media Creator Home, click the Creator Classic link in the Applications Project Window or on the Data tab in the Project List pane.

The Creator Classic window similar to the one shown in Figure 3-9 then appears on your screen. (Note for this particular figure, I have taken the extra steps of adding some graphics files in the Data Disc Project pane to activate its buttons and of selecting an audio file in one my folders in the Select Source pane so as to enable the Tag Editor and Edit buttons at the top of this pane as well as playback controls at the bottom.)

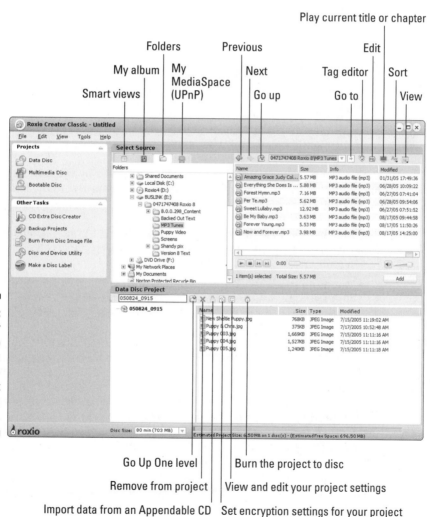

Figure 3-9:
Use Creator
Classic to
create data
disc pro-
jects that
you can
reuse.

As you can see in this figure, the Creator Classic window is divided into three areas:

- **Tasks** pane on the left side (subdivided into **Projects** and **Other Tasks**) where you indicate the type of project to create

- **Select Source** pane on the upper right where you locate the files you want to backup

- **Data Disc Project** pane on the lower right, which shows you all the files you add to the project (this pane changes name if you select a Multimedia Disc or Bootable Disc project as described in the section immediately following)

Opening a new disc project

When you first launch Creator Classic, the program is set to start a new data disc project (that is, a disc that contains only data files). If this is the kind of project that you need to make, all you need to do is start locating the files in the Select Source pane and then add them to Data Project pane.

Data disc projects are not the only ones supported by Creator Classic. In addition to the default Data Disc project, you can create the following audio projects as well:

- **Multimedia Disc** that contains audio, video, or graphics files (or a mixture of thereof) for which you want play lists to be created (see "Making a multimedia disc" later in this chapter)

- **Bootable Disc** that contains enough of the Windows operating system files to enable you to boot your computer from the CD or DVD disc (see "Making a bootable data disc" later in this chapter)

Don't get confused by all this talk about multimedia discs into thinking that your Data Disc projects can only consist of standard data file types like those that contain text, financial data, and the like. If your intention is to back up the music and video clips on a CD or DVD disc (as opposed to playing them in some sort of play list sequence on another device such as a standalone CD or DVD player), you can add any of these file types as data files to your data disc project (provided that the file type is not specifically excluded in the data disc project settings — see "Changing the Data Disc Project Settings" later in this chapter for details). Just keep in mind that the audio or video files saved to the resulting CD or DVD disc that you burn from the Data Disc project can only be accessed by computer programs such as the Windows Media Player when the disc is placed in your CD-ROM drive.

Changing the Data Disc Project Settings

When you start a new Data Disc project, Creator Classic applies certain default settings that you may want to review and possibly change before you start adding files to the project. To review and change the Data Disc Project Settings, click the View and Edit Your Project Settings button to the immediate left of the Burn button (the one farthest to the right with the flames coming out of a disc) at the top of the Project pane. The Project Properties dialog box shown in Figure 3-10 then appears with its three tabs: General, Advanced, and Exclude File Types.

Figure 3-10: Review and change the settings for your new Data Disc project in the Project Settings dialog box.

Project Settings	×

General | Advanced | Exclude File Types

Volume Name: 050824_0915

Type: Data Disc Project
File System: UDF102

Bridge: Joliet Bridge

Note: ISO-9660 is not a valid file system for encrypted or multi-disc projects

Contains: 5 Files, 0 Folders

Used Space: 6.5 MB

☑ Validate source files before recording
☐ Automatically verify File System after recording
☐ Do not split files in multi-disc projects
☐ Enable Compression

Set As Default   OK   Cancel   Help

In addition to displaying information about the type of disc and the number of files and used space currently in the project, the General tab contains the following options that you can modify:

✔ **Volume Name** to change the volume label or name of the disc

✔ **File System** to choose between three file systems: ISO9660 (for discs to be used on diverse platforms including DOS, UNIX, Macs, OS/2, and Windows), Joliet (to support the use of filenames up to 64 characters long — ISO filenames are restricted to the DOS 8.3 naming system), and UDF 102 (for optical discs such as DVDs, especially when burning files larger than 1GB)

✔ **Bridge** to choose between ISO9660 Bridge (to support the UDF and Joliet file system), Joliet Bridge (to support the Joliet, UDF, and ISO file system), and No Bridge (to support no file system other than the one currently selected)

✔ **Validate Source Files Before Recording** when you want Creator Classic to verify that none of the source files have been moved, deleted, renamed, or otherwise modified since you added them (if Creator Classic does find such a file, it prompts you to remove the file from the Disc Project)

✔ **Automatically Verify File System After Recording** to have Creator Classic compare the files burned to the CD with the original source files on your computer system

✔ **Do Not Split Files in Multi-Disc Projects** to prevent Creator Classic from splitting up files when more than one CD or DVD disc is required to accommodate all the data files you've specified to be copied to the data disc

✔ **Enable Compression** to compress the files in the data project as they are copied to the blank CD or DVD

You can't use the ISO9660 file system for any project that you intend to encrypt (see "Encrypting the data disc" later in this chapter) for any project that spans more than one disc (see "Burning a multi-disc data project" later in this chapter).

Note that if you want the modifications you make to these settings on the General tab to be new Data Disc default settings, click Set as Default button at the bottom of the this tab.

The settings on the Advanced tab of the Project Properties dialog box enable you to record various vital statistics about the disc's content such as the name of the disc's publisher and the name of the text file that contains the copyright information and to determine which date to use as the disc's publishing date. Click the Advanced tab to review and change any of these settings:

✔ **Publisher Name** to enter the name of the publisher (up to 64 characters long when using the Joliet file system and 128 when using the ISO9660 file system)

✔ **Prepared By** to enter the name of the person or company who prepared the disc (up to 64 characters long when using the Joliet file system and 128 when using the ISO9660 file system)

✔ **Use Original File Date** option button to timestamp the disc with the date that the disc project is started (this is the date shown in the combo box to the immediate right of the date options)

✔ **Use Date When Disc is Written** option button to timestamp the disc with the date when you burn the disc

✔ **Use This Date** option button to timestamp the disc with the date you select (when you click this button, the date combo box to the right becomes active and you can type in a new date or click the drop-down button and select one on the pop-up calendar that appears)

The Exclude File Types tab on the Project Properties dialog box enables you to indicate what types of data files should not be added to the disc project. Any file types that you indicate on this settings tab are automatically not copied to the Project pane even when you've inadvertently selected them for adding in the Select Source pane. When you click the Exclude tab, the Project Properties dialog box displays a list of all the individual file types you can keep out in the Add Files area. To exclude a particular type of file, simply click its check box to add a checkmark to it.

Below the Add Files area on the Exclude tab you find the following two check boxes and button:

✔ **Exclude All Hidden Files** to automatically exclude all hidden files in any group that you select in the Select Source pane

✔ **Exclude All System Files** to automatically exclude all system files in any group that you select in the Select Source pane

✔ **Select/Clear All** button that you can click to select all the file types in the Add Files area or, alternately, deselect them if they are currently all selected

When you finish changing all the settings on the Project Properties dialog box, click OK to close this dialog box and put your modifications into effect.

Titling the disc project

The first thing you may want to do after starting a new disc project is replace the temporary title that Creator Classic automatically assigns your project (that serial-number type volume label that appears in the Disc Name text box at the top of the Data Disc Project pane) with a volume label of your own. To do this, drag through the serial-number type name in the Disc Name text box to select it and then type in your replacement volume label. When naming the disc project, you need to follow the naming guidelines outlined in the steps on manually formatting a disc for use with Drag to Disc (see "Manually formatting a blank disc" earlier in this chapter).

After you type in the new volume label name in the Disc Name, this new name automatically appears to the right of the Data Project icon in the work area of the Data Disc Project pane below.

Selecting the size of the disc to use

As you add files and folders to a new data disc project, Creator Classic keeps track of the amount of free space by estimating the size of the current project in relation to the total capacity of size of disc currently shown selected at the bottom of the Creator Classic window. This relationship is displayed graphically by the length of the bar to the right of the Disc Size field as well as stated in MB or GB as Estimated Free Space immediately below this bar.

If you ultimately intend to burn your data disc project on a disc that is larger or smaller than one currently shown as the Disc Size, you need to select the correct disc size. To do this, click the currently shown disc size or the drop-down button to the right of the Disc Size field and then click the correct size in the pop-up menu. You can choose between any of the following disc sizes:

- ✔ 21 min (185MB)

- ✔ 24 min (210MB)

- ✔ 74 min (650MB)

- ✔ 80 min (703MB)

- ✔ DVD 4.7GB

- ✔ DVD 8.5GB

As soon as you choose a new disc size, Creator Classic adjusts the bar showing the estimated amount of disc space needed for the number of files added to the project. If more than one disc of the size selected is required in order to accommodate the copying of all the files in the data project, this fact will appear both on the bar and in the status area below.

Adding data files to a disc project

When adding files and folders to your disc project, you have a choice between two similar methods:

- ✔ Using the drag-and-drop method to drag selected files from the Source pane and drop them either on the Disc or Folder icon or directly in file list in the Data Disc Project pane

- ✔ Select the files in the Source pane and then click the Add button and have Creator Classic add them to the Data Disc Project pane for you

I use the first drag-and-drop method when I want to add entire folders (with all of their subfolders and files) to a project. To add an entire folder to a project, I click the Folders button in the Select Source pane and locate the folder in the Folders hierarchy displayed in its own pane in the upper left and drag its folder icon and drop it on top of the Disc icon (representing the entire data disc project) in the Data Disc Project pane.

I happen to prefer the second method using the Add button when adding groups of individual data files to a new project, regardless of whether these files are located using the Smart Views, My Albums, Folders, or My MediaSpace (UPnP) button at the top of the Select Source pane.

When you use the drag-and-drop method to add folders and files to a disc project, you don't have to be concerned about where you drop the folders and files in the Data Disc Project pane. Creator Classic automatically adjusts the list of folders and data files to display all them all in strict alphabetical order.

As you add files to the Data Disc Project pane, Creator Classic not only displays a list of their filenames but also indicates the current estimated project size and the number of discs required. It also displays the free space remaining on the latest disc both in the form of the slider that appears to the immediate right of the Disc Size drop-down list box and in MB or GB free in the Estimated Project Size directly below (see Figure 3-11). Use these stats to determine how many files you can get on a disc and how many discs you need when burning the project.

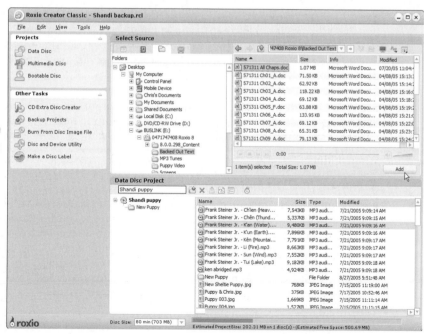

Figure 3-11: As you add data files to a project, their filenames appear in the Project pane along with the estimated project size.

If you try to add a file of a type that is on your excluded files list or that is a normally hidden file or system file that is excluded from copying, Creator Classic displays a Warning dialog box at the time you try to add it. To be able to add the file, you need to click OK to get rid of the Warning dialog box, and then click the View and Edit Your Project Settings button to open the Project Settings dialog box. There, click the Exclude File Types tab and remove the check mark from the type of file that was rejected or from the Exclude All Hidden Files or Exclude All System Files (if the file was either hidden or a system file) before you click OK. After changing the exclude file settings to include the rejected file, you should now be able to add it to the data disc project without any further incident.

Selecting the source of the files for your project

The Select Source pane (see Figure 3-9) contains four tabs: Smart Views, My Albums, Folders, and My MediaSpace (UPnP). These tabs enable you to quickly select a new source for the data files you add to a project:

- **Smart Views** shows you all the media files that Roxio Easy Media Creator 8 has identified on your computer system organized by type (photos, videos, music, and media projects)

- **My Albums** shows you all the media files that you have organized by theme into albums (which can span different disks and folders)

- **Folders** shows you all the drives, folders, and files on your computer system using the familiar Windows Explorer hierarchy of drives, folders, subfolders, and files

- **My MediaSpace (UPnP)** shows you all the media on the computers on your home network and other shared devices (such as a DVD recorder or TiVo connected to the network) to which you have access

See Chapter 4 for more information on these different types of sources, including how to use Media Manager to create and maintain Smart Views, your own albums, and your own MediaSpace using the Universal Plug n' Play standard (which is what UPnP stands for).

Removing files from your project

If you find that you've added folders or files to your data disc project in error, you can easily remove them from the project. Select their folder or filenames in the Project pane and then click the Remove from Project button at the top of the pane. Creator Classic then displays a Warning alert dialog box asking you if you're sure that you want to remove the selected file(s) from the project. To go ahead and remove the files, click the Yes button. If you're not sure that you want to remove the files, click the No button instead.

Keep in mind as well that deleting files from a data disc project only removes them from the Project pane. It does not remove them from your hard disk, so you have no worries should you delete a file from a data project in error. You can always re-add it to the Project pane from its folder on the hard disk in the Source pane.

Encrypting the data disc

If your data disc project contains sensitive data such as personnel records or corporate financial data, you can encrypt and password-protect the CD or DVD so that only those who have the password can decrypt the data and gain access to its files. Just be careful when using this encryption and password-protection feature as you must know the password exactly as you entered it in order to be able to decrypt the disc files (don't lose that password or the data is as good as gone!). Also be aware that the only way to decrypt an encrypted disc so that you can open the data files and have access to their data is by using the Roxio Retrieve utility to retrieve the files to your computer's hard disk (see "Recovering Data with Roxio Retrieve" later in this chapter).

Technically speaking, you can encrypt the files on a data disc without password protecting the disc. In such a case, anyone to whom you distribute the disc must still use Roxio Retrieve to be able to read the files, although they could do so without having to worry about a password. In my view, if the files on the data disc are sensitive enough to encrypt their data, the disc should surely be password-protected as well.

To encrypt the files for the data disc project you're building in Creator Classic, you follow these steps:

1. **Click the Set Encryption Settings for Your Project button on Project pane's toolbar (the one with the open lock that is two to the left of the Burn button at the very end of the toolbar).**

   Creator Classic then opens the Encryption dialog box similar to the one shown in Figure 3-12.

2. **Click the Enable File Encryption (128 bit) check box.**

   This turns on the file encryption that requires the use of the Roxio Retrieve utility to decrypt.

3. **To password-protect the disc, click the Password text box, and then enter a password of at least six characters.**

   In order to complete the password-protection of the disc, you must now re-enter the password in the Re-enter Password text box exactly as you originally entered it in the Password text box.

4. **Press Tab or click the Re-enter Password text box and then retype the password exactly as you originally entered it in the Password text box.**

   If you want, you can hide the display of the filenames on the data disc as well as prevent their use by any unauthorized parties by performing Step 5. If you don't perform Step 5, anyone can get a list of the filenames on the disc using the Windows explorer (or some program like it) but they still can't open any of the files without being able to correctly reproduce the password and then using Roxio Retrieve to copy the encrypted files to their computer's hard disk.

5. **(Optional) Click the Hide File Names on Disc check box to block the display of the filenames in any Windows directory listing.**

6. **Click the OK button to close the Encryption dialog box and put your encryption settings into effect.**

Making a multimedia data disc

Version 8 of Creator Classic offers a new Multimedia Disc option that enables you to create multimedia discs containing any type of mix of audio, video, and graphics files. Multimedia discs differ from regular data discs that contain these same types of media files in that these discs can be played on devices other than your computer.

In order to provide this kind of playback on devices outside the computer such as standalone CD and DVD players, a multimedia data disc conforms to one or both of the two current standard formats for music playlists and video menus: HighMAT and/or MPV (which stands for MusicPhotoVideo).

When you start a new multimedia disc project by clicking the Multimedia Disc link in the Projects pane of the Roxio Creator Classic window, the program automatically enables both these standards for the new project. To deselect either or both of these formats, click the View and Edit Your Project Settings and then select either the Enable MPV and/or the Enable HighMAT check boxes on the General tab of the Project Settings dialog box before clicking OK.

Types of media files supported in multimedia data discs

When the HighMAT and MPV formats are selected for a multimedia disc project, Creator Classic restricts the type of media files that you can add to your project. The program does this by accepting only certains types of audio, video, and graphics files as determined by the type of extension used in their filename (see Table 3-1).

Table 3-1	Types of Media Files Supported by HighMAT and MPV in Multimedia Discs		
Playlist/ Menu Type	**Audio**	**Video**	**Graphics**
HighMAT	.asf, .mp3, .wma	.asf, .wmv	.jpeg, .jpg
MPV	.aac, .ac3, .aif, .aiff, .au, .snd, .mid, .midi, .mpeg4, .mpa, mp1, .mp2, .mp3, .mp4, .m4a, .wav, .wma	.avi, .mov, .mpeg, .mpe, .mpg, .qt, .wmv	.bmp, .gif, .jfif, .jpeg, . jpg, .jpx, .pic, .pjeg, .png, .tif, .tiff

If you try to add a file to the Multimedia Disc Project pane that does not use an accepted filename extension as prescribed by the playlist and menu format(s) you've selected (such as a Word file with a .doc filename extension or a text file with a .txt extension), Creator Classic displays a Warning dialog box listing the extensions for the allowable file formats in the HighMAT and MPV standards and telling you that any file not sporting one of these filename extensions will not be added to the project. Indeed, when you click OK to close this Warning dialog box, you will find that the name of the unsupported file you tried to add has not been added to the list of filenames in the Multimedia Disc Project pane.

Adding tracks from a commercial audio CD

In addition to adding audio, video, and graphics files to your multimedia disc project (in exactly the same manner as for regular data disc projects described earlier in this chapter) already stored on your computer system, you can also add tracks from commercially-produced audio CDs (you know the ones that you purchase). The only trick to doing this is that the tracks that you want to add to the project must first be copied from the CD to one of the drives on your computer and during copying are automatically converted to the MP3 audio file format.

The steps for adding tracks from an audio CD to the multimedia disc project you're creating are as follows:

1. **Insert the audio CD containing the tracks you want to add in your computer's CD drive.**

2. **Click the Folders tab at the top of the Select Source pane and then click the icon representing your computer's CD drive.**

   When you do this, Creator Classic displays a list of the tracks on the Track View tab on the right side of the Select Source pane. If your computer has Internet access, the program will automatically connect to the Gracenote Web site and add the track names to this list. If your computer doesn't have Internet access or the audio CD is not listed in the Gracenote online database, the list on the Track View tab just shows the track numbers rather than their names.

3. **Select the track or tracks that you want included in the multimedia disc project on the Track View tab in the Select Source pane.**

   To select all the tracks, press Ctrl+A. To select a sequential group, click the first track in the group and then hold down the Shift key as you click the last one. To select nonsequential tracks, hold down the Ctrl key as you click the tracks.

   If you want to listen to a track before selecting it, click it on the Track View tab and then click the Play button (the first one with the triangle pointing to the right) in the playback controls that appear at the bottom of the Track View tab. To stop the playback, click the Stop button (the filled-in rectangle).

4. **Click the Add button or drag the selected tracks to the Multimedia Disc Project pane.**

   Note that you can add a single track by double-clicking it.

5. **Click the OK button in the Warning dialog box that appears showing you the allowable HighMAT and MPV file formats.**

   As soon as the Warning dialog box closes, the Copy Tracks from Audio CD – Options dialog box opens (see Figure 3-13). Here, you select the destination, the file type, and the compression settings to use.

   By default, Creator Classic copies the selected tracks to the folder designated as My Music on your hard disk. To change this destination, click the Browse button and select a new folder in the Select Directory dialog box and then click OK.

   By default, the program converts the selected tracks to MP3 files using constant bit rate compression and the 128 kbps (11x compression), in other words, the setting that is almost smack dab in between the smallest size and the best quality. To select a different audio file format, click the new audio type in the File Type drop-down list.

To select compression settings for better quality (and subsequently larger files), you drag the compression rate slider toward Best Quality. To select compression settings for smaller size (and subsequently lesser audio quality), you drag this slider towards Smaller Size.

6. **Change any of the default settings that need changing in the Copy Tracks from Audio CD – Options dialog box and then click its Start Copy button.**

   As soon as you click Start Copy, as Copying Audio Files dialog box showing the progress of the track copying to the destination folder.

7. **When the track copying is complete, click Close button in the Copying Audio Files dialog box.**

   As soon as the Copying Audio Files dialog box closes, the names of the copied tracks now appear in the list of files in the Multimedia Disc Project pane.

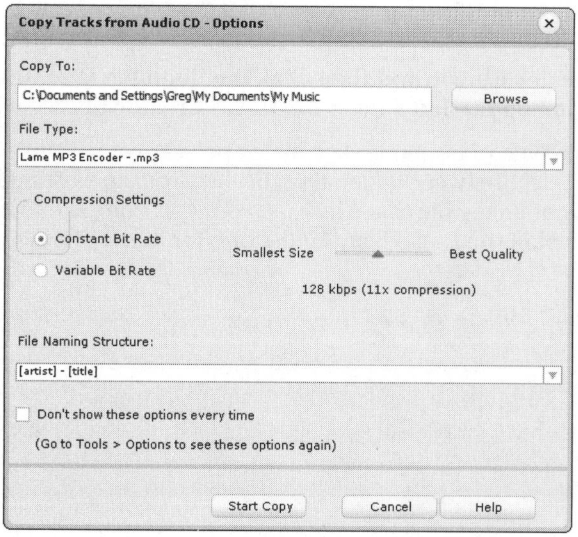

Figure 3-13:
The Copy Tracks from Audio CD – Options dialog box determines the destination, file type, and compression settings for the selected tracks.

Copy Tracks from Audio CD - Options	✕
Copy To:	
C:\Documents and Settings\Greg\My Documents\My Music	Browse
File Type:	
Lame MP3 Encoder - .mp3	▼
Compression Settings	
● Constant Bit Rate Smallest Size ▲ Best Quality	
○ Variable Bit Rate 128 kbps (11x compression)	
File Naming Structure:	
[artist] - [title]	▼
☐ Don't show these options every time	
(Go to Tools > Options to see these options again)	
Start Copy Cancel Help	

Making a bootable data disc

Creator Classic makes it possible to create a bootable CD-ROM. A bootable disc in essence emulates a 1.44 floppy disk drive (the so-called A: floppy drive that is so often missing from today's computer's, especially in laptops which are normally configured with only a CD or DVD disc drive) and that contains the Windows system files necessary to boot your computer. Such a disc enables you to boot your computer from your computer's CD or DVD drive in the event that you experience some kind of glitch with your computer's hard disk that prevents it from using its own Windows system files.

Before you can use Creator Classic to create a bootable disc, you have to ascertain that your computer system's BIOS settings support this feature. While most computers based on the Pentium-class computer chip support this feature, you may still have to check your computer documentation to learn how to access your system's BIOS settings and whether or not you have actually enabled a bootable CD-ROM option.

If your CD or DVD drive is connected to your computer via a SCSI host adapter, it may have its own BIOS. You still need to check the drive's documentation to verify that the SCSI adapter supports the bootable CD-ROM feature and, if so, how to activate it for your drive.

Assuming that your system supports the bootable CD-ROM feature and that you have activated it for your computer, you can then create a bootable CD-ROM using these steps:

1. **Place a blank CD-ROM into your computer's CD or DVD drive.**

    Make sure that this is a new CD-R disc and not one that you've burned before and then later on erased.

2. **Launch Creator Classic and then click the Bootable Disc link in the Projects pane on the left side of the Roxio Creator Classic window.**

    The Choose Type of Bootable Disc dialog box shown in Figure 3-14 opens where you select between generating the disc from an existing floppy disk or from a boot image file that's installed on your computer's hard disk when you install the Roxio Easy Media Creator 8.

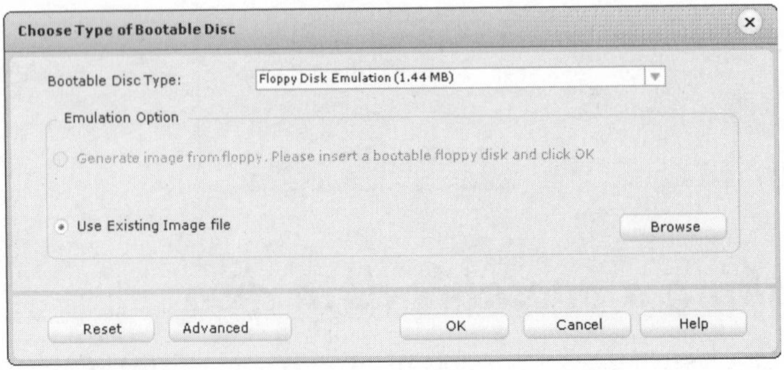

Figure 3-14:
Use the settings in the Choose Type of Bootable Disc dialog box to create a bootable CD-ROM that emulates a 1.44MB floppy disk.

3. **If you have a bootable 1.44MB floppy disk that you want used in making the bootable CD-ROM, make sure that the Floppy Disk Emulation (1.44MB) option is selected in the Bootable Disc Type field. If your**

computer has a 2.88MB floppy, select Floppy Emulation (2.88MB) option on the Bootable Disc Type drop-down list. If your computer has only a CD or DVD disc drive, select Hard Disk Emulation option from this drop-down list instead.

If you select either of the Floppy Disk Emulation options, you must insert the disk in your computer's floppy drive before you click OK in the Choose Type of Bootable Disc dialog box.

If you select the Hard Disk Emulation option but don't want to use the boot image file supplied by Roxio, click the Browse button to its immediate right of the Using Existing Image radio button and then locate and select the image file you want to use.

4. **Click the OK button at the bottom of the Choose Type of Bootable Disc dialog box to close it and have Creator Classic format your CD-ROM and copy the bootable system files to it.**

If you use one of the Floppy Disk Emulation options, an alert dialog box appears prompting you to insert the disk in your computer's A: drive. Click OK to have Creator Classic continue with preparing the disc and copying the necessary files.

After preparing and copying the system files to your CD-ROM disc, Bootable Disc Project – Untitled appears at the top of the Project pane and you can then use Creator Classic to add any additional files that you want burned onto the disc (for example, you might want to add hard disk utilities, application installers, or other backup utilities to the disc in addition to the boot image files).

If you want to access information on your computer from your bootable disc (beyond just starting up the system), be sure to add these files to your Bootable Disc Project. These include the following:

✔ mscdex.exe

✔ cdrom.sys

✔ Device drivers for your computer's CD and/or DVD drives

After burning the files you add to your Bootable Disc Project (see "Saving the disc project and burning the disc" that immediately follows for details, you need to test out your bootable CD-ROM. To do this, restart your computer while the CD-ROM is still in your CD or DVD drive (by clicking the Start button on the Windows taskbar, the Turn Off Computer item on the Start menu, and the Restart button in the Turn Off Computer dialog box). If your computer starts from the CD-ROM rather than from your computer's hard disk, your bootable CD-ROM has all the information it needs to start your system in case of any hard disk problems. Of course, this means that you have now to remove the CD-ROM from your CD or DVD drive to resume normal startup from the hard disk.

Saving the disc project

After you add all the files you want to your data, multimedia, or bootable disc project, you can save it so that you can use it at a later time to burn additional CD or DVD discs without having to go through all that creation rigmarole all over again. To save the project you're working on:

1. **Choose File⇨Save Project on the Creator Classic menu bar or press Ctrl+S.**

   The Save As Project dialog box (looking very much like any other Windows Save As dialog box) appears where you can select the drive and folder in which to save the project and the filename under which to save the project.

2. **Indicate the drive and folder where you want to save the project with the Save In combo box.**

3. **Replace Untitled in the File Name text box with the filename you want to use (just don't delete the .rcl filename extension).**

4. **Click the Save button to close the Save As dialog box and save your project settings on your hard disk.**

Note when you save the project, Creator Classic doesn't actually save the files in the project on your hard disk. This means that if you want to use the project again a later time to burn a disc, the files in the project must be in the same folders and disk locations as they were at the time you saved the project.

Burning the disc

To burn the CD or DVD by copying the files in your project, all you have to do is to put a blank CD or DVD in your computer's recording drive (depending on which type of media is designated in the Disc Size drop-down list box), and then click the Burn button on the right side of the Disc Project pane tool-bar. When you click this button, the Roxio Creator Classic – Burn Setup dialog box appears, showing you the device that will be used in burning your disc. If this is not the device that contains the blank CD or DVD and that you want used in burning your data disc project to disc, you need to click the drop-down button to the left of the current device name and select the correct drive.

Click the Save Disc Image File button and then use the Browse button to select the location and filename for the file on your computer's hard disk that is to contain a complete copy of the disc project. You can then burn this disc image file to a blank CD or DVD disc a later time using Creator Classic (keep in mind that the data files added to the project are not saved as part of this disc image file and therefore must be in the same folder and disk locations on your hard drive as they were when you created the project).

If, however, you want to change any of the default burn settings (such as the write speed or the number of copies), click the plus sign button to the immediate left of the Burn Options to expand the Burn Setup dialog box to include both General Options and Advanced Options (to display the list of Advanced Options, you must click the plus sign button in from of the Advanced Options heading). Figure 3-15 shows the Burn Setup dialog box with all the General and Advanced Options displayed.

As you can see in Figure 3-15, the General Options in this expanded version of the Roxio Creator Classic – Burn Setup dialog box enable you to select a new write speed (if your CD or DVD media support this) and increase the number of disc copies to be made and make the disc read-only so that no more data files can be added even when the disc is rewritable and has free space.

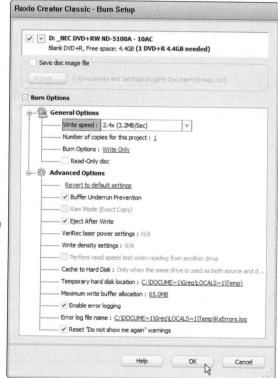

Figure 3-15:
The expanded Burn Setup dialog box showing the General and Advanced Options.

In addition, you can select, deselect, or modify any of the following Advanced Options:

- ✔ **Revert to Default Settings** link to reset all the Advanced Options back to their original settings

- ✔ **Buffer Underun Prevention** check box to enable or disable buffer prevention for your CD or DVD drive that creates a buffer in the memory to ensure that the data is recorded to the disc without any interruptions (this option is disabled for older drives that don't support this feature)

- ✔ **Raw Mode (Exact Copy)** check box to enable or disable the burning of a single-session data disc that can't be burned using normal burn settings (available only when both source and destination driver support it)

- ✔ **Eject Discs After Write** check box to ensure or prevent Creator Classic from automatically ejecting each CD or DVD disc after it finishes recording all its data files

- ✔ **VariRec Laser Power Settings** to adjust the amount of laser power to use in burning the disc (available only when using CD-R media and imposes a recording speed of 4x)

- ✔ **Write Density Settings** to increase the recording capacity by a new percentage value (available only when using CD-R media and imposes a recording speed of 4x and makes it read-only)

- ✔ **Perform Read Speed Test When Reading from Another Drive** check box to enable or disable the testing of the actual speed of the source disc and then adjusting the write speed or caching options to suit

- ✔ **Cache to Hard Disk** drop-down list box to select an option indicating when to cache data before burning

- ✔ **Temporary Hard Disk Location** link to change the locations where your project is cached

- ✔ **Maximum Write Buffer Allocation** link to change the maximum amount of memory to allocate for buffering the files being burned

- ✔ **Enable Error Logging** check box to turn on and off the creation of an error log when burning the disc

- ✔ **Error Log File Name** link to change the location and/or name of the error log file (generated when the Enable Error Logging check box is selected)

- ✔ **Reset "Do Not Show Me Again" Warnings** check box to enable or disable burn setup warnings that appear during the burn process

After adjusting all the necessary options in the Burn Setup dialog box, click the OK button to close it and begin recording your files. The Roxio Creator Classic – Progress Information dialog box (similar to the one shown in Figure 3-16) then appears. This dialog box is updated to a Disc 1 of x (where *x* is the total number of discs required to copy all the files in your disc project). The Progress Information dialog box also shows you the progress of the data recording both in terms of the tracks and overall disc progress. It also contains a Create a Label Creator button that you can click to launch the Label Creator application for creating a custom label for your CD or DVD disc(s) after the recording is completed (see Chapter 9 for details).

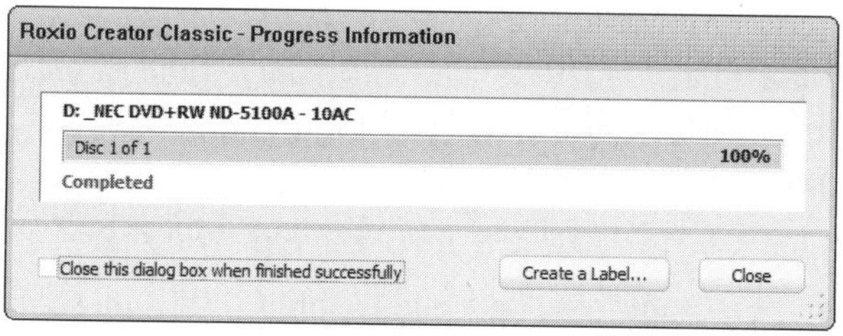

Figure 3-16:
The
Progress
Information
dialog box
keeps you
informed of
the progress
of your burn.

> **Roxio Creator Classic - Progress Information**
>
> D: _NEC DVD+RW ND-5100A - 10AC
>
> Disc 1 of 1   100%
> Completed
>
> ☐ Close this dialog box when finished successfully   Create a Label...   Close

If you don't want to make a label for your disc after the files are burned onto it, simply click the Close button to close the Roxio Creator Classic – Progress Information dialog box and return to the Creator Classic window.

If you've added more files to your disc project than can be burned on a single CD or DVD, Creator Classic indicates the number of discs required along with the total size of the project at the bottom of the Project pane. When you burn the project, Creator Classic prompts to insert a new disc in the destination drive after it finishes copying as many files as fit on the current disc. This continues until all the files are copied. Because Creator Classic can split data in a single file across more than one disc, you need to use the Roxio Retrieve utility in order to access files burned on such a multi-disc project (see "Recovering Data with Roxio Retrieve" later in this chapter for details). Just be sure to label the discs in a multi-disc project sequentially (1, 2, 3, and so on) so that you identify each disc when using this tool to recover their files.

Adding files to an existing CD or DVD disc

Provided that a rewritable CD or DVD disc you've burned still has space free for additional files and was not recorded with the Read-Only Disc option (see "Saving the disc project and burning the disc" earlier in this chapter for details), you can append files to the disc by taking the following steps:

1. **Launch Creator Classic by clicking the Creator Classic link in the Applications Project Window of the Easy Media Creator Home window.**

2. **Put CD-ROM disc to which you want append additional files in your computer's CD or DVD drive.**

   Remember that in order to add files to this CD-ROM, it must have sufficient free space and it must *not* have been originally burned as a Read-only disc.

3. **Choose File⇨New Project⇨Data Disc, Multimedia Project, or Bootable Disc.**

   Creator Classic starts a new project of the type you select.

4. **Click the Import Data from an Appendable CD button on the Project pane's toolbar (the one the third from left of the Burn button with an arrow pointing downward).**

   Creator Classic responds by importing the list of files on the CD or DVD disc in your computer's drive to which you can now add additional files.

5. **Add the other folders and files on your hard disk that you want recorded on the disc as you normally would (refer to "Adding data files to a disc project" earlier in this chapter for details).**

   If you think you might ever reuse this new project, name the project by replacing the numeric name in the Disc Name text box and then choose File⇨Save Project (Ctrl+S) on the Creator Classic menu bar.

6. **Click the Burn button at the right of the Project pane's toolbar; then select the appropriate burn options in the Roxio Creator Classic – Burn Setup dialog box (see "Saving the disc project and burning the disc" earlier in this chapter) and click its OK button.**

Note that you don't have to burn the new data disc project to the same disc. If you want to burn it to a new CD or DVD disc, replace the one from which you imported most of the data with a blank disc before you click the Burn button on the Disc Project pane's toolbar.

Getting the Lowdown on a Disc

You can use the Disc and Device Utility to get all kinds of information about the discs that you burn with Creator Classic or Drag to Disc. You can also use this utility to erase and reformat discs so that you can reuse their media for burning other data disc projects.

To launch this handy utility from Creator Classic window, click the Disc and Device Utility link in the Other Tasks pane on the left. If Creator Classic isn't running at the time you want to use the Disc and Device Utility, you can get the same type of information from within the Easy Media Creator Home window itself by clicking the Disc Information link on the Tools tab of the Project List pane.

Figure 3-17 shows Disc and Device Utility window opened from Creator Classic. When you first open this dialog box, it shows you only condensed information about the disc in your CD or DVD drive and the drive itself. To get more information on the disc, including as detailed Session and Disc properties, click the Expand button (the one with the plus sign) in front of the disc's description. To get detailed information about the drive, click its Expand button instead.

To erase or reformat the disc, click media's icon in the Disc and Device Utility dialog box and then click the Erase/Format button (this button may be grayed out and unavailable until you click the disc's icon). The Disc Erase/Format Confirmation alert dialog box then appears giving you the opportunity to choose between the Quick Erase/Format (selected by default) and the Full Erase/Format option button.

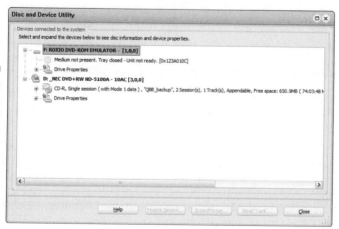

Figure 3-17:
Use the Disc
and Device
Utility to get
information
about a CD
or DVD
you've
burned.

If you want to ensure that all the data on the disc is erased before the disc is formatted, click the Full Erase/Format option button before you click the Start button. If you're not worried about a full erase and want to be able to use the disc quickly, leave the default Quick Erase/Format option button selected when you click the Start button.

Recovering Data with Roxio Retrieve

You can use the Roxio Retrieve utility to recover files from the data disc projects you burn onto multiple discs or to recover files on discs that you have encrypted (see "Encrypting the data disc" earlier in this chapter).

Unlike the data disc projects burned onto a single CD or DVD where all the files are on that disc (and which you can readily access in any standard window opened with the Windows File Explorer), the data in some of files in a multi-disc project can actually be split across more than one physical disc. Because of this, you must use the Roxio Retrieve tool in order to copy such files to your computer's hard disk or some other network disk to which you have access.

Don't try to use the Windows Explorer to access files that are split across discs in a multi-disc project. Doing so can render the files on the discs in the set unusable. Therefore, always use the Roxio Retrieve tool to restore any of the files from a multi-disc project to your computer's hard disk.

To recover files from a multi-disc project with Roxio Retrieve, follow these steps:

1. **Put whatever disc of the multi-disc set into your computer's CD or DVD drive you think contains the files you want to restore.**

   Whenever you put in a disc from a multi-disc set, Roxio Retrieve shows you all the folders and files on the disc set along with the number of the disc on which they're stored.

2. **Launch the Roxio Retrieve utility by clicking the Retrieve link under the Utilities column in the Applications Project Window of the Roxio Media Creator Home window.**

   A Roxio Retrieve window similar to the one shown in Figure 3-18 then opens. This window shows the name of the disc with its navigation tree in the pane on the left and the names of all the folders and files at the current level along with its source disc number in the pane on the right. If the disc is encrypted, you will be prompted to enter the disc's password. If the disc is part of a backup disc project (see "Creating a Backup project" earlier in this chapter for details), the Roxio Retrieve window shows the backup history in the Backup History list. You can then choose the backup history you want to use (usually the most recent one, unless you're looking for an earlier version of a file before certain editing changes were made).

Figure 3-18: Use the Roxio Retrieve utility to recover files from multi-disc projects by copying them onto your computer's hard disk.

3. **Scroll up and down the navigation tree in the left pane and through the folder and file list in the right pane until you locate the files you want to copy to your hard disk.**

   To open a folder and displays its contents, click its icon in the navigation tree to the left. To return to the previous level in the tree and display its folders and files, click the Up One Level button on Roxio Retrieve window's toolbar. Note that Roxio Retrieve indicates the location of all folders and files in the set by displaying the number of its disc in the set in the Source Disc column. When a file is split across two discs, its Source Disc information shows the numbers of both discs as is 1-2, to tell you that part of the information is on the disc 1 and part is on disc 2.

4. **Click the check box before the names of all the folders or files that you want copied to your hard disk so that each of its boxes contains a checkmark.**

   To copy all the files on the disc, click the check box in front of the disc's name in the pane on the left. Once you finish marking all the folders and files to copy, you're ready to start the copy procedure and indicate where the folders and files are to be copied.

5. **Click the Click to Copy Selected Files and Folders button on the Roxio Retrieve window's toolbar (the one the farthest to the right).**

   The Choose Destination dialog box shown in Figure 3-19 appears. By default, Roxio Retrieve selects the Alternate Destination option button to save the selected files in the directory whose path is shown below. You can accept this default directory, change it with the Browse button, or have the files copied to their original directories by selecting the Original Location(s) option button.

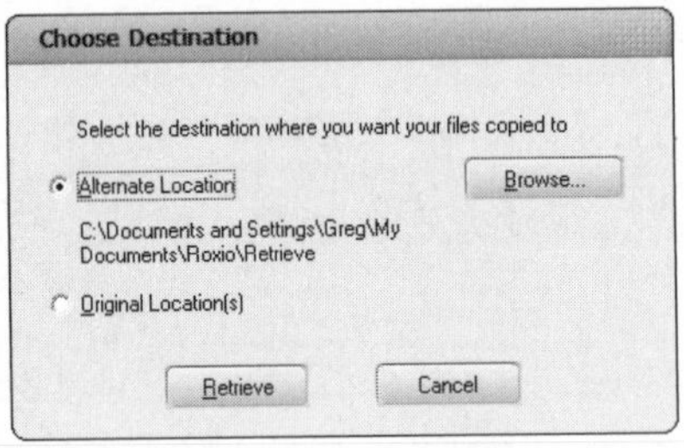

Figure 3-19:
Use the
options in
this dialog
box to tell
Roxio
Retrieve
where to
copy the
selected
files.

6. **Indicate where you want the selected folders and files copied in the Choose Destination dialog box and then click its Retrieve button.**

   As soon as you click the Retrieve button, Roxio Retrieve starts copying the selected folders and files to your designated location on your computer system. When copying a file that's not on the disc currently in your CD or DVD drive or one that's split across discs, Roxio Retrieve automatically ejects the current disc and prompts you to replace it with the number of the disc that contains the files or part of the file in question.

   When Roxio Retrieve finishes copying all of the files, the utility displays a Roxio Retrieve alert dialog box indicating that the Retrieve process has been successfully completed.

7. **Click the OK button the Roxio Retrieve alert dialog box indicating the completion of the copying operation to close it and then click the Close button in the upper-right corner of the Roxio Retrieve window to close this utility.**

Note that you can re-sort the files displayed in the right pane of the Roxio Retrieve window by clicking on their column heading. For example, to sort the files by their Source Disc number in descending order (from highest to lowest), click the Source Disc column heading once. To then re-sort the files by Source Disc number in ascending order (lowest to highest), click the Source Disc column heading a second time.

You can also use the Search for Files and Folders on the Disc Set button to locate particular files on the disc set. Simply enter the complete name of the file (including its filename extension) you want to find in the Named text box and click the Search Now button in the Search for Files and Folders dialog box that appears. Roxio Retrieve then expands the Search for Files and Folders dialog box to show you the number of the disc that contains your file.

Creating a Backup Project

The Roxio Backup application enables you to create a special Data Disc project called a Backup project. A Backup project differs from a regular Data Disc project in that you get to specify not only what files are copied to disc but how often. Backup projects are perfect for backing up files such as personnel or financial data files that require routine and regular backups as you add to and edit their contents during the course of business.

When creating a Backup project, you not only determine which files are backed up, how they are backed up, and whether or not they are encrypted, but also how often you should be prompted to use the Backup project to burn the backup discs.

To start a new Backup project, you follow these steps:

1. **In the Roxio Media Creator Home window, click the Applications link on the Home tab of the Project List, and then click the Roxio Backup link in the Applications Project Window.**

   The Roxio Backup window appears (see Figure 3-20). This window is updated to show all the Backup projects you've created in the Backup Projects pane on the right and listing the individual Backup Tasks at the top of the Tasks pane on the left.

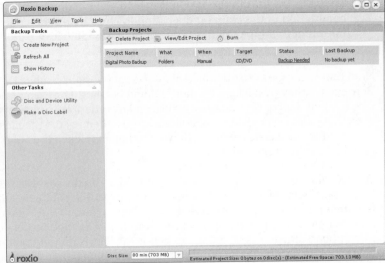

Figure 3-20:
The Roxio
Backup
window
showing all
the backup
projects
you've
already
created.

2. **Click the Create New Project link at the top of the Backup Tasks pane.**

   The first Backup Options dialog box entitled What Files to Want To Back Up opens (Figure 3-21) where you name the project and indicate what folders or types of files to include in the backup. Note that indicating which files to backup, you have a choice between selecting files by the folders in which they reside or by the type of files.

3. **Type a name for the new Backup project in the Project Name text box.**

   Note that you can't later change the project name that you enter here.

4. **To select individual folders to back up, leave the Select Folder(s) on Your Computer option button selected. To select the files to back up by their file type, click the Selected Files Based on File Types option button instead.**

   When the Select Folder(s) on Your Folder option is selected, you select the folders to back up by clicking the check box in front of their folder names.

   When the Selected Files Based on File Types option is selected, you select the types of files to include in the backup by clicking the check box in front of the category names (along with the filename extensions included) listed in the File Categories list box. To add a category of your own, click the Add button and then enter a new category name in the Category Name text box and click the check boxes in front of the various filename extensions and types in the Add Category list box before clicking the Save button.

Figure 3-21:
This Backup
Options
dialog box
enables you
to name the
project and
select the
files to be
included.

5. **Indicate what folders or file types to include in the Backup project.**

   After indicating what files to backup, you may want to designate which files not to backup with the Exclude File Types button and display an estimate of the size of the backup project using the files you've selected by clicking the Check button.

6. **Click the Next> button to display the second Backup Options dialog box entitled Where Do You Want to Back Up the Files (Figure 3-22) and indicate a disc or hard drive destination for the backup, whether to do a full or incremental backup, and, when making the backup to discs, whether or not to first erase a rewritable CD or DVD disc and to allow files to be split across discs.**

   When selecting the options for where you back up the files, you have the following choices:

   • Click the Hard Drive option button under Destinations and then click the Browse button and select the drive in the Select Backup Directory dialog box and click OK to back up the files on a drive rather than discs.

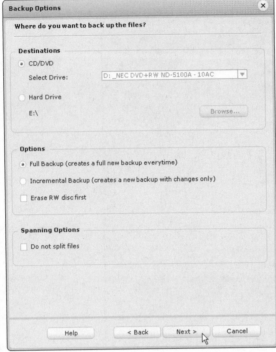

Figure 3-22:
This Backup
Options
dialog box
enables you
to indicate
the desti-
nation and
choose
between
a full and
incremental
backup.

- Click the Incremental Backup (Creates a New Backup with Changes Only) option button under Options to have only new and modified files backed up.

- Click the Erase RW Disc First check box to have Roxio Backup delete all the files on rewritable CDs or DVDs used in making the backup.

- Click the Do Not Split Files check box under Spanning Options if you don't want Roxio Backup to split files across discs so that you can then use the Windows operating system as well as Roxio Retrieve to restore the files onto your computer.

7. **Click the Next button to open the third Backup Options dialog box entitled When Do You Want to Start the Backup (see Figure 3-23) where you choose between a manual and automatic backup, and in the case of an automatic backup, indicate the backup interval, start time, and how soon before the start time to be reminded.**

    - Click the Automatic Backup options button under Method to have the Roxio Backup program make backups on a regular basis (if you leave the default Manual Backup option button selected, it's up to you to remember to launch the Roxio Backup program and use this backup project to backup your files).

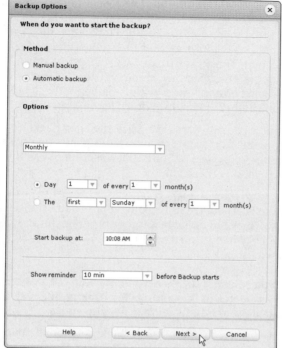

Figure 3-23:
This Backup
Options
dialog box
enables you
to determine
whether the
backup is
manual or
automatic.

- To change the interval from weekly when doing an automatic backup, click the Weekly drop-down list button and then select Daily or Monthly on the drop-down list.

- To have the program make a backup every other week when using the Weekly interval, replace 1 in the Recur Every text box with 2 or every third week, with 3.

- To change the day of the week from Sunday when using the Weekly interval, click the name (Monday through Saturday) of its check box.

- To change to every other day when using the Daily interval, replace the 1 in the Every text box with 2 or to every third day, with 3 (and so on).

- To have the program only make daily backups on work days when using the Daily interval, click the Every Weekday (Monday Through Friday) option button.

- To change the day of the month from the first day when using the Monthly interval, replace the 1 in the Day drop-down list box with the appropriate value (between 2 and 31).

- To change the monthly interval, select the appropriate value (between 2 and 12) in the Month drop-down list box.

- To make monthly backups on a particular day of a monthly interval (such as the second Saturday of every other month), select the option button in front of the settings indicating the first Sunday of every month as the interval and then adjust the ordinal of the day (First, Second, Third, Fourth, or Last) in its drop-down list box, the day of the week (Sunday, Monday, Tuesday, and so on) in its drop-down list box, followed by the number of the monthly interval (between 2 and 12) in its drop-down list box.

- To set a new backup start time, click the Start Backup At text box and then enter a new start time by entering the number of the hour and minutes, along the AM or PM designation or use the spinner buttons to modify these values.

- To have Roxio Backup display a reminder sometime before the time the backup is scheduled to begin (giving advance notice you can use to save work you're doing in another program, for example), select the number of minutes (between 5 and 45) in the Show Reminder drop-down list box.

8. **(Optional) If you selected the Automatic Backup options button, make any necessary changes to the settings for backup interval, backup start time, and show reminder before backup starts.**

9. **Click the Next> button to open fourth Backup Options dialog box entitled How Do You Want to Back Up the Files (see Figure 3-24) where you indicate whether or not to compress and encrypt the files and to have the program verify the source files before making the backup and the destination after making it.**

   By default, Roxio Backup neither compresses nor encrypts the files. To save disc space, click the Compression check box. To encrypt the files, click the Enable File Encryption (128-bit) check box, and then type a password in the Password text box and re-type it exactly in the Re-enter Password text box.

   Remember that if you encrypt the disc with a password, you must be able to produce the password exactly as you assigned it or you have no access to the disc and can just kiss the data goodbye.

   Roxio Backup also automatically validates all the source files before actually backing them up on disc (or to a new hard drive, if you're using that option). To forgo this step, click the Validate Source Files Before Backing Up check box to remove its checkmark. If you want the program to verify the files after making the backup, click the Verify Destination After Backing Up check box.

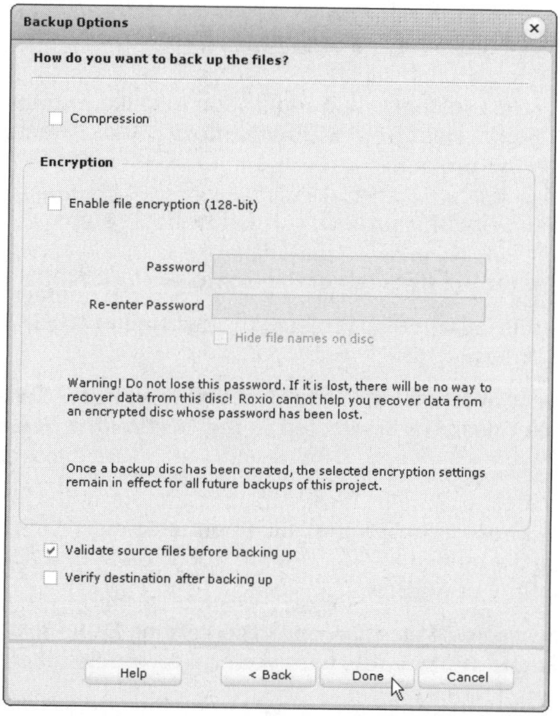

Figure 3-24:
This Backup
Options
dialog box
enables you
to determine
whether or
not to com-
press and
encrypt the
backup files.

10. **Click the Done button to save your Backup project and return to the Roxio Backup window.**

When you return to the Roxio Backup window, the Backup Projects pane now lists your new Backup project. This list includes the project name, type of project, and the status of the project, that is, whether or not the backup is needed (it is always needed when you first create the project).

To burn a Backup project listed in the Backup Projects pane, make sure that it's selected and then click the Burn button at the top of this pane. If you need to review or make changes to a particular Backup project, select the project in this pane and then click the View and Edit the Selected Backup Project's Settings button on the Backup Projects toolbar (the button to the immediate left of the Burn button). If you want to delete a particular Backup project instead, click the Delete the Selected Backup Project (the one with the red X at the beginning of the Backup Projects toolbar).

Creating a Data Disc Project

Instead of launching the Creator Classic application to make your disc backups, you can create data discs right from within the Roxio Media Creator Home using the new Data Disc project.

To create a data disc using this project, you follow these steps:

1. **Click Data Disc on the Data tab of the Roxio Media Creator Home.**

   When you do this, a Data Disc Project Window similar to the one shown in Figure 3-25 opens.

2. **Insert a blank or appendable CD or DVD disc in your CD/DVD drive and make sure that this drive is selected in the Destination Selection pane.**

   Remember that an appendable disc is one that is not write-protected and one that, although it contains files, still has room for more. To display a list of the files already copied onto an appendable disc, click the Load Disc button to the immediate right of the Add Data button at the top of the Data Disc Project window.

3. **To change the name of the disc, click the Volume Label text in its drop down list box and replace this with your own volume label.**

   Now you are ready to designate the data to include on the disc. You have a choice between adding individual files and folders that you select, and adding files of a particular type that Roxio selects:

   - To select files, click the Add Data button and then click Add Files on its pop-up menu to open the Add Files dialog box, and then select the drive and folder containing the files you want to add in the Look In drop down list box and select their filenames or icons before clicking the Add Files button.

   - To select folders, click the Add Data button and then click Add Folders on its pop-up menu to open the Browse For Folder dialog box where you select the name and icon of the folder to add in the hierarchy showing all the components of your computer system.

   - To have Roxio select files of a certain type, click the Quick Scan button to open the Quick Scan pane (see Figure 3-25), and then click the check box in front of all the types of data you want added. To see what filename extensions are included in any of the various categories, position the mouse pointer over the category name.

   - To change the source folder from My Documents, click the My Documents drop-down button and then click Browse in the pop-up menu. Roxio then opens a Browse For Folder dialog box where you select the new folder to scan before clicking OK.

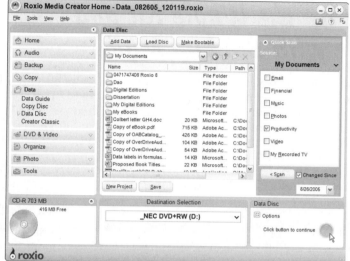

Figure 3-25:
The Data
Disc Project
Window
enables you
to create a
data disc in
the Roxio
Media
Creator
Home.

- To include only files that have changed since a certain date, click the Changed Since check box and then click the drop-down arrow that appears to the right of the text with the current date. Roxio opens a mini calendar from which you can select the cut-off date for the files of the type(s) you've selected.

After designating the file types, their source, and optionally their cut-off dates, click the Scan button to have Roxio scanned the designated source folder for all files meeting your criteria. These names of these files are automatically added to Data Disc list.

4. **Designate all the folders and files you want included in the Data Disc project.**

5. **(Optional) To save the Data Disc project so that later on you can burn other discs using its file list, click the Save button to open the Save As dialog box and then select the folder and enter the filename for the data disc project (just be sure not to delete the .roxio filename extension) before clicking the Save button.**

6. **Click red button marked Click Button to Continue in the Action panel of the Control pane to begin burning your data disc.**

As Roxio burns your new disc, Project Running with stats on the burning appears in the Project Window and a progress bar appears in the Input panel (which is now labeled Progress).

7. **When the burn is completed and the last disc is ejected from your CD or DVD drive, click the Label Disc button that now appears in the Project Window to launch the Roxio Label Creator (see Chapter 8) or click the Done button to return to the Data Disc Project Window.**

Backing Up the Whole Kit and Kaboodle with Backup MyPC

Backup MyPC is a new utility in the Roxio Media Creator 8 suite that enables you to backup your entire computer system either onto CD or DVD discs or onto a removable drive you have connected to it. That way, should you ever experience a hardware failure of your computer's hard drive, you can easily restore the programs and data files you had on it.

The Backup MyPC window (launched by clicking the Backup MyPC link in the Applications Project Window in the Roxio Creator 8 Home window and shown in Figure 3-26) contains the four options:

- ✔ **Backup Wizard** to backup all the files and folders on all the local drives on your computer or just selected files, folders, and drives onto CD or DVD discs or onto a removable drive

- ✔ **Restore Wizard** to restore files and folders on the local drives of your computer from either from a set of CD or DVD discs or from a removable drive

- ✔ **Automatic Data Protection** to set up a schedule for regular backups of the files and folders on your computer

- ✔ **Disaster Recovery Preparation** to create a Disaster Recovery Set of discs that you can use to restore your computer in the event of a crash and hardware failure of your computer's hard disk

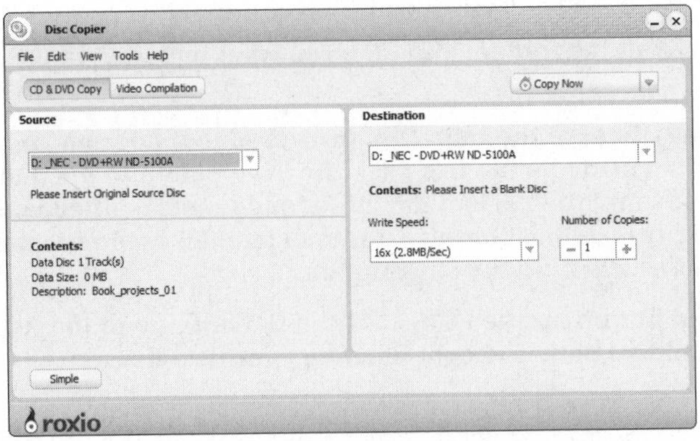

Figure 3-26:
Backup
MyPC
enables you
to backup
your entire
computer
system on
disc or on a
removable
drive.

If you're using a laptop computer that you routinely take out into the field, I highly recommend that you use the Disaster Recovery Preparation link in Backup MyPC to create a Disaster Recovery Set for its hard disk. I know from experience how easy it is for a laptop's hard disk to fail and how long and painful a process it is to re-install all of its software!

Disc Copies in a Jiffy

The Roxio Disc Copier enables you to make duplicates of any noncopy-protected CD or DVD even if your computer system has only a single CD or DVD drive. This nifty application is especially useful when you need to make additional copies of CD or DVD discs that you burned either with Drag to Disc or Creator Classic.

To make a disc copy with Disc Copier, you follow these easy steps:

1. **Put the CD or DVD disc which you want copied in your computer's CD or DVD drive.**

   Now you're ready to launch the Roxio Disc Copier application.

2. **Click Applications on the Home tab of the Roxio Media Creator Home, and then click the Disc Copier link in the Applications Project Window.**

   The Roxio Disc Copier alert dialog box then appears warning you that unless you own the copyright or have the explicit permission of the copyright holder to copy the disc, you may be violating the Copyright law and be subject to legal penalties (such as fines and even perhaps damages). As soon as you click the OK button to close this alert dialog box, the Roxio Disc Copier window appears. This window is divided into a Source pane on the left and a Destination pane on the right.

3. **Click the Advanced button to expand the Roxio Disc Copier window to show information on the disc you want to copy and source and destination drive.**

   An expanded version of Roxio Disc Copier window similar to the one shown in Figure 3-27 then appears. This version shows the type of disc to be copied as well as the recorder and write speed and enables you to change these settings as well as to increase the number of copies to make.

4. **(Optional) If your computer has more than a disc drive (such as a CD-ROM and a DVD recorder), select the drive with the disc you want to copy on the Drive drop-down list in the Source pane and the drive that contains the blank disc to which the files are to be copied on the Recorder drop-down list in the Destination pane.**

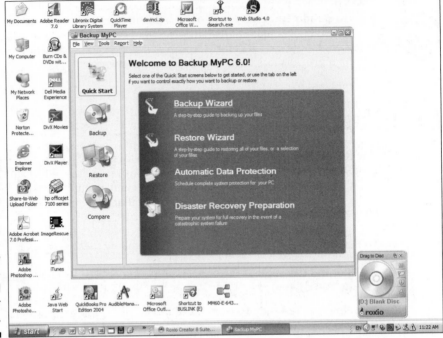

Figure 3-27:
Use the
Roxio Disc
Copier to
make dupli-
cates of any
noncopy-
protected
CD or
DVD disc.

5. Click Copy Now button to begin the disc copy operation.

The Roxio Disc Copier – Progress Information dialog box then appears, keeping you apprised of the copy operation by displaying Finished and Disc Progress sliders showing you the percentage completed and the elapsed time.

If your computer has only one CD or DVD drive which acts both as the source and destination, after copying all the disc files to a temporary location on your hard disk, the Roxio Disc Copier automatically ejects the disc you're copying and displays a message that prompts you to replace the ejected disc with a blank disc of the same media type. After you click OK, Select Write Speed dialog box may appear, enabling you to select a new write speed for the disc copy (to use the same write speed, simply click the Continue Recording button in this dialog box). When Completed appears under the progress bar that has now reached 100% in Roxio Disc Copier – Progress Information dialog box, the program ejects the copied disc and you can then either launch the Label Creator application to design and print a label for the newly copied disc (see Chapter 9) or close the Roxio Disc Copier application.

6. **To create a label for the disc copy, click the Create a Label button. To close the Roxio Disc Copier – Progress Information dialog box and return to the Roxio Disc Copier window, click the Close button instead.**

If you don't choose to make a label for your new disc copy, you can then close the Roxio Disc Copier application by clicking its Close button in the upper-right corner of the window.

Making and Burning Disc Image Files

The files that you add to the data disc projects you create in Roxio Creator Classic or as Data Disc project in Roxio Media Creator Home can be converted into a single file called a *disc image*. You can then use this single image file to burn copies of all the data files on CDs or DVDs.

Roxio Easy Media Creator supports two types disc image file formats: the Global-Image (with the file extension .gi) and the ISO Image (with the file extension .iso) formats. Image files using the Global-Image format save the contents of the data files along with additional information such as their folder structure and their read and write properties. The ISO Image format, however, is more universal than the Global-Image (despite the name) so that you would want to use this format for your disc image file if you intend to create CD and DVD discs from the file that will be used on computer systems that don't run the Roxio Easy Media Creator suite.

Using disc image files in Roxio Creator Classic

To create a disc image file from the data project that you've created in Creator Classic, you click Save Disc Image File check box in the Roxio Creator Classic – Burn Setup dialog box opened when you click the Burn the Project to Disc button in the Data Disc Project pane. Doing this activates the Browse button, which you may then click to specify the location, name, and type of disc image file to create in the Save As dialog box before you click the Save button. Then, when you return to the Roxio Creator Classic – Burn Setup dialog box, you click the Cancel button to return to the Roxio Creator Classic window.

To burn a CD or DVD disc set from a disc image file in Roxio Creator Classic, you click the Burn From Disc Image File link in the Other Tasks pane of its program window. Then you select the disc image file in the Burn from Disc Image File dialog box before clicking the Open button.

Using disc image files in Data Projects in Roxio Media Creator Home

To create a disc image file from a data project that you've created in the Roxio Media Creator Home, you click the drop-down list button in the Input Panel (with the heading, Destination Selection), and then click Browse on the drop-down list to open the Select the Destination Drive or Folder dialog box. Here, you specify the location, name, and type of disc image file to create before you click the Save button.

When selecting the type of disc image file to create from the Save as Type drop-down list box in the Select the Destination Drive or Folder dialog box, be sure to select not only the desired format (Global-Image or ISO Image) but also the type of disc (CD or DVD) that matches the kind of disc you intend to use when you do burn the data project. Keep in mind that you cannot burn a DVD disc from a CD image file just as you cannot burn a CD disc from a DVD image file. Therefore, to create a disc image file using the Global-Image format from which you intend to burn CDs, you select CD Global-Image (*.gi) on the Save as Type drop-down list. To create an image file for CDs using the ISO Image format, you select CD ISO Image (*.iso) instead. To create an image file using the Global-Image format for burning on DVDs, you select DVD Global-Image (*.gi). To create an image file for DVDs using the ISO Image format, you select DVD ISO Image (*.iso) on the Save as Type drop-down list in its place.

To burn a CD or DVD disc set from a disc image file that you create in the Roxio Media Creator Home window, click the Burn Image link on the Copy tab of the Project List. Then click the Browse button that appears in the Burn to Disc Project Window and select the image file in the Select Image dialog box before you click the Add button. Finally, click the red button in the Action panel of the Control pane entitled Click Button to Continue.

Using disc image files in Disc Copier

To create a disc image file from a CD or DVD in the Disc Copier application, you select Disc Image in the Destination drop-down list box and then specify the location, filename, and type of disc image file in the Save As dialog box before clicking the Save button.

To burn copies of a CD or DVD disc set from a disc image file in Disc Copier, you click the Source drop-down button and then click Browse for Disc Image/ DVD-Video Folder to open the Media Selector dialog box where you select the disc image file to use before clicking OK.

Chapter 4

Organizing Your Media Files

· ·

· ·

*M*edia Manager is the place to go when you need to organize or find the various types of media files used in the creation of the various projects you build with the Roxio Creator 8 Suite. These media files include photos, video clips, audio files, music tracks as well as the actual Roxio project files themselves.

This chapter gives you the lowdown on using Media Manager to keep tabs on the many types of files even when they're saved on widely divergent locations on computer system. As you find out, you can use Media Manager both to organize and quickly find and review all the different media files stored on various drives and on media (including CDs and DVDs) throughout your computer system.

This chapter also covers using Media Manager to make it possible to quickly locate particular types of media files by enabling you to assign keywords to them that you can then use in the searches you conduct for media files of a particular kind (you can even create media file collections based on your search results). Last but not least, you get vital information on using Media Manager to make backup copies of all your media files by burning them to CDs or DVDs (which then enables you to free up much needed space on your hard disk).

Making the Most of Media Manager

To launch Media Manager from the Roxio Creator 8 Home window, you click the Organize link on the Organize tab of the Project List or you can click the Media Manager link in the Applications Project Window after clicking the Applications link on the Home tab.

Either way you go about it, when you launch Media Manager, a window very similar to the one shown in Figure 4-1 opens. This window contains a Browse area that is divided into two sections: a navigation pane on the left in which you select a media view and a contents pane on the right in which all the media files and folders for the currently selected view are displayed.

When you first open Media Manager, the All Photos view on the My Media tab is selected, showing you all the graphics files that Media Manager has automatically identified and classified according to their graphics file type and any keywords that you've assigned.

To switch to any other of the other three views — My Albums, Folders, or My MediaSpace (UPnP) — you click their tab buttons at the top of the navigation pane.

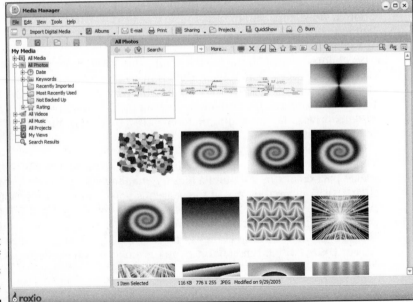

Figure 4-1:
Use the
Media
Manager to
keep track
of and
organize all
the different
types of
media files
you use.

Meandering through My Media

Roxio Creator 8 uses its new *smart views* feature to automatically catalog all the media files on designated folders on your computer system into different categories, including photos, videos, music, and Roxio Creator projects. When you first select the My Media tab of the Media Manager navigation pane, the All Photos category is selected. To display all the media files identified on your system, you click the All Media link at the top of the navigation pane. This mega category includes every media file identified on your computer system arranged alphabetically by name.

Most of the time, you will find it much easier to locate a particular media file by selecting the appropriate media category by clicking its icon (All Photos, All Videos, All Music, or All Projects) on the My Media tab than by perusing the All Media category (which can contain literally thousands of entries).

In addition to these automatically maintained media categories, you can also create your own smart views from the results from a media search that you perform in Media Manager (see "Finding Wayward Media Files" later in this chapter). These custom smart views are then added to the My Views category near the bottom of the My Media navigation pane.

Each of the different categories listed on My Media enables you to filter their files by selecting from a number of different criteria, such as the date they were created, imported, last used, or backed up. In addition to date-related filtering criteria, you can filter the files by ratings that have been assigned to the files as well as media-specific criteria such as the genre, artist, and album in the case of music files, video file types in the case of video files, and application-specific projects in the case of media projects.

To filter the files in a media category, click the the expand button (the one with a plus sign in front of its name) and then click the desired criteria. Some criteria such as Date have their own expand button that, when clicked, display their own filtering categories. Figure 4-2 shows the Media Manager window after expanding the Date filter in the All Photos category and selecting the Last Week filter. Also note in this figure that I have also expanded the 2005 filter to display the individual months that I added photos to my computer system. So, for example, to display all the photos that I added in the merry, merry month of May, all I have to do is click the May filter icon on the My Media tab.

As soon as you select the type of media and filter the category as desired, the contents pane of the Media Manager shows you thumbnails of all the media files that meet your criteria. In the case of photos, the thumbnails show a small version of the actual image. In the case of videos, the thumbnails show either the first frame of the video. In the case of music and Roxio Media projects, the thumbnails show a generic audio and project file icon.

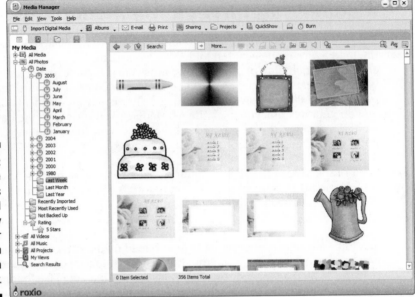

Figure 4-2:
Viewing the
graphics
files that I
added to my
computer
last week in
the Media
Manager.

 Drag the Thumbnail Slider (located on the Options bar at the top of the contents pane) to the left to reduce the size of the media file thumbnails so that as many files as possible can be displayed together in the Media Manager window.

To get information on a particular media file that's displayed in the contents pane of the Media Manager window, position the mouse over its thumbnail or file icon. A tooltip then appears at the mouse pointer giving you scads of information about the selected media file.

If this info in this tooltip is not sufficient for you to identify a particular photo, audio, or video file, you can preview it. Simply double-click its thumbnail or file icon in the contents pane or click the thumbnail or file icon and then click the Preview Selected Item(s) button on the Option bar at the top.

When you preview a photo, Media Manager displays it in its own Preview window (see Figure 4-3). This Preview window contains buttons that you can use to do simple editing tasks such as cropping and rotating the image. If these simple edits are not enough, you can open the photo in the PhotoSuite 8 application by clicking the Edit button.

When you preview an audio file, it opens in a Preview window that contains standard playback controls along with an Edit button (just like the one identified in Figure 4-3). If you find that you need to edit the start or end points of the audio file after playing it in this Preview window or that you need to add a simple fade-in or fade-out effect to it, click the Edit button to open the audio file in a Quick Sound Editor window.

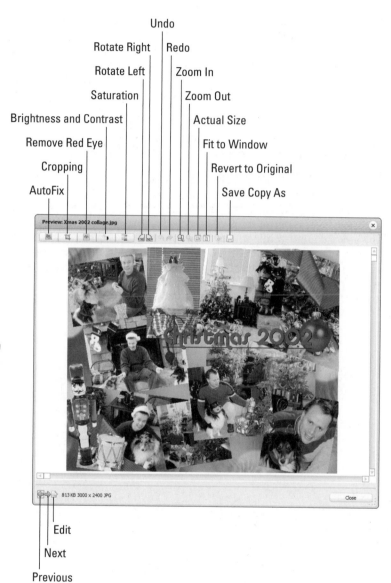

Undo

Rotate Right | Redo

Rotate Left | Zoom In

Saturation | Zoom Out

Brightness and Contrast | Actual Size

Remove Red Eye | Fit to Window

Cropping | Revert to Original

AutoFix | Save Copy As

Figure 4-3:
Previewing
a photo
displayed in
the contents
pane of the
Media
Manager
window.

Edit

Next

Previous

If you try to edit an audio file for which you don't have a license for editing (usually because it's a track that you didn't purchase as a commercially produced CD or from an online music service), an error message dialog box opens to inform you that you don't have the editing rights for the music file after clicking the Edit button. After you click the OK button to clear this Message dialog box, the Quick Sound Editor window opens sans the song you wanted to edit.

When you preview a video file, the Media Manager plays the video in a separate Preview window that contains a set of playback controls along with an Extract Image, Set as Thumbnail, and Edit button. If you need to edit the contents of the video file such as trimming the video by setting new start and end points, you can open the video file up in a VideoWave 8 window by clicking this Edit button.

Ambling through My Albums

When you click the My Albums tab button (the one with the picture of tiny blue album book with the Roxio icon on it) in the navigation pane of the Media Manager window, the My Media pane changes to the My Albums (see Figure 4-4). The My Albums pane enables you to browse the contents of all the special media collections files (referred to as *albums*) on your computer system (see "Creating Your Own Albums" later in this chapter for details on creating collections), search for items within your collections and assign keywords, comments, and sounds to media files in collection to make them easier to search.

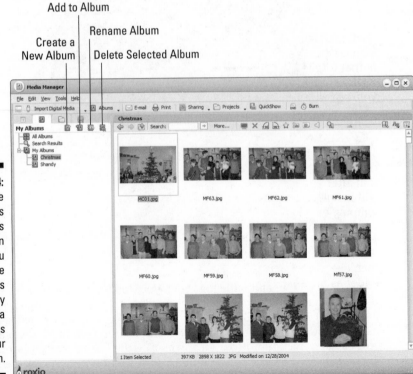

Figure 4-4: Using the My Albums tab's navigation tree, you can explore the contents of any media collections file on your system.

When you select the My Albums tab, the following buttons appear at the top:

- ✔ **Create New Album** to start a new album to which you can add media files

- ✔ **Add to Album** to add new media files to new and existing albums

- ✔ **Rename Album** to change the name of the album selected on the My Albums tab

- ✔ **Delete Selected Album** to remove the album selected on the My Albums tab (note that deleting an album does not affect the media files in any way — they remain safe and sound in their respective folders after removing any of the albums to which they have been assigned

Finding your way around your folders

The Folders navigation pane in the Media Manager window enables you to explore your media files using the folders on your computer's hard disk, removable media in your computer's CD and DVD drives, as well as the other drives on your network to which you have access. To display the media contents of a particular drive or folder on your system, click the Expand button (the one with the Plus sign) in front the Desktop, My Computer, My Documents, or My Network Places system folder icons to display the drives and folders they contain. Then, to display the contents of a drive or folder contained within one of these system folders, click its drive or folder. Media Manager responds by displaying all the folders and files on that drive or in that folder in the Contents pane on the right. You can continue in this manner, expanding folders within folders to peruse their files and reacquaint yourself with the folders on your drives and their hierarchical relationship.

Figure 4-5 shows you the Media Manager after I expanded the My Documents system folder on my hard disk and then expanded the My Pictures folder and selected the Crater Lake 6-05 folder. Media Manager responds by displaying thumbnails of all the digital photos in this folder in the Contents pane. Note that after you use the Folders navigation tree to descend several levels deep within a particular drive or system folder, you can then ascend the tree, jumping back one level at a time by clicking the Up One Level button until you reach the very top of the tree (the Desktop in this case).

After you select a folder you want to explore in the navigation pane, you can then use the following buttons at the top of Folders tab to manipulate the folder as follows:

- ✔ **Create a New Folder** to create a new subfolder within the current folder that you can name

- ✔ **Rename Selected Folder** to select the name of the currently selected folder so that you can replace it with a new folder name

- ✔ **Delete Selected Folder** to delete the current folder and everything within it (be careful with this button)

Rename Selected Folder

Create a New Folder | Delete Selected Folder

Figure 4-5:
Using the
Folders
navigation
tree, you
can explore
the contents
of any part
of your
computer
system.

Keep in mind that you can use the options on the View As drop-down list to change how media files are displayed in the contents pane

Moseying through My MediaSpace

Media Manager enables you to view media files located other computers and media devices connected to a home network provided that you have access to these computers and that the devices support the recent Universal Plug and Play technology (UPnP for short). To view these media files, you click the MyMediaSpace (UPnP) tab at the top of the Media Manager's navigation pane.

The first time you click the MyMediaSpace (UPnP) tab, the Enable My MediaSpace (UPnP) Browsing dialog appears (although an alert dialog box asking you if you want to unblock this program may come up first if your system is on a network and protected by a firewall). In a nutshell, the rather longwinded text of this dialog box is telling you that in order to browse digital content from other computers and devices on your home network, these machines must have Universal Plug and Play technology enabled and, in the case of computers, have authorized the sharing of this digital content.

In order to turn on UPnP sharing to share smart views or albums on your computer with other computers on your network, you launch Media Manager and then choose Tools⇨Start Sharing with MediaSpace(UPnP) on the Media Manager menu bar.

To manage the sharing, you choose Tool⇨Manage My MediaSpace(UpnP) on the Media Manager menu bar. Doing this opens the Manage My Media-Space(UPnP) dialog box that contains the following options for choosing the devices with which you want to share your media files as well as the albums you want to share:

- ✔ **Start Sharing/Stop Sharing:** Click this button to start or stop sharing your media files with other devices on your home network.

- ✔ **Disabled/Enabled:** Click this button to turn on or off sharing with the selected devices.

- ✔ **All My Albums to All Enabled Devices:** Click this button to share all your albums with all enabled devices.

- ✔ **Selected Collections to Selected Devices:** Click this button to share only certain albums with certain devices. When you click this button, you can use the following buttons to manage which albums to share with what devices:

  - • **Add** to add the Smart Views or albums to the list of Smart Views and albums that are being shared

  - • **Delete** to remove a Smart View or album from the list of Smart Views and albums that are being shared

  - • **Devices with Access To** to grant access to only the devices that you select by clicking the check boxes in front of their names

After you select the albums to share in the Manage My MediaSpace(UPnP) dialog box, you can then peruse their media by selecting their albums on My MediaSpace(UPnP) tab just as you would select albums on your own computer system on the My Albums tab. When you select an album on the My MediaSpace(UPnP), Media Manager shows you thumbnails or file icons for all the digital media it contains in the contents pane on the right.

You're being watched!

The first time you launch Media Manager, the program displays a dialog box informing you that your default watched folders (My Documents and the Desktop) are about to be scanned for the first and that this scanning proce-dure may take a few minutes (see Figure 4-6). To have Media Manager pro-ceed and scan the default folders for all of its media files, click the Close button in this dialog box.

Welcome to Media Manager   ✕

Your default Watched Folders (My Documents and Desktop) are being scanned for the first time.
This may take a few minutes as this is the first time you have run Media Manager. Thank you for
your patience.

If you would like to change your default Watched Folders, click Watched Folder Settings below.

> Watched Folder Settings   Close

If you have other folders on your computer that contain media files that you want to add to the watched folders list, follow these steps instead:

1. **Click the Watched Folder Settings button in the Welcome to Media Manager dialog box.**

   Media Manager opens the Watched Folder Settings dialog box (similar to the one shown in Figure 4-7) where you specify which folders on your computer system are to be watched. Note that you can also open this dialog box anytime after this by choosing Tools⇨Select Watched Folders on the Media Manager menu bar.

   In this dialog box, all Watched Folders (including all of its subfolders) are indicated by green boxes that contain check marks. All folders (including subfolders) that are not currently watched are indicated with red boxes that contain Xs.

2. **Click the red box in front of any drive or folder that you want added to the Watch list.**

   As soon as you click the red box, it turns to green and the X becomes a check mark, indicating that it is now added to the Watch list. Note that if you add a drive to this list, all its folders and subfolders are automatically added as well.

   By default, the Show Folder Watching Icon in System check box is selected meaning that a Folder Watching icon appears in the Systems Tray on the right side of the Windows taskbar that you can click to open the Watched Folder Settings dialog box and change which folders are watched.

3. **(Optional) Click the Show Folder Watching Icon in System check box to remove its check mark if you don't want a Watched Folders icon added to the System Tray on your taskbar.**

   By default, the Show Notifications check box is not selected. Select this check box when you want notification message dialog boxes to appear anytime you change the watched folder settings or some other change that affects a watched folder takes place.

4. **(Optional) Click the Show Notifications check box to be notified when changes occur to folders on your Watched list.**

   By default, the Filter Small Files check box is selected so that all media files added to the Smart Views in the folders on the Watched list are filterable, regardless of how small they are. Click this dialog box if you don't want to include small files when filtering Smart Views by media.

5. **(Optional) Click the Filter Small Files check box to remove it check mark if you don't want to have small files filtered.**

6. **Click the OK button to close the Watched Folder Settings dialog box and return to the Media Manager.**

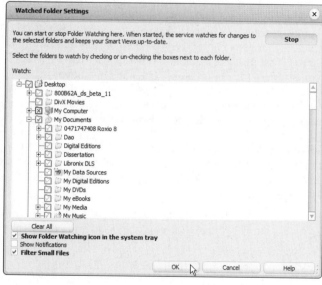

Figure 4-7:
Use the settings in this folder to determine which folders are watched for changes in keeping your Smart Views current.

When you click OK, Media Manager scans all the folders on your Watched list for all the designated file types and adds them to the appropriate Smart View on the My Media tab of the Media Manager.

Media files in folders on your Watched list will go missing if you rename, delete, or move them to another folder using the Windows operating system or some other Windows program. If you try to access a missing file in the Media Manager, the Cannot Find Required Files dialog box appears. If the files in question have been deleted, you must use the Skip button. If you have moved them, you must use the Browse button and then locate their new folders. If you have renamed them, you must use the Locate File button and then select the renamed file before you click Connect.

Instant movies, slideshows, and playlists thanks to QuickShow

You can use the QuickShow link on the Media Manager Task Bar to make a selection of video clips into a quick-and-dirty movie, photo images into an off-the-cuff slideshow, or audio files into a spur-of-the-moment track playlist. All you have to do is open a Smart View, album, or folder that contains a bunch of the same type of media files (video, graphic, or audio) and then select their files in the contents pane in the order in which you want to them to play in the impromptu show. Then click the QuickShow link on the Media Manager Task Bar.

Media Manager then switches to full-screen mode and plays the media in the selected files. This show screen contains toolbar with a simple playback controller that initially appears in the center at the top of the screen and then disappears (you can always make this toolbar visible simply by positioning the mouse pointer somewhere in this area). You can click the Play/Pause button in this toolbar (see Figure 4-8) to pause and then continue the show. You can use the Next and Previous File buttons to advance to next or return to the previous video, photo, or music track in the show.

When the slideshow is paused, you can click the QuickShow Settings button to display a pop-up menu containing the following options:

- ✔ **QuickShow Settings** to open the QuickShow Setting dialog box where you can change settings for photo slideshows including the slide duration, applying motion effects to the slides, and select background music to play during the show

- ✔ **Save As Slideshow Project** to save your impromptu photo slideshow on disk as a slideshow project that you can open and edit with the VideoWave 8

- ✔ **Edit in VideoWave** to open the impromptu photo slideshow in VideoWave 8 where you can further edit it by adding different transitions and effects

- ✔ **MyDVD Express** to burn the impromptu photo slideshow to CD or DVD disc using the MyDVD Express application

You can also change the settings for your impromptu photo slideshows before you generate them by choosing Tools➪Options on the Media Manager menu bar and then clicking the QuickShow tab in the Options dialog box.

Rotate 90° Left

Next | Rotate 90° Right

Play/Pause | Rating

Previous File | Hide Pane

Seek to Beginning | Quick Show Settings

Figure 4-8:
The
QuickShow
feature
enables you
to view
selected
videos,
photos, and
music
tracks.

Creating Your Own Albums

Media file collections known affectionately as albums are a key element in the struggle to organize and keep on top of the many media files of different types that you use in the various projects you create with the Roxio Creator 8 suite. Albums enable you to associate different types of media that you might want to use together in a particular project (such as a DVD movie as described in Chapter 12).

The great thing about albums is that you don't have to physically move or copy all the media files you want to associate with one another into the same folder. An album can keep track of all the different files regardless of where they're actually located on your computer system. This includes files saved in folders on your hard disk, files saved in folders on a network drive to which you have access, and files saved in folders on backup CD and DVD discs (that you can actually initiate from Media Manager — see "Backing Up Media Files on Disc" later in this chapter for details).

To create a new album, follow these steps:

1. **Launch the Media Manager and then click the My Albums tab in the navigation pane.**

   Media Manager displays the contents of the last selected album in the contents pane of the Media Manager window.

2. **Click the album icon in the album hierarchy under which you want the new album to appear, then click the Create a New Album button at the top of the My Albums tab.**

   Media Manager adds a New Album icon (which you need to rename) in the album hierarchy in alphabetical order under the album that you originally selected, while at the same time displaying an empty album in the contents pane on the right.

3. **Replace New Album by typing your own album name and then pressing Enter.**

4. **Click the Add to Album button at the top of the My Albums tab.**

   The Add to Albums window opens where you open the folder that contains the media files you want in the album collection and then select them.

5. **Select the folder in the folders' hierarchy in the Folders pane of the Add to Albums window that contains the media files you to add and then select all the files to add from that folder in the contents pane before you click the Add button.**

   When you click the Add button, Media Manager closes the Add to Album window and then adds thumbnails and file icons for all the media files you selected for adding.

6. **Repeat Steps 4 and 5 until you have added all the media files you want in the new album.**

Figure 4-9 shows a new Halloween album that I added to the My Albums tab in Media Manager. The photos for this album come from file folders saved on networked rather local drives on my computer system.

Add to Album

Create a
New Album

Rename Album

Delete Album

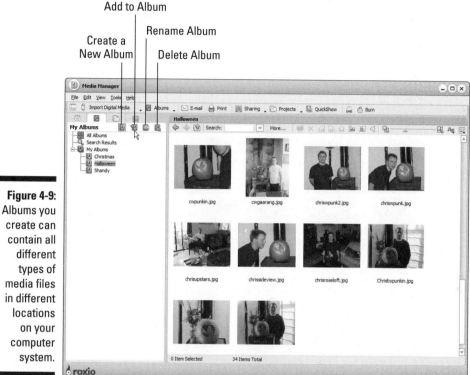

Figure 4-9:
Albums you
create can
contain all
different
types of
media files
in different
locations
on your
computer
system.

Creating albums from searches

Although you can create new albums from scratch as outlined in the previous section, you need to be aware that you can also create them by doing an advanced search and then turning the search results into an album. All you have to do is run an advanced search (see "Finding Wayward Media Files" later in this chapter for details).

When the search is complete and you have the media files that you want in the new album, you click the Save as New Album button at the top of the Search Pane. Next, you enter a name for the new album in the Save As New Album dialog box and select its location before clicking the Save button.

When the Save As New Album dialog box closes, the name of your new album with all the searched for media files will appear on My Albums tab of the Media Manager window.

Arranging the files in an album

Media Manager makes it easy to modify the order in which media files appear in your albums. To re-sort the thumbnails in a selected album, click the Sort By button near the end of the Option bar at the top of the My Albums tab, then select among the options on its pop-up menu:

- **Name** to sort files alphabetically by filename

- **Size** to sort files by their file size

- **Date Created** to sort files by the date they were originally created

- **Date Modified** to sort files by the date they were last modified

- **Type** to sort files by their file type

- **Rating** to sort files by their ratings

- **Custom Sort** to sort files using a custom order based on the other sort settings you select

- **Ascending** to select an A to Z, smallest to largest, least recent to most recent sort order

- **Descending** to select an Z to A, largest to smallest, most recent to least recent sort order

- **Show in Groups** to group files by other selected sort categories such as Type and Rating

Keep in mind that you can change the way individual media files are displayed in the contents pane of the Media Manager window as well as sort them. To change the display from the default thumbnail view with filename below, click the View As button (to the immediate right of the Sort By button) and then select Thumbnails, Details, Information, or List on its pop-up menu.

Tag, You're It!

The My Media and My Albums views of the Media Manager enable you to tag their media files (see "Creating Your Own Albums" earlier in this chapter) so that later you can more easily identify their contents or search for them. The program supports three different types of tags:

- **Keywords** that enable you to find related groups of files when doing searches in Media Manager (see "Finding Wayward Media Files" that immediately follows)

> ✔ **Comments** that enable you to add text notes that describe the contents of a media file (such as adding the location where a photo was taken and the names of the people who are in it)
>
> ✔ **Sounds** that enable you to add audio notes that describe the contents of a media file

To check a media file for tags, right-click its file icon and then click Properties on its shortcut menu. Then click the Tags tab in the Properties dialog box. This tab displays all the keywords, the text of any comments added to the file, as well as the name of any sound file associated with the media file.

Adding keywords to your albums

To add keywords to the media files in an album in Media Manager, follow these steps:

1. **Click the My Albums button on the Media Manager toolbar.**

   The My Albums pane appears.

2. **If necessary, expand My Albums in the navigation tree and then click the name of the album with files you want to tag.**

   Now you need to select the media file to which you wish to assign the same keyword.

3. **Select the thumbnails and file icons for all the media files to which you wish to assign the same keyword in the contents pane.**

   Media Manager opens the Assign and Manage Keywords portion of the Collections pane with its own toolbar of three buttons (see Figure 4-8).

4. **Click the Keywords button to open the Assign and Manage Keywords options at the top of the contents pane.**

   Now you're ready to select the keyword(s) to assign to the selected files.

5. **Click the check boxes in front of all applicable keywords listed at the top of the contents pane (see Figure 4-10).**

   If none of the currently listed keywords applies, you can create a new keyword(s) to apply.

6. **(Optional) Click the Add New Keyword button and then type in the keyword in the blank box and press Enter.**

   If you add a new keyword in Step 6, then you still need to take the next step to apply it to the selected files.

7. **(Optional) Click the check box in front of the new keyword you just added to apply it to the files selected in the contents pane.**

8. **When you finish assigning keywords to the media files in your various albums, click the Keywords button again to hide the Assign and Manage Keywords options at the top of the contents pane.**

To remove a keyword that you've applied to a file, all you have to do is to click the Keywords button to display the Assign and Manage Keyword options and then click the keyword's check box to remove its check mark.

Adding comments to your albums

In addition to or instead of keywords, you can add explanatory comments to a media file that help you identify its contents. To add a comment to a media file, make its album active in the My Albums navigation pane and then select its thumbnail or file icon in the contents pane. Next, click the Comments button on the Option bar at the top of the contents pane.

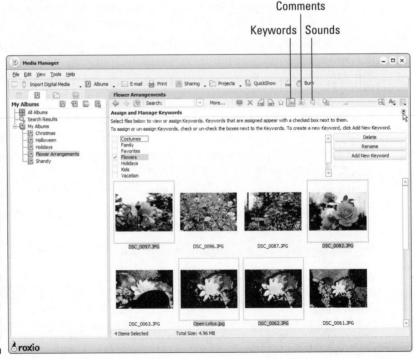

Figure 4-10: Use the Assign and Manage Keywords portion of the contents pane to add keywords, comments, or sounds to your media files.

Doing this opens the View and Edit Comments portion at the top of the contents pane. Click the list box area that contains the text "Type a comment for the selected file" and then type the text of your comment.

To add a comment to another media file in the same album, click its thumbnail or file icon and repeat this process of replacing the "Type a comment for the selected file" in the View and Edit Comments list box with your own text.

When you are finished adding comments to the media files in your album, close the View and Edit Comments list box either by clicking it Close button or by clicking the Comments button on the Options bar again.

Adding sound tags to your albums

In place of a written comment, you can add a sound tag to a particular media file that explains something about the file's contents or how the file should be edited or used in any of the other projects you create with the Roxio Media Creator 8 suite. The process for assigning a sound tag is very similar to that for assigning a comment except that instead of clicking the Comments button on the Options bar, you click the Sounds button to its immediate right.

When you click the Sounds button, the Associated Sounds controls appears at the top of the contents pane. These controls include a Select a File to Play or Associate a Sound drop-down list box (where you can select audio files with sound notes that you've already recorded for other media files) along with a Play, Select, and Record button.

To select an audio file that is not already listed on the Select a File to Play or Associate a Sound drop-down list, click the Select button and then select the audio file in the Open File dialog box before you click the Open button.

To record a new sound note, click the Record button to open the Roxio Media Import window where you can select audio recording device and then record and save your audio message (see Chapter 10 for details on recording sound with the MediaImport application). After you finish recording you're audio message you can listen to it by clicking the Play button attached to its sound file icon.

When you are satisfied with the note, click the Done button at the bottom of the Roxio Media Import window to return to Media Manager. Then click the Select button and select the newly recorded audio file in the Open File dialog box before you click the Open button. A speaker icon then appears in the lower-right corner of the media file's thumbnail or file icon, indicating that you have attached an audio file to it.

To listen to the sound note that you've assigned to a media file, select the thumbnail or file icon when the Associated Sounds controls are displayed and then click the Play button. To close the Associated Sounds controls, click the Sounds button on the Options bar at the top of the contents pane.

To remove a sound note from a selected media file, click the Select Sound drop-down button when the Associated Sounds controls are displayed at the top of the contents pane and then click the None item at the top of this box's pop-up menu.

Finding Wayward Media Files

Media Manager enables you to find just the media files you want to work with by searching all the Smart Views or albums on your computer system. When searching for media files, you can do the search on the name of the file as well as on keywords that you've assigned to the files and even the text of comments that you assigned to them (see "Tag, You're It!" earlier in this chapter for details on assigning keywords and comments to your media files).

Media Manager supports two kinds of media searches:

- ✔ **Simple search** in which you just enter search text and Media Manager then searches for it in all media filenames, keywords, and comments in all the media files scanned on your computer system (see "You're being watched!" earlier in this chapter)

- ✔ **Advanced search** in which you specify all types of search criteria including where to search on your computer system, the types of media files to search for, the dates when they were last modified, their file size, keywords assigned to them, as well as special properties unique to particular types of media file

Doing a simple search

To conduct a simple search, you follow these simple steps:

1. **Click the Search text box in the Options bar at the top of the contents pane.**

2. **Type the text to search for in the names of your albums or filenames they contain and in the keywords and comments you've assigned to these files in the Search text box.**

    The search text that you enter can be just part of an album name (such as **vacation** to find both the album called Europe vacation and Last summer's vacation) or media filename.

3. **Click the Start Searching button or press Enter to initiate the search.**

Media Manager then displays all the icons for the collections and thumbnails for the media files that contain the search text either in their album name or filename or in their keywords or comments. These matching albums, thumbnails, and file icons appear in the Search Pane under the Options bar.

Doing an advanced search

To perform an advanced search, you click the More button (to the immediate right of the Search text box) on the Options bar at the top of the contents pane when the My Media or My Albums are selected in the Media Manager.

Clicking the More button opens the Advanced Search dialog box shown in Figure 4-11 where you can specify all the criteria to use in the search:

1. **Enter the file or album name to search for in the Enter All or part of the File or Album Name Text box.**

   You can then narrow the search by selecting which types of media files to include in the search.

2. **(Optional) Click the check boxes in front of the types of media files that you do *not* want included in the search in the Search For section to remove their check marks.**

   You can even further narrow the search by selecting what albums to include in the search.

3. **(Optional) Click the Look In drop-down button and click the name of the album to include in the search on the Look In drop-down list box.**

   To search all the albums on your computer, click My Albums in Look In drop-down list and be sure that the Search All Sub-Albums check box remained checked. To search all media files in the Watched list that Media Manager scans on your computer system, click All Media instead.

4. **Specify any additional search criteria on the General, Keywords, and/or Special Properties tabs.**

   The search options on the General tab enable you to search for files containing specific comment text, search for files that have created or modified within a certain time period, or are of a certain file size.

   The search options on the Keywords tab enable you to select the check boxes for all the keywords you want included in the search.

   The search options on the Special Properties tab enable you to search criteria specific to particular types of media files, including Photos Files, Audio Files, Video Files, PhotoSuite Projects, and MyDVD 8 Projects. To specify media-specific criteria, click one of these file types to expand its criteria options, and then select the check boxes for the type of criteria to use and the associated drop-down list boxes to specify the range of values to apply for that criterion.

5. **Click the Search button to conduct the advanced search using all your search criteria.**

As with the Simple Search, Media Manager displays all the albums and media files that match your search criteria in the Search Pane on the right side of the Media Manager window.

If you want to make all the albums and media files displayed in the Search Pane into its own album, click the Save as New Album button at the top of the Search Pane, then give a new name for the album in the Save as New Album dialog box and select its location in the album hierarchy before clicking the Save button.

Figure 4-11: Use Media Manager's advanced search feature to locate specific types of media files in the albums on your computer system.

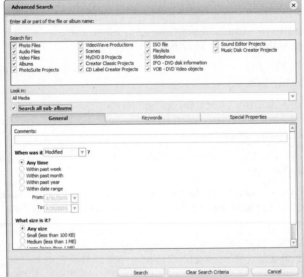

Printing Your Photos

The best thing about Smart Views and albums is that they enable you to easily print all or some of your photos. To print the contents of a Smart View or album containing photos, you have only to select its icon in the My Media or My Albums tab, and then select the thumbnails of the photos you want printed in the contents pane, before you click the Print button on the Media Manager Task Bar.

When you click the Print button, the Print dialog box (similar to the one shown in Figure 4-12) appears. There you select all the necessary print settings including the printer to use, orientation of the photos, how many photos to print on each page, which pages to print, and the number of copies to print before sending the job to the printer by clicking the Print button.

Figure 4-12:
Printing
your photos
from the
Media
Manager is
snap using
the options
offered in
this Print
dialog box.

Sharing Photos Online

The Media Manager gives you two ways to share your photos online with friends and family. The first way is to simply e-mail them. To do this, select the photos in their Smart Views and albums before you click the E-mail button on the Media Manager Task Bar. Doing this opens the E-mail Assistant dialog box where you select which e-mail client to use (Microsoft Outlook, Yahoo!, and so forth), whether or not to convert the photo files to JPEG, and, if so, what size to make them — Small (640), Medium (800), Large (1024), or Original Size.

After selecting the e-mail options and clicking OK, Media Manager opens the e-mail program you selected with a new message with all the photos embed-ded in the text area of the message. There, you use the e-mail client's options to specify the recipients of the message, along with its subject, and message text you want to add to the photos before sending the message.

The second way to share photos online is with Roxio's LiveShare feature. This new feature enables you to share the photos saved in the Smart Views and albums in the Media Manager by saving them in an ad hoc Web page which the people you invite by e-mail can then visit anytime your computer is running and connected to the Internet.

Once at this impromptu Web page, the visitors you've invited can print the photos you save there as well as download them to their own computers.

To add photos to a new LiveShare Web page, first select their thumbnails in the Media Manager window, next click the Sharing button on the Task Bar, and finally click the Share Now Using LiveShare item on the Sharing pop-up menu. Media Manager then opens a Create LiveShare dialog box where you specify the name of the Web page in the LiveShare Name text box before you click the Share Now button.

Media Manager then opens a new e-mail message. This message contains stock text that invites your recipients to view your photos online. This message text also contains a hyperlink that, when clicked, takes your e-mail message recipients directly to the LiveShare page containing your photos. All you have to do is specify the e-mail addresses of all the people who you'd like to view your photos and specify a subject for the message before sending it as you would any other message.

To manage a LiveShare page from within the Media Manager, you choose Tools⇨Manage My LiveShares on its menu bar. Doing this opens the Manage My LiveShares dialog box. The controls in this dialog box enable you to add a new album to a LiveShare Web page, remove some of its content, as well as to rename, and ultimately to delete it.

Click the Preview button in this dialog box to open your LiveShare Web page with your computer's own Web browser so that you can see the photos that are available online. You can also click the Invite button to open a new e-mail message with links to the Web page so that you can invite more people to come and see your photos.

Backing Up Media Files on Disc

The Media Manager makes it really easy to back up the media files in your albums on CD or DVD disc. All you have to do is select the media files in that album in the Media Manager window and then click the Burn button on the window's Task Bar.

The Media Manager then responds by launching the Creator Classic application and opening a new data disc project in this program that contains all of the media files in the selected album. Then all you have to do is name the volume, select the type of disc to use, and click the Burn button in the Creator Classic window to go ahead and burn all the media files to disc (see Chapter 3 for details on building data projects in Creator Classic and burn them to disc).

Part III
Creating Audio CDs and Photo Projects

The 5th Wave   By Rich Tennant

"You know kids – you can't buy them just any media creation software."

In this part . . .

Undoubtedly, the digital audio and digital photos that Part III deals with represent some of the most fun media to work with (who doesn't love a good tune and the memories that photos of our favorite activities engender?). This part begins with Chapter 5, which covers the mixing of digital audio clips, from live recordings as well as tracks on audio CDs and DVDs you own in Sound Editor. Chapter 6 is the place to go for information on acquiring, editing, and using your digital photos. Part III concludes with Chapter 7, which gives you the ins and outs of compiling and burning Audio CDs, MP3/WMA Discs, and DVD MusicDiscs, and Chapter 8, which covers Roxio Label Creator that makes it as easy as can be to design and print disc labels and case inserts for all your CDs and DVDs.

Chapter 5

Editing Audio with Sound Editor

In This Chapter

▶ Getting familiar with Sound Editor's interface

▶ Adding audio clips to your Sound Editor project

▶ Recording audio clips for your Sound Editor project

▶ Importing tracks from an audio CD or DVD for your Sound Editor project

▶ Applying special audio effects to an audio mix

▶ Exporting an audio clip or mix as a separate sound file

As you find out in this chapter, Sound Editor is the place to go when you need to preview, edit, or enhance audio files (assuming that they're non-licensed files which are not copy-protected) that you want to use in various projects you create with Roxio Creator 8.

Sound Editor in the Roxio Creator 8 suite is essentially an audio mixer that enables you to arrange audio clips from a variety of sources into your own audio mix. This program then lets you save your mix in a variety of different audio formats and compression settings. Because Sound Editor can open audio files saved in any of these formats and then save them back out in any of these formats, you can also use the Sound Editor to convert audio tracks that you receive saved in one audio format into another more compressed or manage-able format for use in your other Roxio projects. You can also use Sound Editor to burn the edited audio clips in the final mix to standard audio CDs or MP3 discs or use them in audio projects you create with Audio CD, Jukebox Disc, and DVD Music Disc, all available on the Audio tab of the Project List in Roxio Creator 8 Home (see Chapter 7 for details).

Adding Clips to Your Audio Mix

You launch Sound Editor from the Roxio Creator 8 Home window by clicking the Sound Editor link in the Applications Project Window (opened by clicking the Applications link on the Home tab of the Project List).

An empty Sound Editor window then opens where you can record new audio file clips, import tracks from a CD or DVD as clips, or add existing audio files already saved to disk as clips for the new sound project. This window is divided into the following panes: Add to Project, Export, Project View, Clip Editor, and Mix Editor.

To open existing audio files as clips for a new audio project, you click the Add Audio File link in the Add to Project pane. Then locate the audio file to add to the Sound Editor project in the Media Selector dialog box and click the OK button.

When you add an audio clip to the sound project, Sound Editor represents its sound visually as a waveform in the Clip Editor pane (as shown in Figure 5-1). This waveform shows the relative amplitude of the sound (that's volume to you and me) with its different spikes, peaks, valleys, and dips over time.

These left- and right-channel dB scales measure the voltage gain of the amplifier against the strength of its original signal (indicated by the baseline that runs through the middle of each scale). When the audio file's waveform rises above this baseline, the scales measure how much stronger the audio signal is than the original carrier signal. When the waveform dips below this baseline, the scales measure how much weaker the audio signal is when compared to the original carrier signal.

Figure 5-1:
The Sound
Editor
visually
represents
each audio
file you add
as a wave-
form that
shows the
relative
amplitude of
the sound
over time.

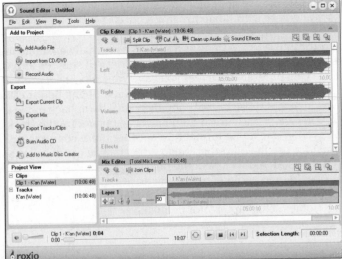

In the lower-right corner of the Sound Editor window, peak meters appear for both the left and right channels (marked L and R). These meters indicate how close the recording level comes to the zero dB clipping point where the sound literally goes off the chart (indicated by the gray squares on the right side of the meters). Volumes in the safe zone are indicated by blue bars to the left of these squares and sounds that actually approach this point where sounds are clipped are indicated in yellow, with red bars indicating clipped sounds that actually exceed these squares.

The Mix Editor pane immediately below the Clip Editor shows all the layers in your sound project. When you start a new project in Sound Editor, it contains only a single layer (identified as Layer 1) onto which all your audio clips go in succession. If you need to, you can add up to eight additional layers (labeled Layer 2 through Layer 8) in the Mix Editor onto which you can add audio clips. You can then overlap sections of the individual layers for the final audio mix.

At the very bottom of the Sound Editor window beneath the Project View and Mix Editor panes, you find a mute button, volume control along with standard playback controls.

Figure 5-2: These controls at the bottom of the Sound Editor enable you to play back the clips in your audio mix.

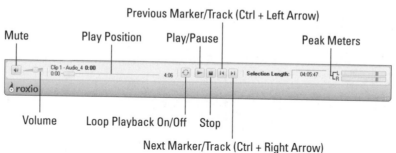

Recording and Editing Audio

Recording your own audio clips

You can record your own clips for your Sound Editor projects. You can make these recordings using a microphone connected to your computer or some other device such as cassette or record player that connects to the sound input (microphone) port on your computer. You can also record audio clips directly from your computer's sound card, so that, for example, you could record the music or sound effects that are playing with another computer program such as the Windows Media Player.

To record audio clips from the Sound Editor, you follow these steps:

1. **In the Sound Editor window, click the insertion point at the place in the waveform in the Clip Editor pane where you want the clip you're about to record to be inserted. If you want to lay the new recording down over an existing audio clip, click that clip's waveform in the Mix Editor pane to select its layer as well.**

   If the audio you're about to record is the first clip in the sound project, you can disregard Step 1. If your project contains clips and you want the new recorded audio appended to the end of them, click the insertion point at the end of the last clip's waveform in the Clip Editor.

   If you want Sound Recorder to play back an existing audio clip as you record your new audio (presumably using your computer's microphone), click the insertion point at the place in the clip where you want the recording to start in the Clip Editor, and then click its waveform in the Mix Editor before proceeding on to Step 2. Note that this technique is useful when you want to record a narrative voiceover on top of a background track that you then add to a slideshow or video production.

2. **Click the Record Audio link in the Add to Project pane of the Sound Editor window.**

   The Sound Editor opens a Record Audio dialog box similar to the one shown in Figure 5-3.

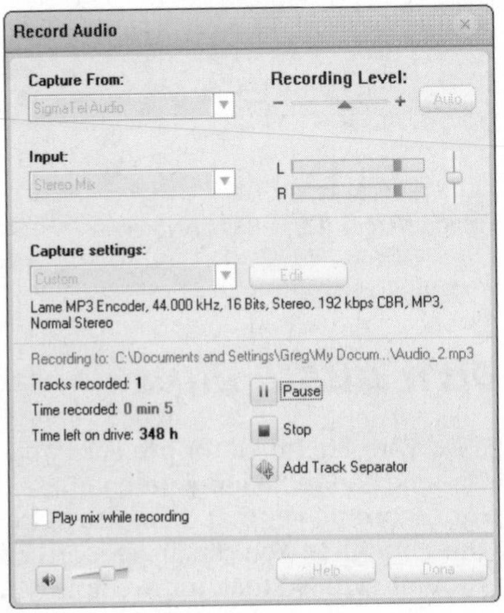

Figure 5-3:
The Record
Audio dialog
box lets you
record clips
for your
sound
projects.

3. **If the name of your sound card does not appear in the Capture From combo box, click its drop-down button and then click the name of your sound card on the drop-down menu.**

4. **Click Input drop-down button and then click the name of your computer's recording source on the drop-down menu.**

   For example, if you're recording through a microphone connected to your computer's sound input, click Microphone on this drop-down menu. If you're recording through your computer's sound card, click Stereo Mix on this menu. If you're recording through a line connected to an analog device such as a cassette recorder, click the option on this submenu that mentions Line or Line In (the actual items on this submenu vary according to the sound card your system uses).

5. **Click the Capture Settings drop-down button and then select the audio file format to use in making the recording on the drop-down menu and then click the Edit button to open the Capture Settings dialog box where you change any necessary settings before clicking OK.**

   By default, the Sound Editor selects the WAV audio file format for capturing the new clip. While this format gives you top-notch audio quality, it also takes a lot of disc space as it is not compressed. To save disk space, select one of the other capture options on the drop-down list: MP3 (Good Quality) at 192 Kbps, MP3 (Low Quality) at 96 Kbps, WMA (Good Quality) at 128 Kbps, WMA (Low Quality) at 64 Kbps, or Custom to define your own format, encoder, and bit rate settings on the File Format tab and track detection settings on the Track Detection tab of the Capture Settings dialog box.

   If you want to change the folder in which the Sound Editor saves the temporary audio file after you finish recording it, click the button to the immediate right of the Save To text box on the General tab of the Capture Settings dialog box and then select a new folder in the Select Folder dialog box (by default, the program saves all recordings in a Recorded Tracks folder inside your My Music folder). While you're at it, you can edit the default Audio filename prefix given to all the files you record (as in Audio1, Audio2, and so on) by clicking the File Name Prefix text box and then entering your own prefix before clicking OK.

   If you want to set a limit on the recording time, click the Limit Recording To check box on the General tab and then enter the number of minutes to set as a limit in its text box to the immediate right.

   If you want to enable the auto pause feature whereby the recording automatically pauses if a silence is detected (very useful if you don't intend to monitor the recording at all times), click the Auto Pause check box on the General tab and then designate the number of seconds for the pause in the Length of Silence text box. If the noise made contain some noise (as with an older LP), click the Silence May Contain Noise check box as well.

6. **To set the recording level manually, drag the Recording Level slider to the desired position. If you want Sound Editor to automatically adjust the recording level to avoid clipping, click the Auto button.**

   When setting the recording level manually, it is a good idea to play some of the music track you intend to record or speak a few words in the microphone to see what effect this has on the peak meters.

   If the peak meters reach or go past the squares indicating the clipping points, reduce the recording level by dragging the triangle in its slider to the left and then test the audio level again.

7. **If you are recording an existing music track as opposed to recording live with a microphone, cue up the LP record or cassette to the point at which you want to start recording in Sound Editor.**

   If you're recording tracks on an LP, place the needle near or at the end of the track previous to the one you want to record and then when the record player reaches the silence in between the tracks, proceed to Step 8. If you're recording a track on cassette, cue up to the silence in between the two tracks and immediately after you follow Step 8, press the Play button on the cassette player.

8. **(Optional) To record the new clip while an existing one plays in the background, click the Play Mix While Recording check box.**

   Note that this check box only appears in the Record Audio dialog box if you clicked the waveform in the Mix Editor before opening the dialog box as indicated in Step 1.

9. **Click the red Record button to start recording.**

   As Sound Editor begins to record your audio, the Time Recorded indicator shows you the recording time in minutes and seconds and the Time Left on Drive indicator the amount of recording time left on the disk where the temporary recording is saved in hours and minutes. In addition, the Play button changes to Pause and the Stop and Add Track Separator buttons become active.

   If you need to pause the recording to switch the tape or turn over the LP, click the Pause button (which then becomes Play again). To begin recording again, you click the Play button again.

10. **(Optional) To insert a track separator at the end of the audio clip you're recording, click the Add Track Separator button.**

    Take this step when you intend to record additional tracks before closing the Record Audio dialog box.

11. **(Optional) If you enabled the Limit Recording To option and then need to extend the recording time, click the Plus button (+) to the right of the Time Left to Record indicator for each additional minute you want to add.**

12. **Click the Stop button when you finish recording your audio clip and then click the OK button in the Audio alert box.**

    The Audio alert dialog box that appears lets you know the name of the temporary audio file you just recorded and its locations via its path name.

    Now, you can record another audio clip by repeating the previous steps or, if you're finished recording clips, proceed to Step 13.

13. **Click the Done button when you're finished recording all the audio clips you need with Record Audio.**

The Record Audio dialog box closes and you return to the Sound Editor window where the waveform of the recording you just made appears.

If you selected an existing clip in the Mix Editor pane before recording the audio clip, its waveform will appear on its own layer in the Mix Editor pane beneath the one that was selected before you started recording the new clip.

Importing your clips from CDs and DVDs

You can easily import tracks from audio CDs and DVDs to use as audio clips in your audio mix in Sound Editor. To do this, you follow these steps:

1. **In the Sound Editor window, click the insertion point at the place in the waveform in the Clip Editor pane where you want the imported track to be inserted. If you want to lay this track down over an existing audio clip, be sure to click that clip's waveform in the Mix Editor pane to select its layer as well.**

2. **Insert the audio CD or DVD into your computer's drive.**

3. **Click the Import From CD/DVD link in the Add to Project pane in the Sound Editor window.**

    The Media Selector dialog box opens.

4. **Select the icon for the drive containing the audio CD or DVD in the Folders pane of the Media Selector dialog box.**

    The audio tracks on the selected CD or DVD then appear on the Track List tab in the Media Selector. If you have access to the Internet and you're importing from a commercially produced CD, Sound Editor will automatically contact the Gracenote only database and replace the track numbers with the track names.

5. **Select the track or tracks to import into your audio mix and then click OK.**

To listen to a track before importing it, click its track number or name and then click the Play button on the playback controls at the bottom of the Track View tab. To select more than one track for importing, hold down the Ctrl key as you click the track numbers or names.

When you click OK, the Media Selector dialog box is replaced by the Save Audio Tracks to File dialog box where you select the output settings and the folder in which to save the track(s).

6. **Make any necessary changes to the Output Settings and Save To option in the Save Audio Tracks to File dialog box before you click the Save button.**

By default, the Sound Editor selects the uncompressed WAV audio file format for capturing the new clip. To select a compressed audio file format, select one of the other capture options on the drop-down list: MP3 (Good Quality) at 192 Kbps, MP3 (Low Quality) at 96 Kbps, WMA (Good Quality) at 128 Kbps, WMA (Low Quality) at 64 Kbps, or Custom to define your own format, encoder, bit rate, and compression settings on the File Format tab of the Output Settings dialog box.

If you want to change the folder in which the Sound Editor saves the track, click the Browse button to the immediate right of the Save To text box and then select a new folder in the Select Folder dialog box (by default, the program saves all recordings in a Recorded Tracks folder inside your My Music folder).

Recording clips with analog equipment

You can use the Record Audio link in the Sound Editor to record audio clips from analog sources such as LP records and audio cassettes or you can record your clip using the LP and Tape Assistant (opened by clicking the Convert LP/Tapes link on the Audio tab of the Project List pane of the Roxio Creator 8 Home).

In either case, before you start the recording, you must first connect your analog audio equipment to your computer's sound input with the appropriate cables. Most of the time, this cable will be a y-shaped cable with one red and one white stereo-jack connector on one end that come together in a single earphone- or microphone-type connector on the other. You then connect the red and white stereo-jack connectors to the left and right-channel line out connections on your analog audio equipment (tape deck, stereo receiver, and so on). On most personal computers that aren't equipped with a special analog-to-digital converter (see Chapter 2), you then connect the other connector to the microphone connection on your personal computer so that this acts as the sound input when recording your LPs or cassette tapes with Sound Editor.

Note that when record audio clips from a record player, you must take the line out of a stereo receiver or some other type of amplifier to which the record player is connected (if you were to cable the record player directly to your computer's sound input, the audio would be too weak for Sound Editor to record it).

As soon as you click the Save button, the Media Selector dialog box is replaced by the Copying Track dialog box that keeps you informed of the progress of the copy. As soon as the track copying is completed this dialog box is replaced by an Audio alert dialog that displays the file name and location (by path name) of the copied track(s). Click OK to close the alert dialog box (or boxes) and to have the imported tracks loaded as clips in the Sound Editor window.

Editing Your Audio Mix

After you have all the audio clips that you want in your mix, you are ready to begin editing. The Sound Editor provides you with a number of nifty enhancements that you can apply to the project, including fade ins and fade outs, filters to clean up a less-than-perfect audio clip, and a whole bunch sound effects that run the gamut from converting a stereo recording to mono all the way to giving the singer a Munchkin-type voice or make you think the recording was made in Westminster Abbey.

 Keep in mind when editing your audio mix in either the Clip Editor or the Mix Editor that you can temporarily maximize the editor you're working in by collapsing the other editor's pane. For example, if you're editing a clip in the Clip Editor, you can enlarge its waveform by clicking the Collapse Mix Editor button to minimize this pane (simply click the same button a second time to restore the Mix Editor pane to normal). So too, if you're working with clips on different layers in the Mix Editor, you can enlarge and display all its layers in this pane by clicking the Collapse Clip Editor button.

Zoom, zoom, zoom. . .

When editing your audio mix, you will often need to apply your editing to some portion of a particular clip. You can use the zoom controls at the top of the Clip Editor and Mix Editor panes in the Sound Editor window to zoom in and out to find the exact place you want to edit in their waveforms:

- ✔ **Zoom to Selection (Shift+1)** to zoom in just the portion of the audio waveform that you've selected in the Clip Editor or Mix Editor pane

- ✔ **Zoom Out Full (Ctrl+1)** to zoom out on so that the waveforms of all the clips in the sound project are visible in the Clip Editor or Mix Editor

- ✔ **Zoom In (+)** to zoom in on the waveform so that you can see more detail of the waveform over less time in the Clip Editor or Mix Editor

- ✔ **Zoom Out (-)** to zoom out on the waveform so that you can see less detail but over more time in the Clip Editor or Mix Editor

As you click the Zoom In and Zoom Out buttons, the scale on the time track in between the left and right channel waveforms in the Clip Editor and beneath single waveform in the Mix Editor change to show the how much of the recording's waveform is currently displayed in the respective pane of the Sound Editor window (this timescale shows the number of minutes and seconds that have elapsed from the start of 0:00.0).

When you zoom all the way out on the audio file, the recording's entire waveform is displayed in the Clip Editor or Mix Editor pane of the Sound Editor window and the Zoom Out button becomes grayed out (indicating that it's temporarily unavailable). As you zoom in on the recording and not all of its waveform is displayed in the Sound Editor window, the scroll bar that appears at the bottom of each pane no longer extends the entire width of the window. You can then drag this scroll bar to the left and right to bring different parts of the recording's waveform into view.

To zoom in on just a particular portion of the waveform, click the mouse pointer at the starting place in the waveform and then drag through the waveform until you've selected through the entire of portion of the waveform you want to examine up close. Then click the Zoom to Selection button or press Shift+1 (that's the number 1 and not function key F1) to display just the selected section of the waveform in the Sound Editor window. To return to the previous view of the waveform, click the Zoom Out button once. To deselect the waveform selection, click the mouse pointer anywhere in the waveform (a position cursor indicated by a thin vertical line replaces the waveform selection at the place you click).

You can use the plus (+) and minus (–) keys on your keyboard to zoom in and out on a recording's waveform. In fact, by pressing the plus key you can actually zoom out on the waveform many times more than by clicking the Zoom Out button until only fractions of a second of the recording is displayed in the Clip Editor of the Sound Editor window and the left and right channels of the waveform appear as very spaced-out waves extending above and below the dB scale's baseline.

Playing with the playback controls

As you make editing changes to the audio clips in your mix (especially after applying special effects to them), you will want to play them back to determine whether or not you want to keep the changes you made to them.

You can use the playback controls at the bottom of the Sound Editor window in conjunction with the Clips selector in the Project View pane to play any of the clips in the audio mix. Simply make sure that the Clip Editor pane is active (by clicking the Clip Editor title bar) before you click the Clip number in the Project View pane and then click the Play button in the playback controls.

When you click the Play button, Sound Editor begins to play back the selected clip form its beginning. If you want to begin playback later in the clip, click the Position indicator (the thin, blue vertical line that moves across the wave-form from left to right as you play back the audio) at the desired place in its waveform in the Clip Editor before you click Play. Sound Editor will then play the clip from the selected position

As soon as you click the Play button to start the audio playback, this button changes to a Pause button, which you can then click to pause the playback. To the immediate right of the Stop button, you find a Previous Marker/Track button that you can click to move the Position indicator to the beginning of the current clip for replay. You can click the Next Marker/Track button to advance to the beginning of the next track in the recording (or to the very end of audio file if it has only a single track).

Drag the Volume slider to control the volume (drag left to reduce the volume and right to increase it). If you need to temporarily mute the volume altogether, click the Mute/Unmute button to the immediate right of the Volume slider. The first time you click this button, Sound Editor mutes the playback. The second time you click this button, the program removes the muting, returning to the original playback volume. Table 5-1 gives you a list of the most common key-stroke shortcuts that you can use to control the playback of a recording in Sound Editor. You can use any of these keystrokes instead of having to click the controls at the bottom of the Sound Editor window.

Table 5-1	Sound Editor Playback Keystroke Shortcuts
Keystroke	*What It Does*
Space	Play/Pause
Enter	Pause/Play
Shift+Space	Play from the beginning of selected clip
F8	Mute/Unmute
F9	Decrease volume
F10	Increase volume

Removing silences from a recording

One of the first edits you may want to make (after saving your new audio project to disk — File⇨Save Project) is to remove any leading or trailing silences that you may have recorded in the clips you added. You will get a leading silence if you have a delay between the time you cue up the analog audio, click the Record button in the Record Audio dialog box, and actually start playing the LP or cassette tape that you want to record. You will get a trailing silence if you have a delay between the time the LP or tape finishes playing and the time you click the Sound Editor's Stop button to stop the recording.

To get rid of a recording's leading or trailing silence, take these steps:

1. **Select the silent area in the waveform in the Clip Editor by clicking and dragging from its start to end.**

   Use the zoom controls in the top right corner of the Clip Editor pane to enlarge the waveform (silences appear flat in the waveform).

2. **To play back the selection marked for deletion to ensure that it doesn't contain any audio you want to retain, click the Play button in the playback controls at the bottom of the Sound Editor.**

3. **Press the Delete key or choose Edit⇨Delete on the Sound Editor menu bar.**

If you delete a leading or trailing silence only to suddenly realize that you need to retain that silence in this recording (perhaps to act as a track break when combining this recording with another audio track in one of your Easy Media Creator projects), press Ctrl+Z to Undo your deletion of the silence and put it back in your file before you do any more editing. Then click the mouse pointer anywhere in the recording's waveform to remove the selection.

Inserting silences into a recording

Should you find that you need a silence in a recording, you can insert it by following these two steps:

1. **Select the place in the waveform in the Clip Editor where you want the silence to be inserted and then drag to the right to indicate how long a silence to insert.**

2. **Right-click the selected portion of the waveform and then click the Insert Silence option on its shortcut menu.**

The Insert Silence option on the waveform's shortcut menu can come in real handy after you've used the Insert Recorded Audio option to record a new clip or the Add Audio File or Import From CD/DVD links in the Add to Project pane to insert another track or recording into your current audio mix and need a gap between the two to mark and separate the individual tracks.

Adding and deleting markers

The Sound Editor enables you to add markers to the audio clip you're editing so that you can quickly and easily find places in the audio that need editing or are of a special interest.

You can use markers to denote places in the timecode of audio clip to which you want to be able to return quickly. To identify the place for the marker, press lowercase letter P on the keyboard to turn on the display of the current timecode as a tooltip at the mouse pointer's position (note that pressing lowercase P again turns this tooltip off).

Use this timecode tooltip to locate the exact place in the audio where you want a marker. When you locate the timecode in the waveform, click the mouse pointer to position the cursor there before you press lowercase letter M. Sound Editor inserts a marker indicated by a downward pointing triangle at the top of the waveform.

After inserting markers in an audio clip, you can click the Next Marker/Track button (or press Ctrl+→) and the Previous Marker/Track button (or press Ctrl+←) to jump the cursor right to them in the waveform in the Clip Editor.

To remove a marker in an audio clip, go to it in the waveform and then press lowercase M to remove it.

Adding and deleting track separators

If the audio clip that you recorded with the Record Audio option in the Sound Editor had more than one track and you didn't remember to use the Add Track Separators button to insert them, you can use easy add them to the clip in the Clip Editor pane by following these steps:

1. **Select the clip in the Project View pane into which you need to insert a track separator and then click the Clip Editor pane to make it active.**

2. **Use the Play/Pause button at the bottom of the Sound Editor window to play back the clip until you reach the place in the audio where a new track begins.**

3. **Click the Add a New Track Separator to Define a New Track button (the first one with the plus sign on the Clip Editor pane's toolbar) to insert a track separator at the position in the waveform containing cursor.**

The end of the first track and the beginning of the new track is shown by a track separator indicator (two opposing triangles back to back) above the waveform. The Sound Editor also precedes that track designation with the next available number as in 2 Audio_3, indicating the second track in the third audio clip or 2 Speed of Sound Coldplay, indicating the second track in the Coldplay's "Speed of Sound" single.

Note that you can have Sound Editor automatically locate the tracks in a particular clip and add all the necessary track separators provided that the tracks in the clip have silences in between them. To do this, choose Tools⇨Track Detection on the Sound Editor menu bar or press Shift+Ctrl+D. This opens the Track Detection dialog box where you specify the minimum length in seconds of each silence that signals a new track, the maximum number of tracks to create, and whether or not the silences to be used in locating the tracks contains noises before you click OK.

After inserting a track separator in an audio clip, you can click the Next Marker/Track button (or press Ctrl+→) to jump the cursor right to it in the waveform in the Clip Editor. You can also click the Previous Marker/Track button (or press Ctrl+←) to jump to the start of the first track.

To remove a track separator, all you have to do is select the new track created when you inserted the separator (in other words, the one that follows) in the Clip Editor by clicking the area that contains its track designation and then click the Remove the Currently Selected Track button (the one with the minus sign on the Clip Editor pane's toolbar).

Splitting a clip at its track separator

Sometimes in addition to adding a track separator to an audio clip, you need to split the clip as well. By splitting a clip at a track separator, you can move the track to a new layer in the audio mix (see "Working with different layers" later in this chapter).

To split a clip, you click the Split Clip button on the Clip Editor pane's toolbar and then drag the split bar to the place in the waveform where you want the split to occur.

After splitting an audio clip, you can then select the new smaller clips for editing with the Edit⇨Select Next Track or the Edit⇨Select Previous Track commands on the Sound Editor menu bar. You can also reposition any of the new clips on their current layer or move onto another layer as you need (see "Working with different layers" later in this chapter).

Joining two clips into one

If, after splitting a larger audio clip, you find that you no longer want the split, you can join them the smaller clips made from the larger one back together. Simply select the clips to be joined in the Mix Editor pane by holding down Ctrl as you click their waveforms and then click the Join Clips button on the Mix Editor pane's toolbar.

The Sound Editor then joins the selected clips, leaving only a marker at the spot where the split once was. You can then remove this marker if you want by moving the cursor to it in the Clip Editor and then pressing lowercase letter M.

Adjusting the volume and balance

You can easily adjust the volume of part or all of an audio clip in your sound project. Not only can you adjust the overall volume but you can add fade-in or fade-out effects at the beginning and end of a clip so that sound builds in and out over time. Of course, if you are working with clips on different layers in the Mix Editor, you can create a cross-fade effect by fading out the audio in a clip on one layer at the same time as you fade in the audio for an overlapping clip on another layer.

The Clip Editor pane of the Sound Editor window shows any changes that you make to the volume of the current clip in the line diagram in the Volume indicator box located directly beneath the waveform representing the audio's Right channel. The current volume of the clip is represented by the straight blue line in the middle of the Volume indicator box. Changes you make to the volume in portions of the audio clip are indicated by drawing nodes (that appear as tiny square) that divide the otherwise straight line into diagonal segments that can extend above (indicating increases in the volume) or below (indicating decreases in volume)

The same principle holds true for the display of any balance adjustments you make to portions of the audio clip in the Balance indicator box located immediately beneath the Volume box. However, in this case, the straight green line in the middle of diagram represents equal balance between the left and right channels at 100% of their volume. Here, any *decrease* to the volume of the right channel is represented by segments of the green line above this straight line just as any *decrease* to the left channel is represented by segments extending below it.

Please adjust that volume!

To adjust the volume of an entire audio clip, select the clip in the Project View pane, and then double-click its waveform in the Clip Editor pane to select its entire waveform before you click the Fading & Volume button on the Clip Editor pane's toolbar and then select from among these options on its pop-up menu:

- **Fade In and Out** to fade the audio at the beginning and out at the end of the clip the number of seconds you specify in the Seconds text box in the Fade In and Out dialog box
- **Maximize Volume** to increase the overall volume as much as possible for the entire clip

To apply just a fade-in effect to the first part of an audio clip, go to the beginning of the clip and then drag through the first part of the waveform, representing the amount of time over which the fade-in is to take place before clicking the Fading & Volume button and the Fade In option on its pop-up menu.

To apply just a fade-out effect to the last part of an audio clip, go to the end of the clip and then drag through the last part of the waveform, representing the amount of time over which the fade-out is to take place before clicking the Fading & Volume button and the Fade Out option on its pop-up menu.

If you want to slowly increase or decrease the volume over just a portion of the audio clip, drag through that part of the waveform where this volume adjustment is to take place and then click the Fading & Volume button followed by the Adjust Volume option on its pop-up menu. The Sound Editor opens the Volume Fading dialog box (shown in Figure 5-4) that contains two slider controls:

✓ **Fade From** to set the percentage above or below normal (100%) from which the sound increase or decrease is to begin

✓ **Fade To** to set the percentage above or below normal (100%) at which the sound increase or decrease is to end

Figure 5-4:
Use the
Fade From
and Fade To
controls to
increase or
decrease
volume in a
portion of an
audio clip.

To create a volume increase over the time represented by the selected portion of the audio clip, you must set the Fade To percentage in the Volume Fading dialog box so that it is higher than the Fade From percentage. Conversely, to decrease the volume over in the selected audio, you must set the Fade From percentage higher than that of the Fade From percentage.

To create a wave in an audio clip whereby the volume increases from normal before reaching a new high and then returning back to normal, you need to create back to back volume adjustment effects: the first effect creates a volume increase by raising only the Fade To percentage in the Volume Fading dialog box and the second effect, abutting the first, creates a volume decrease by setting only the Fade From percentage the same as the Fade To percentage in the first effect. To create a wave whereby the volume decreases to a low and then builds back to normal, you two back to back volume adjustments with just the opposite settings (change only Fade To below 100% in the first and change only Fade From to the same percentage below 100% as the first).

Normalizing the volume over several audio clips

Sometimes you create a mix from clips recorded at vastly different volumes and need to set a common volume for the entire sound project. To do this, join all the audio clips in a single layer of the sound project and then select their combined waveform in the Mix Editor. Click the Fading & Volume button on the Clip Editor pane's toolbar and select Normalize on its pop-up menu. Sound Editor opens the Normalize dialog box with a level slider that you can use to set how many times the current volume to normalize the selected clips (between 1 and 10x).

After setting a new level with this slider, click the Play/Stop button in the Normalize dialog box to play back the mix at the new volume level to make sure that it's not too loud. When the level is just right, click OK to have Sound Editor normalize the volume (and add a Normalize band to the Effects area of the Clip Editor).

To reset the volume level after applying the Normalize effect or to remove it entirely, right-click somewhere in the Normalize band in the Effects area and then on its shortcut menu select Effects Properties to re-open the Normalize dialog box or Delete to remove the normalization.

When it's a matter of balance

By default, all recordings you make yourself and sound files you import into your mix are given a left and right channel in the Clip Editor, regardless of whether or not the clip's recording is really recorded as two-channel stereo.

For those audio clips that really are stereo and do have a different left and right channel, you can adjust the balance between the two by clicking the Fading & Volume button and then selecting Adjust Balance on its pop-up menu. Sound Editor opens the Balance Fading dialog box, which just like its Volume Fading counterpart contains a Fade From and a Fade To slider.

Both the Fade From and Fade To sliders in the Volume Fading dialog box are set smack dab in the middle, indicating that both the left and right channels are set at an equal 100% level. To decrease the percentage of the volume in the right channel, you drag the slider button upward in either the Fade From or the Fade To slider. To decrease the percentage of the volume in the left channel, you drag the slider button downward in either of these two sliders.

When you drag a slider button upward, Sound Editor shows you the percentage of decrease in the right channel volume at the top of slider. Likewise, when you drag a slider button downward, the program shows you the percentage of decrease in the left channel volume at the top of the slider. To adjust the left/right balance for a section of an audio (most usually at the beginning of the clip), drag through its waveform in the Clip Editor before opening the Balance Fading dialog box and using its controls.

For example, to create the effect wherein all the sound comes from the right channel when the clips starts playing and then gradually during the first minute of play comes up in the left channel as it finally normalizes in both, you drag through the timecode at beginning of the clip's waveform in the Clip Editor up 'til 1:00:00, the time at which this balance effect is to end. Then, in the Volume Fading dialog box, you drag the button in the Fade From slider all the way down (so that the left channel is set at L0%, essentially muted it and the Fade To remains at 100%) before you click OK.

When you click the Play button in the Sound Editor to listen to the effect (preferably through stereo headphones), watch the peak meters as well as the Clip Editor: when the audio starts playing only the Right meter registers any activity and gradually the Left meter comes alive as the cursor moves across the timecode in the waveform.

After you make balance adjustments in the Balance Fading dialog box, Sound Editor displays the results using segments and nodes in the green line diagram in the Balance indicator box (between Volume and Effects) in the Clip Editor. Figure 5-5 shows you the Balance diagram after applying the effect whereby the left channel is muted at the start of play and the sound normalizes in the left and right channels during its first minute.

Figure 5-5:
Audio clip with adjusted balance wherein all sound comes from the right channel and gradually moves to both.

As you can see in this figure, this balance effect requires only two nodes with a single diagonal segment between them. To remove this effect using this diagram, you would have only to drag the first node up to until the line is once again straight. To further modify this effect so that the sound goes entirely from the right to left and then normalizes in both channels, you could insert another node by right-clicking in the middle of the diagonal segment and then selecting Insert Node on the shortcut menu, effectively bisecting the original diagonal line segment. Then you would drag the new node up to the top of the Balance area so the segment on its left goes from the very bottom of the box (no left channel) to the very top (no right channel) and the segment on the right goes back down to meet the straight line in the middle of the box (both channels at a hundred percent).

Keep in mind that you can remove any adjustment that you've made to the volume or balance for the currently selected audio clip anytime you decide you don't want it. Simply, click the Fading & Volume button and then select Reset Volume Envelope to reset the volume or Reset Balance Envelope to reset the balance between the left and right channel.

Working with different layers

The Sound Editor in the Roxio Creator 8 suite is a true audio mixer in its support of multiple layers in its Mix Editor (you have up to eight maximum). You can use layers (also referred to as audio tracks) in your mix to overlay audio clips to great effect.

For example, you can overlay the end of one audio clip in one layer with the beginning of another clip in the next layer and then apply a fade-out effect to end of the clip in the first layer and a fade-in to the one in the next layer, creating a cross-fade effect whereby as the music of the first clip fades, the music of the second comes up. You can also use layers to add background music to a narration, an audio effect which really enhances a slideshow or video movie project with the narration providing the information about the visuals while the music sets the proper mood.

Adding new layers

Each new project you launch in Sound Editor has a single layer named Layer 1 and all the audio files you bring into the sound project are added to this layer (the only exception to this is when you record open the Record Audio dialog box immediately after selecting the Mix Editor pane — see "Recording your own audio clips" earlier in this chapter).

The easiest way to add a new layer to your project is by clicking the Add Layer Below button (the one with the plus sign) in the toolbar area of an existing layer. Sound Editor then inserts a new layer beneath the one whose Add Layer Below button you clicked.

To add or record an audio file for a new layer, you need to remember to click that layer to make it active (indicated by highlighting its name and toolbar) before you select the Add Audio File, Import from CD/DVD, or Record Audio options in the Add to Project pane.

Don't forget that you can maximize the Mix Editor pane to display all the layers you're working with by clicking the Collapse Clip Editor button (with the upward-pointing triangle) in the upper-right corner of the Clip Editor title bar.

Manipulating layers

In addition to the Add Layer Below button, each layer you add to a sound project has the following toolbar controls that you can use to control the layers:

- ✔ **Delete Layer** button to remove the layer including all its audio clips and effects applied to them

- ✔ **Mute On/Off** button to temporarily mute all audio clips added to the selected layer when you play the mix (click this button a second time to turn mute off in the current layer)

- ✔ **Solo On/Off (Mute All Other Layers)** button to temporarily mute the audio clips in all layers except for the one currently selected when you play the mix (click this button a second time to turn mute off in all the other layers)

- ✔ **Adjust Layer Weight** slider and text box to adjust the relative volume of all audio clips in the currently selected layer (adjust upward toward 100 for a higher relative volume and downward toward zero for a lower relative volume)

Use the Adjust Layer Weight controls in your respective layers to make one set of clips more prominent than another. In the example overlaying a narrative track on top of background music, you could set the relative weight of the layer with the narration audio clip up to something like 75 and the layer with background music clip down to something like 25 to ensure that narration is clearly in the forefront and the background music stays in the background where it belongs.

After adding clips to a particular layer you can arrange them by dragging them to new positions on that layer. You can also use drag-and-drop to move a clip to a new layer in your project. Note that when you try drop a clip on top of a clip already on the layer that has a blank space in front of it, Sound Editor inserts the clip you moved in front of the existing clip by moving it to the right on the layer. If, however, you try to drop the clip you're moving on an existing clip where there is no blank space in front of it (it either abuts another clip or the beginning of the layer), Sound Editor inserts the clip you're moving after the existing clip (even if it has to move a clip that otherwise abutted its end before the move).

Figure 5-6 shows the Sound Editor window after collapsing the Clip Editor pane and adding clips to three different layers. In this particular example, the audio in Clip 1 in Layer 1 contains a piece of background music that starts playing immediately, Clip 4 in Layer 2 contains a narrative track that then comes up after a few seconds, and Clip 2 in Layer 3 (the one currently selected in this figure) contains another piece of background music that comes up towards the end of the narration and conclusion of the first piece.

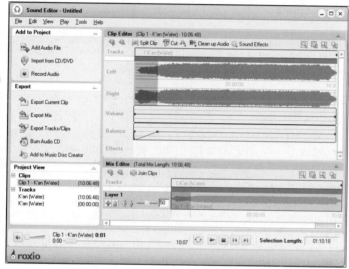

Figure 5-6:
Sound
Editor win-
dow after
collapsing
the Clip
Editor pane
to display all
the layers
in the Mix
Editor.

Enhancing audio in the mix

Sound Editor supplies you with a multitude of different kinds of audio effects that you can apply to the clips in your mix. These audio effects are arranged on two different menus: audio clean up effects on the Clean Up Audio pop-up menu and special audio effects on the Sound Effects pop-up menu.

To apply an audio clean up effect to the portion of the clip selected in the Clip Editor (remember you can press Ctrl+A to quickly select a clip's entire waveform), click the Clean Up Audio button on its toolbar and then select among these menu options:

✔ **Clean** to open the Clean dialog box where you can use its Declicker, Decrackler, Denoiser, and Noise sliders to adjust the intensity of clicks, crackling sounds, and both the threshold and intensity of hiss and rumbles (noise) in the clip

✔ **Enhancer** to open the Enhancer dialog box where you can use its Bass or Excite option buttons and its Level slider to enhance either the bass or make the audio brighter

✔ **Equalizer** to open the Equalizer dialog box with a 10-band equalizer that enables you to boost or cut the amplitude (volume) for ten bands of sound frequencies by dragging their respective frequency sliders (note that this equalizer contains a Master slider that you can use to adjust overall volume for the selected audio)

To apply special effects to the portion of the clip you've selected, click the Sound Effects button on the Clip Editor pane's toolbar and then select among these menu options:

✔ **Alienizer** to add metallic and alien synthesized effects to your audio by dragging the Alien 1 and Alien 2 sliders in the Alienizer dialog box

✔ **Devoicer** to remove a voice from the selected clip by adjusting its intensity in the Devoicer dialog box (this effect is only effective on music with one, prominent singing voice)

✔ **Digital Hall** to add different types of reverberation audio effects on the selected audio: Box, Room, Church, or Space to simulate these various environments as reverberation chambers (note that for any of the four options you choose, you can adjust the amount of reverberation and echo by adjusting the Reverb Time and Echo Level sliders) — click the Play button in this dialog box to hear the result on the selected audio of your Box, Room, Church, or Space Option button selection and any adjustments you make to the Reverb Time and/or Echo Level sliders before clicking OK to apply them

✔ **Maturizer** to adjust the quality of the selected audio (especially LPs recorded from older "vintage" equipment) in the Maturizer dialog box by adjusting the Intensity slider for any or all of five different check box options: Noise (for tapes that have a lot of noise), Hum, Crackle, and Click (for 33 rpm or 78 rpm LPs)

✔ **Mono to Stereo** to adjust the Intensity slider to simulate stereo in a mono recording in Mono to Stereo dialog box

✔ **Parametric Equalizer** to open the Parametric Equalizer dialog box containing a 4-band equalizer that enables you to boost or cut the gain (amplitude) and bandwidth (Q) for four bands of sound frequencies by selecting their channel and then dragging their nodes in the line graph to adjust their frequency, quality, and gain (note that this equalizer contains a Master slider that you can use to adjust the overall gain for the selected audio)

✔ **Pitch** to adjust the pitch of the selected audio without affecting the speed in the Pitch dialog box by adjusting its Pitch slider (0 being the original pitch of the audio clip)

✔ **RoboVoice** to add metallic and robotic synthesized effects (similar to the Alienizer) to your audio in the RoboVoice dialog box by dragging the Harmonize and Metallize sliders (note that you can also click the Spread check box to increase the perceived separation of the left and right channels of a stereo recording)

✔ **Stereo Enhancer** to open the Stereo Enhancer dialog box where you can adjust its Intensity slider to increase or decrease the perceived separation between the left and right channels of stereo audio

As you add various effects to the audio clip displayed in the Clip Editor, Sound Editor adds a band identifying the effect in the Effects area. To modify an effect, right-click its band and then select Effect Properties on its shortcut menu to open its dialog box showing the current settings. To remove an effect, click the Delete option at the top of this shortcut menu instead.

Keep in mind that Sound Editor's audio effects are cumulative, that is, they are layered on top of the other. This means that you need to test each effect as you apply it by listening to the result before applying another effect. That way, if you find that you goofed up and really don't like the audio effect you just applied, you can remove it by choosing Edit⇨Undo on the Sound Editor menu bar or pressing Ctrl+Z (remember that you can also reapply an effect that you remove with the Undo command by immediately choosing the Edit⇨Redo command or pressing Ctrl+Y).

Exporting a Sound Editor Project

When you save the audio mixes you create with Sound Editor as a sound editor project (File⇨Save Project), the program saves the audio mix in a special DMSE (Digital Media Sound Editor) file format. This format includes references to all the audio files add to the mix, information about all the effects that you applied to its clips as well as information about these clips are organized into tracks and layers.

The DMSE file, however, is not suitable for sharing with others or for using outside of the Sound Editor program itself. Sound Editor does, however, include several export options that enable you to save particular clips in project or even the entire audio mix in commonly used audio file formats.

To export an audio clip, you select it in the Mix Editor and then click the Export Current Clip link in the Export pane. To export the entire audio mix with all its clips, you simply click the Export Mix link instead.

When you click Export Current Clip, Sound Editor opens an Export Current Clip dialog box (similar to the one shown in Figure 5-7) where you specify the name of the new audio file, where to save, and what file formatting settings to use. When you click Export Mix, the program opens an Export Mix dialog box that uses the very same layout and options as the Export Current Clip dialog box.

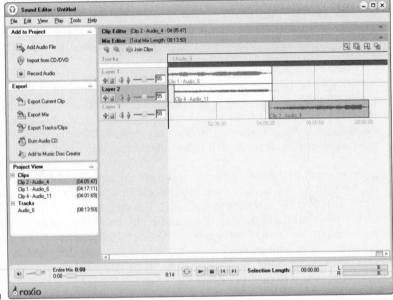

Figure 5-7:
Use the options in this dialog box to save the current audio clip in a commonly-used audio file format.

When specifying the Output Settings in Export Current Clip or Export Mix dialog box you have a choice of the following audio formats:

- ✔ **Custom** to save the clip in a format of your own definition, including audio file type, encoder, bit rate, and compression settings on the File Format tab of the Output Settings dialog box opened by clicking the Edit button

- ✔ **Wav (Recommended)** to save the clip or mix as an uncompressed Windows Audio File

- ✔ **MP3 (Good Quality)** to save the clip or mix as an MP3 file with a compression rate of 192 Kbps

✔ **MP3 (Low Quality)** to save the clip or mix as an MP3 file with a compression rate of 96 Kbps

✔ **WMA (Good Quality)** to save the clip or mix as a Windows Media Audio file with a compression rate of 128 Kbps

✔ **WMA (Low Quality)** to save the clip or mix as a Windows Media Audio file with a compression rate of 64 Kbps

If you're dealing with an audio mix in which you have several clips or tracks created from clips that you want to save as standalone audio files, click the Export Tracks/Clips link in the Export pane and then select all the tracks or clips you want to export in the Export Tracks/Clips dialog box.

In addition to exporting your clips or audio mix to readily-recognized audio files that are saved on your computer's hard disk, you can also export them directly to an audio CD by clicking the Burn Audio CD link in the Export pane. Selecting this option opens a Burn Audio CD dialog box where you can select all the tracks or clips you want on the CD as well as select the audio CD and burn settings (see Chapter 7 for details).

Last but not least, you can export the audio mix in your Sound Editor project directly to a new Audio CD project in the Music Disc Creator application simply by clicking the Add to Music Disc Creator link in the Export pane. Once added to an Audio CD project in this program, you can then burn it along with other files you add to the CD project in the Music Disc Creator program (see Chapter 7 for details).

Chapter 6

Managing Digital Photos

*W*orking with digital photos has become one of the more important functions of today's computer software. In the PhotoSuite application in the Roxio Creator 8 suite, you have one of the most powerful tools for fixing and editing your digital photos. Coupled with the capacity of the suite's Media Manager tool for organizing your digital photos (see Chapter 4) and the ability of its VideoWave application to arrange photos into a slideshow (see Chapter 11), you have at hand all the software you need for maintaining and arranging all your digital photo collections from now on.

In this chapter, you find out how to use the PhotoSuite application to fix, edit, and enhance your digital photos. You also discover how easy it is to use PhotoSuite to print your photos either individually, in groups on a single page, or as a contact sheet. In addition, this chapter covers sharing your digital photos with your friends and family. As you see in this chapter, with PhotoSuite you not only can send your photos in the body of your e-mail message, but you can also package a group of them into a slideshow that your recipients can then play in sequence. Alternatively, you can upload them to an online album on the Snapfish Photo Album Web site.

Launching PhotoSuite Your Way

If you have the Roxio Creator 8 Home window open, clicking the PhotoSuite link in the Applications Project Window after clicking Applications on the Home tab of the Project List is the easiest way to launch the program. It is, however, not the only way to launch PhotoSuite from Roxio Creator Home. You can also launch the program by clicking the Fix & Enhance link on the Photo tab of the Project List.

If the Roxio Creator 8 Home window is not open and you have a photo to edit, you can launch PhotoSuite and load the photo from Windows. Right-click the photo's file icon and then position the mouse pointer over the Open With option to displays its submenu. The first time you display the Open With submenu, PhotoSuite 8 will not be listed as a program for opening the selected photo file.

To add PhotoSuite to the list of programs, follow these steps:

1. **Click the Choose Program option at the bottom of the Open With submenu.**

   Windows displays the Open With dialog box.

2. **Click the Browse button.**

   Windows opens a second Open With dialog box where you locate the PhotoSuite program file.

3. **Click the My Computer button on the left side of the dialog box and then double-click the Local Disk (C:) icon to open it.**

4. **In the Local Disk (C:) folder, double-click the Program Files icon to open it.**

5. **In the Program Files folder, double-click the Roxio folder icon to open it.**

6. **In the Roxio folder, double-click the Easy Media Creator 8 folder icon to open it.**

7. **In the Easy Media Creator 8 folder, double-click the PhotoSuite folder icon to open it.**

8. **In the PhotoSuite folder, click the PhotoSuite8.exe program icon and then click the Open button.**

   Windows returns you to the original Open With dialog box where PhotoSuite 8 is not only added to the list of programs but is already selected.

9. **Click the OK button to launch PhotoSuite with the selected photo opened and ready for editing.**

After adding PhotoSuite 8 to the program list by following these somewhat elaborate steps, the next time you want to open a photo for editing in it, you have only to right-click the photo file icon, mouse over Open With to open its submenu, and then click PhotoSuite 8 on it.

Getting Familiar with PhotoSuite 8

When you launch PhotoSuite with a photo to edit (as outlined in the steps in the preceding section), a PhotoSuite 8 window similar to the one shown in Figure 6-1 appears. When first opened, this window displays three panes: the Task pane with Common and Edit tabs on the left, Canvas pane at top right, and Open File(s) pane right beneath Canvas.

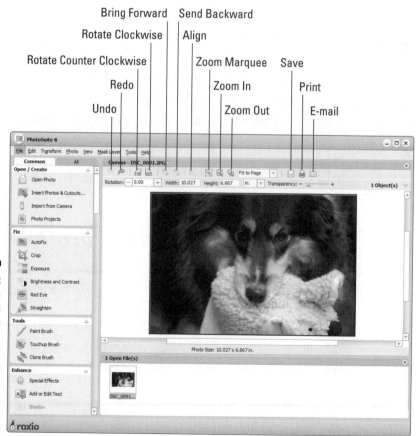

Figure 6-1: The PhotoSuite 8 window offers its many editing options on the two tabs of its Task pane.

Note that you can control which panes are displayed in the PhotoSuite window by selecting them on PhotoSuite's View menu. When a pane is displayed, a check mark appears in front of its name on this menu. To hide a currently displayed pane, click its name on the View menu.

The Common tab contains the following panes:

- **Open/Create** pane contains links that enable you to open photos for editing as well as import photos directly from your digital camera into PhotoSuite

- **Fix** pane contains links to the most commonly used editing options including adjusting the exposure, color, and sharpness; cropping; removing red eye;, and straightening

- **Tools** pane includes links to a variety of brushes that you can use to touch up a photo

- **Enhance** pane contains links to a wide range of special effects (including black and white) and to those that enable you to add text to a photo

The All tab of the Task pane contains a full list of the editing options available (not just the most commonly used ones) arranged in the same four categories.

Note that each of the panes on the Common and All tabs contains its own collapse button (a triangle pointing upward) on its right side that changes to an expand button when clicked (a triangle pointing downward). You can click a category's collapse button to temporarily hide its options to make room in the Task pane for the options in the categories you are using. To redisplay the options in a collapsed category, just click that category's Expand button.

PhotoSuite's Supported File Formats

PhotoSuite makes it a snap to fix damaged digital photos, edit their contents, and enhance their overall look with the program's extensive editing features. PhotoSuite can open and edit photos saved in any of the following graphics file formats:

- **BMP** (Bitmap) with the .bmp, .rle, or .dib filename extension

- **JPEG** (Joint Photographic Experts Group) with the .jpg, .jpe. or .jpeg filename extension

- **PNG** (Portable Network Graphics) with the .png filename extension

- **TIFF** (Tagged Information File Format) with the .tif or .tiff filename extension

BMP or Bitmap is the Microsoft Windows' standard graphics file format. Bitmap files come in 2, 16, 256, and 16.7 million (24-bit) color and most use no compression. The so-called RLE or Run-Length Encoded variation of the basic Bitmap does use some modest compression. RLE files use 16 or 256 colors and are primarily used in saving graphics used as Windows desktop wallpaper and background images.

The JPEG file format is one of the most popular graphics file formats for digital photos (many digital cameras save their photos as JPEG files). This graphics file format uses a *lossy* compression scheme that attempts to reduce the overall file size by reducing detail in certain areas. This often results (especially in photos with lots of detail) in a slight degradation of the overall picture quality. JPEG is an especially good format to use for photos that you intend to display on Web pages.

The PNG file format was developed as an alternative to the GIF (Graphics Information Format), the ever-popular file format for displaying Web page graphics. PNG files come in 256-color, True Color, and 32-bit color varieties and use a lossless compression scheme to cut down on the overall size.

The TIFF file format was developed as a portable format for bitmap images. TIFF files come in monochrome, 16-color and grayscale, 256-color and grayscale, and 16.7 million-color (24-bit) varieties. This file format gives you the highest quality in terms of bitmap images, but the files are notoriously large — especially for high-resolution images.

Although PhotoSuite can open for editing and also save edited photos in the Bitmap, JPEG, PNG, or TIFF file format, the program's native graphics file format is something known as DMSP (using the .dmsp filename extension). This file format was developed for editing photos in PhotoSuite and developing photo projects using the program's templates (see "Playing with PhotoSuite Projects" later in this chapter for details). This file format supports the use of a layer scheme (somewhat akin to that used in Adobe Photoshop) that enables you to undo changes made to specific graphics objects (even when you've combined multiple photos and other objects together in a collage).

When editing photos originally saved in the other supported graphics file formats with PhotoSuite, open the photo and use the File➪Save As command to save the file in PhotoSuite's DMSP format. You do this by selecting PhotoSuite Format (*.dmsp) in the Files of Type drop-down list in the Save As dialog box before clicking the Save button. Then, after you finish making all your editing changes to the photo in PhotoSuite, you can save the final edited version in its original graphics file format (BMP, JPEG, PNG, or TIFF) for distribution to others.

The process of saving the original file as a DMSP file for the editing process and then saving it back out in its original file format when the editing's done is especially important when it comes to dealing with JPEG photos. That's because continually saving the editing changes made to a JPEG photo in PhotoSuite contributes to the overall degradation of its quality (especially when the photo has a lot of detail).

Photos saved in PhotoSuite's native DMSP file format can only be opened with PhotoSuite. For this reason, never send a DMSP photo to anyone you aren't completely certain has PhotoSuite installed on his or her computer. Also, photos saved in PhotoSuite's DMSP native file format can't be opened on the Internet (always save photos bound for the Web either in the JPEG or PNG file formats).

Fixing, Editing, and Enhancing Photos

To edit a photo in PhotoSuite, click the Open Photo link at the top of the Open/Create pane. The Open Files dialog box, similar to the one shown in Figure 6-2, then opens. Here, you can select the Smart View, album (see Chapter 4 for details), or folder that contains the photo you want to edit.

My Album

My Media | Folders

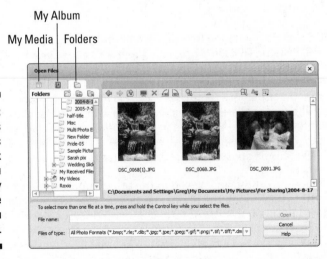

Figure 6-2: PhotoSuite's Open Files dialog box enables you to easily select the photo you want to edit.

When you locate the photo you want to edit in the Open Files dialog box, click its thumbnail and then click the Open button. The selected photo then appears in the Canvas pane on the right side of the PhotoSuite window, along with thumbnails of it in the Object(s) pane to the right (which contains all project objects displayed in the Canvas, including photos, clip art, paint strokes, and text used in editing) and the Open Files pane below.

Fix me up

The Fix pane on the Common tab contains but a fraction of the fix options available to you in PhotoSuite 8. (To see a complete list, choose Photo⇨Fix on the menu bar and look at the list of options on its submenu. Or, you can click the All tab button and then click the Fix pane's expand button.)

The most commonly needed options on the Fix pane include

- ✔ **AutoFix** to have PhotoSuite figure out and then automatically fix any exposure, saturation, and sharpness problems in the photo
- ✔ **Crop** to trim the photo to a desired size and shape
- ✔ **Exposure** to enable you to manually adjust the exposure of the photo
- ✔ **Brightness and Contrast** to enable you to adjust the brightness and contrast of the photo
- ✔ **Red Eye** to remove red eye from the subjects in your photo
- ✔ **Straighten** to enable you to select a horizontal or vertical line that is less than true in the photo and have PhotoSuite use it in straightening the image. (After straightening, you can use the Crop feature to trim the photo to remove any of the white areas now included within the original size and shape of the photo.)

AutoFix to the rescue

As all photographers know, you can't always take your shot in the most optimal lighting conditions. The worst lighting conditions, of course, are those outdoor settings where it's way too bright, as when shooting right into the sun rather than having the sun at your back, and those indoor settings where it's way too gloomy, as when taking a shot in a dimly lit room and the flash doesn't go off. As a result, like it or not, the quality of many of the pictures you shoot ends up being compromised by the presence of some really overexposed or underexposed areas.

Fortunately, digital photo editing often enables you to compensate for most extreme lighting conditions, making it possible to return a certain amount of balance and detail to your favorite photo. This is especially true in the case of grossly underexposed photos where the color and detail is washed out throughout. It also works pretty well with photos that are generally overexposed. Where digital photo editing is not so successful is with digital photos that suffer from both extremely over- and underexposed areas. In these cases, you usually have to split the difference and settle for a certain amount of improvement in toning down the washed out effect in overexposed areas and in bringing back a little of the color and detail to the underexposed ones.

To instantly improve the quality of a digital photo, you can turn to the AutoFix feature. AutoFix automates the process of trying to find the correct exposure, saturation, and sharpness settings for a photo that suffers from either some underexposure or overexposure.

To have PhotoSuite diagnose and attempt to cure your photo's ills, click the AutoFix link in the Fix pane. This opens the AutoFix dialog box, where you can click the AutoFix button. PhotoSuite attempts to diagnose problems in the photo's exposure, color saturation, and sharpness, and then proceeds to reset them. After transforming the photo, the AutoFix dialog box indicates what areas (Exposure, Saturation, and Sharpness) have been adjusted (see Figure 6-3).

Figure 6-3:
After
PhotoSuite
finishes
fixing the
photo, the
AutoFix
dialog
box shows
what areas
have been
modified.

If you don't like the results (and often, you won't), click the Reset button in the AutoFix dialog box. If you like what you see and want to retain the modified photo, click the Close button in the upper-right corner of the AutoFix dialog box and save the changes to the file (Ctrl+S). Of course, if you take the added precaution of working on a copy of the original digital photo, you can always fall back to opening the original photo in PhotoSuite.

Exposure, color, and sharpness

If AutoFix isn't able to cure what ails your photo, you can try using one or more of the individual controls — Exposure, Brightness & Contrast, Saturation, Sharpness, and Tint — to fix the problems.

The Exposure, Saturation, and Sharpness dialog boxes (opened by clicking their respective options on the All tab in the Task pane) each contain their own AutoFix button. You can click this button in the hope that PhotoSuite will correctly diagnose and fix the respective problems with the photo's exposure, color saturation, and sharpness settings.

Don't forget that the Common tab contains only the links to the Exposure and Brightness & Contrast options. To access the Saturation, Sharpness, and Tint options, you must click the All tab and then expand the Fix pane.

I often find that I get better results by fiddling with the Exposure, Saturation, and Sharpness controls individually and in the order of their appearance on the All tab, rather than by using the AutoFix option. After making corrections in each of these areas, I very seldom, if ever, have to go on and fool with the Brightness & Contrast control as well.

In addition to their AutoFix buttons, the Exposure, Saturation, and Sharpness dialog boxes also have their own sliders that you can use instead to manually achieve the amount of correction your photo needs:

- **Exposure** dialog box contains Dark Areas, Midtones, and Bright Areas sliders that enable you to adjust the exposure in just the darker or brighter areas of the photo or only in the mid ranges in between

- **Saturation** task pane contains a Saturation slider for adjusting the overall saturation of color in the photo and a Midtones slider for adjusting color saturation in just the mid ranges of the photo

- **Sharpness** task pane contains an Amount slider for adjusting the amount of contrast in the photo's edge pixels, a Radius slider for adjusting the number of pixels radiating from the edge pixels that you want to sharpen, and a Threshold slider for adjusting how different pixels must be to be considered as the edge pixels for sharpening

Just a tint of color

The controls in the Tint dialog box enable you to correct the overall hue and balance of color in a photo. It's useful when you're dealing with an old photo print that shows yellowing from age that carries over into the digital photo during scanning. To change the tint of a photo, open the Tint dialog box and with the eyedropper mouse pointer click the area of the photo that should be white or gray. PhotoSuite automatically adjusts the tint of the photo.

In some cases, you're not trying to get rid of yellowing by restoring the whites and grays, but rather you want to "tint" the photo in a particular color (often to add a mood to it). You can use the Tint Color slider to select the color you want to tint the photo and the Tint Balance slider to increase or decrease the amount of color tinting applied.

Making it bright and crisp

The Brightness & Contrast dialog box pane, as its name implies, enables you to modify the amount of brightness and contrast in the photo by manipulating its Brightness and/or Contrast sliders. This dialog box does not offer any control for automatically selecting the optimal brightness and contrast settings. Here, you have to manipulate the appropriate slider(s) to make any modifications.

The Exposure, Saturation, Sharpness, Tint, and Brightness & Contrast dialog boxes all contain Show Preview check boxes that are all automatically checked so that you immediately see the effects of all the modifications you make with the various sliders. You can use this check box to compare the changes you've made to the original photo. Simply click the Show Preview check box to remove its check mark and display the original photo; then click this check box again to reapply its checkmark and display the modifications you've just made.

Here we come a cropping

The Crop option in the Fix pane enables you to cut out whatever parts you consider extraneous in the photo so that it concentrates on what you consider to be the photo's primary subject or subjects. Cropping is one of the most used editing tools for photos. When you click the Crop link, a Crop dialog box opens and crop marks (indicated by dashed lines with resizing handles shown as circles at each corner) surround the perimeter of the photo, as shown in Figure 6-4.

Figure 6-4:
Drag the crop marks surrounding the image to cut out all extraneous portions of the photo.

The Crop dialog box enables you to select a crop shape (other than the default rectangular shape matching the proportions of your original photo). You can then drag the crop marks so that only the part of the photo you want is within the dotted lines (referred to as "the area of interest"). PhotoSuite also indicates which part of the photo will be cropped and which part is in the area of interest (and will be retained). PhotoSuite shows you this when you finish the cropping procedure (by clicking the Close button in the Crop dialog box) by making the display of the cropped area fairly transparent while continuing to display the area of interest as normal.

This differentiation is important when using any non-rectangular crop shape as the program continues to display the crop marks that you manipulate as a rectangle that contains the crop shape you select. This means that when you use a non-rectangular crop shape, you need to pay attention to which areas are transparent and which are in the area of interest (which no longer correspond to the crop marks) in order to tell what is going to be cropped and what is going to be retained.

When defining the area of interest with the crop marks, keep these techniques in mind:

- ✔ Drag anywhere on the vertical or horizontal dashed crop lines to move them individually.

- ✔ Drag the resize handles at a corner to resize both the vertical and horizontal lines extending from that corner, while at the same time maintaining the current aspect ratio.

- ✔ Press and hold down the Shift key when dragging a resize handle when you want to move the vertical and horizontal lines extending from it without maintaining the current aspect ratio.

- ✔ Drag the entire area of interest within the photo by positioning the mouse pointer somewhere within this area and then dragging the open hand mouse pointer.

To select a new proportion for the crop marks, click the new proportion setting from the Select a Dimension for the Crop Area drop-down list. The proportion refers to the comparative relation of width to height (when the default Portrait option button is selected) or height to width (when the Landscape option button is selected).

To see how your photo will appear when the area indicated for cropping is cut out (without actually going ahead with the cropping), click the Hide Cropped Area check box to put a checkmark in it. PhotoSuite then temporarily removes all but the indicated area of interest until you click the Hide Cropped Area check box again to remove the checkmark. If you're happy with the results and want to go ahead with the cropping, click the Close button in the upper-right corner of the Crop dialog box. If you decide you don't like the way you've cropped the image, restore the photo by pressing Ctrl+Z or clicking the Undo button on the Canvas pane's toolbar.

Get the red out!

Red eye is a prominent problem in portraits (often caused when the subject's eyes reflect light from a flash). To take care of red eye in the photo all you have to do is click the Red Eye link in the Fix pane to open the Red Eye dialog box (see Figure 6-5). You can then click the AutoFix button to try and have PhotoSuite take care of the problem automatically.

If the AutoFix button doesn't take care of the problem, you can still take the red out of the eyes of particular subjects in the photo by following this manual procedure:

1. **Click the Zoom In button on the Canvas toolbar and then drag the vertical and horizontal scroll bars to bring the subject whose red eye you want to fix into view on the screen.**

   Repeat Step 1 until you've zoomed in on the subject's eyes so that they're clearly visible on the screen and big enough to manipulate.

2. **Position the mouse pointer (which assumes a circular shape with a crosshair in the middle) over one of the subject's red eyes.**

   The mouse pointer must be the same size as the eyes you're going to treat (see Figure 6-5) before you can go ahead and click the mouse button to replace red eye with blue coloring.

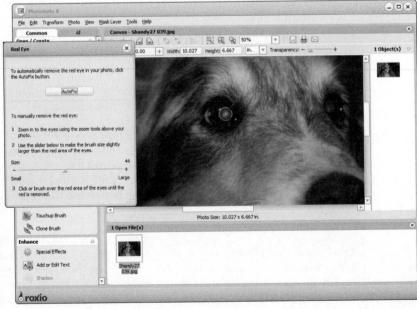

Figure 6-5: Zoom in and then use the brush size slider in the Red Eye task pane to manually remove red eye from subjects in a photo.

3. **Drag the brush Size slider in the Red Eye dialog box to the left (to decrease the diameter of the mouse pointer) or to the right (to increase the diameter of the mouse pointer) until the mouse pointer is the same size or just slightly smaller than the subject's eyes.**

   Now you're ready to replace the red eye by clicking the mouse button.

4. **Position the mouse pointer so that it covers one of the subject's eyes and then click the mouse button.**

   When you click the mouse button, PhotoSuite replaces the red in the eye with blue pixels.

5. **Repeat Steps 2 through 4 to remove the red from the subject's other eye.**

After you finish manually removing red eye from the subjects in the photo you're editing, click the Close button in the Red Eye dialog box.

Flip me over and set me right

The Rotate, Flip, Straighten, and Resize editing features enable you to quickly put the photo into its correct orientation or modify its overall size. Of these four, the Rotate options are probably the most important, given that whenever you turn the camera up to get a tall, vertical shot, this photo appears as a picture in landscape mode (as though it were laying on its side) that needs to be rotated either ninety degrees counterclockwise (to the left) or clockwise (to the right).

When you open the Transform menu on the PhotoSuite 8 menu bar, you find the following three rotate options you can use to quickly correct the orientation of most photos:

✔ **Rotate Left** to rotate the photo ninety degrees counterclockwise (the same as clicking the Rotate Counter Clockwise button on the Canvas toolbar)

✔ **Rotate Right** to rotate the photo ninety degrees clockwise (the same as clicking the Rotate Clockwise button on the Canvas toolbar)

✔ **Rotate 180 Degree** to rotate the photo so that it's completely turned upside down

If you want to rotate the photo to any other angle, you can do this from the Rotation combo box on the Canvas pane's Option bar. After selecting the current rotation setting in this box, you can replace it by typing in the new value (representing the number of degrees between 1 and 359 that the photo should be rotated in a clockwise direction). You can also select the number of degrees to rotate the photo by clicking the combo box's Plus (+) or Minus (–) button until the desired number of degrees is displayed in the combo box.

The Flip options on the Transform menu enable you to reverse the orientation of your photo. The Flip options include:

- **Flip Vertical** so that what appears at the top in the original photo now appears on the bottom (this is equivalent to rotating the photo 180 degrees)

- **Flip Horizontal** so that what appears on the right in the original photo now appears on the left

- **Flip Both** so that the photo is flipped both horizontally and vertically

Can you straighten this out?

The Straighten option enables you to straighten your photo (something I always seem to need help with). To use this feature, click the Straighten link on the Fix pane to open the Straighten dialog box and then follow these simple steps:

1. **Click the mouse pointer at one end of some object in the photo that should be perfectly horizontal or vertical.**

   You now need to draw a horizontal or vertical line that PhotoSuite can use as a guideline when straightening the photo (see Figure 6-6).

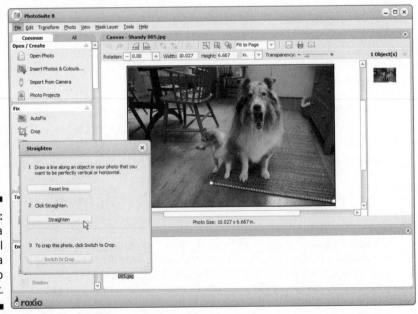

Figure 6-6: Using a horizontal line in a photo to straighten it.

2. **Drag the mouse pointer along the object to draw the guideline to be used in straightening the photo horizontally or vertically.**

   Now you're ready to have PhotoSuite actually straighten the picture.

3. **Click the Straighten button in the Straighten dialog box. If the straightened photo requires cropping, proceed to Step 4. Otherwise, click the Close button in the Straighten dialog box.**

4. **(Optional) Click the Switch to Crop button, then click the Yes button in the dialog box asking you to flatten the object to open the Crop dialog box.**

5. **Crop the photo as required (see Figure 6-7) and then click the Close button in the Crop dialog box.**

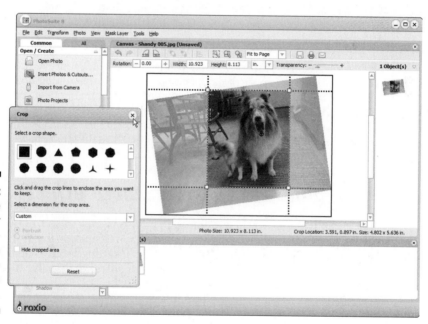

Figure 6-7:
Cropping the photo after straightening it to remove the extraneous white areas.

When it's a matter of size

The Width and Height text boxes on the Canvas pane's Option bar indicate the current size of the photo in inches. (To change the units for these text boxes, click the drop-down button to the right of in. and then select cm. for centimeters or pixel on its drop-down list.) To resize a photo, all you have to do is click in either the Width or Height box and then select the current value and replace it by typing in a new value (in the currently selected units).

When you press the Enter key or click the mouse pointer somewhere in the image in the Canvas pane after entering a new value in the Width or Height text box, PhotoSuite automatically adjusts the value in the other text box to maintain the original proportions of the image.

If you want to resize a photo without maintaining these proportions, you must do it from the Resize dialog box opened by clicking the Resize link in the Fix pane on the All tab. Then, click its Maintain Proportions check box to remove its check mark before you replace the values in both its Width and Height text boxes.

When you resize a photo from the Resize dialog box, PhotoSuite puts sizing handles all around the image in the Canvas pane. You can manually resize the image by dragging one of these handles. You drag a corner handle to change the width and height of the image at the same time while maintaining the original proportions (providing that the Maintain Proportions check box is still selected).

Unless you're sure you know what you're doing, don't remove the check mark from the Maintain Proportions check box in the Resize dialog box before you start resizing the photo — either manually or by entering new values into the Width or Height text boxes. By resizing a photo without regard to the aspect ratio between the width and the height (that's the proportions that are being maintained), you can end up with a photo that's really distorted.

Achieving that perfect photo effect

PhotoSuite is the best when it comes to easy-to-apply special effects. In addition to the ready-made special effects you have to choose from, you can also lighten a photo by increasing its transparency setting or give the photo a real old-fashioned look by using the Edge Fading control to dissolve its edges.

In addition to applying these filters, transparency, and edging effects, you can also add text to your photos, paint and draw on them, and even add cutouts that remove particular shapes from the photo (a really handy technique when combined with non-rectangular crop shapes where you want to cut off the white areas that fill in the original rectangle that are left behind after cropping the photo to the new shape).

Dazzling special effects for every mood

PhotoSuite includes a wide array of special effects that can really change the look of your photo. To have a gander at all the effects and experiment with what they do (or don't do for your photo), click the Special Effects link in the Enhance pane on the Common or All tab of the Task pane.

PhotoSuite then opens the Special Effects dialog box. This dialog box contains a drop-down list box at the top where you can select the category of effects (Adjust Color through Warp) you want to work with. All Effects is selected by default in this drop-down list box so that every special effect available in PhotoSuite is listed in the list box area below. To apply a special effect to the current photo displayed in the Canvas pane, you simply click the effect's thumbnail in this list box (see Figure 6-8).

When you click one of the special effect thumbnails, PhotoSuite immediately applies that special effect to the photo in the Canvas pane. If you don't like the effect, you can just go ahead and choose another in the Special Effects dialog box (PhotoSuite's special effects are *not* cumulative so you don't have to cancel one effect before trying another).

Note that many of the special effects enable you to adjust their settings, usually in the form of sliders (for example, the Cool Color 1 effect shown in the Special Effects dialog box in Figure 6-8). When you've got the special effect that you want to stay with, click the Apply button at the bottom of the dialog box before you click its Close button (if you click Close before you click Apply, the previewed effect is not applied to the image and it returns to the state it was in before you opened Special Effects).

Figure 6-8:
Applying the
Cool Color 1
effect to
my photo
of the Blue
Mosque in
Istanbul.

Adding text to your photos

PhotoSuite makes it easy to annotate your pictures with text. You can use this feature to add titles to your photos. To do this, click the Add or Edit Text link in the Enhance pane on the Common or All tab. PhotoSuite then displays the Add or Edit Text dialog box like the one shown in Figure 6-9 where you can enter the title or whatever label you want to add and then select the text color, font, font size, font attributes, and alignment for it.

Figure 6-9:
You can add titles to your photos using the controls in the Add or Edit Text task pane.

To annotate your photo with text in the Add or Edit Text dialog box, follow these steps:

1. **Type the text you want to appear in the photo in the Select a Text Object and Edit Its Text Below list box.**

   To add line breaks to the title or comments you're typing, press the Enter key.

   Now you're ready to adjust the text settings beginning with the text color. By default, PhotoSuite selects black as the text color that only works when placing the text on a very light background in the photo.

2. **(Optional) Click the Color drop-down button and then click the text color you want to use on the pop-up palette.**

If you want to use a color that appears in the photo, click the eyedropper icon in the lower-right corner of the color palette and then click the color you want to use in photo. If you want to mix a sample color, click the More Colors button in the lower-left corner of the color palette and then create a new color by entering the appropriate Red, Green, and Blue values or by dragging the crosshairs in the Hues and Shades sample boxes before clicking OK.

By default, PhotoSuite picks Tahoma as the font in which to display the text. If you wish, you can select another font to use from a wide variety of fonts that PhotoSuite makes available.

3. **(Optional) Click the Font drop-down button and then click the name of the font you want to use in the drop-down list.**

If you want, you can select a larger or smaller font size to use for the text.

4. **(Optional) Type a new point size in the Font Size combo box or use its Plus (+) or Minus (–) buttons to select a new point size.**

In addition to adjusting the font and font size, you can also change the alignment of the text in its text box (which is left-justified horizontally and top-justified vertically by default), add the bold, italics, or underlining attribute to the text, and even scrunch up or spread out the text in the text box by modifying the Horizontal Scaling percentages (percentages below 100% bring the text closer together and percentages above 100% spread it out).

5. **(Optional) Make any necessary adjustments to the text alignment, text attributes, or horizontal scaling.**

PhotoSuite positions the new text box in the dead center of the photo. Most of the time, you'll want to move the text box to a more appropriate location in the photograph.

6. **Position the mouse pointer inside the text box and when the pointer changes to an open hand, drag the text box to the desired position on the photo.**

In addition to repositioning the text box in the photo, you may also want to re-orient the text by rotating the text box.

7. **(Optional) Position the mouse pointer on the rotation handle (the larger ball in the middle at the top of the box). When the mouse pointer turns into a circular arrow, drag it until the text is oriented just as you want it to appear in the final photo.**

When you have the text positioned and oriented the way you want it, you're ready to set it.

8. **Click the Close button to close the Add or Edit Text dialog box. Then click somewhere in the white space outside the image in the Canvas pane to remove the box's outline as well as its sizing and rotation handles.**

After adding text to a photo, a text object (indicated by an A on blank page) appears in the Object(s) pane. If you need to edit the text, double-click this text object and PhotoSuite will not only reselect the text box but the Option bar will now display text controls — Color, Font, Bold, Italic, Underline, Size, Horizontal Scaling, Align Left, Align Center, Align Right, Align Top, and Align Middle. You can use these controls to change the attributes of the text (to edit the text, you must click the Add or Edit Text link in the Enhance pane when the text box is selected).

Touching up your photos with painting and drawing

You can use PhotoSuite's painting and drawing tools to touch up your photos or even add either freehand or predefined shapes to your photos. These tools include a Paint Brush tool that you can use to add brushstrokes to your photo, a Flood Fill tool that fills particular areas of the photo with color, and a Touchup Brush tool that adds color to the photo by actually painting on it (when you use the Paint Brush and Flood Fill tools, you create and add new graphic art objects to the photo, which means that you can continue to edit it because the object is on its own layer).

In addition to adding painting and drawing to your photo, you can also add standard shapes such as circles, squares, triangles, and the like with the Predefined Shapes tool as well as create custom shapes of your own design with Custom Shapes. Note, however, that you will mostly want to reserve the adding of shapes to photo projects where they can combine with the photos you're adding rather than literally overshadow them (see "Playing with PhotoSuite Projects" later in this chapter for information on creating projects).

In the Paint Brush dialog box (opened by clicking the Paint Brush link in the Tools pane on the Common or All tab), select the brush shape and paint color. You can then use the two sliders to refine your brush settings:

- **Thickness** to increase or decrease the width of the brush

- **Softness** to set the amount of blurring at the edges of the stroke and how much the stroke blends into the background

After you finish setting your brush settings, you can drag the mouse pointer to paint strokes on the photo. All the strokes that you make with a particular set of brush settings are adding to a single brush object in the Objects pane. If you make a mistake and want to erase a particular stroke, click the Undo button on the Canvas toolbar to remove it.

If, after painting on the image, you decide that a brush stroke needs modification, click the Edit and Existing Paint Stroke button at the top of the Paint Brush dialog box. PhotoSuite then selects the brush stroke (indicated by the bounding box with sizing handles all around it and a rotation handle at the top). You can then change the brush shape, color, thickness, and/or softness settings in the Paint Brush dialog box and these changes will immediately appear in the selected brush stroke object in the Canvas pane.

Note that working with the Touchup Brush in the Tools pane is similar except that you can select not only your brush shape, paint color, and brush size, but also modify the Transparency and the Edge Fading setting (which works like the Softness setting in the Paint Brush dialog box). In addition, you need to select a particular style of the Touchup Brush that determines what kind of painting you do. These brush style selections include a wide variety of effects which the PhotoSuite attempts to illustrate through the use of butterfly thumbnails displayed in the Select a Touchup Brush list box at the top of the dialog box.

Note that the function of most of the brush styles in this list is far from evident from their thumbnails. You should experiment with them to see just what effects they produce, as some are quite surprising. For example, the Lighten brush style actually lightens the colors of whatever object you paint with it rather than putting down the paint color you've selected. So too, the Transparency brush style actually removes all color, acting like an eraser function found in other paint programs.

When you paint with the Touchup Brush using the settings you've chosen, PhotoSuite does not put down each stroke as a separate brush object — indicated by the lack of a new brush object in the Object(s) pane. This does not mean that you can't delete a brushstroke made with the Touchup Brush (you do this by clicking the Undo button on the Canvas toolbar), but it does mean that you can't do any more editing to the brushstroke, such as move or rotate it after you've finish painting with this brush (something you *can* do when using the regular paint brush).

Getting ready to use the Flood Fill tool in the Flood Fill dialog box (opened by clicking Flood Fill in the Tools pane on the All tab) is very similar to getting ready to use the Touchup Brush tool in that you must select a fill style in the Select a Fill Style list box (using the exact same list of styles illustrated with the very same butterfly thumbnails as in the Select a Touchup Brush list box), as well as fill color, transparency, and edge fading.

Instead of setting the brush size as you do in the Touchup Brush dialog box, in the Flood Fill dialog box, you indicate how the pixels in the photo are selected for filling by using the Tolerance slider. If you set a low tolerance with this slider, PhotoSuite fills the pixels area you click with the paint bucket mouse pointer that are the same color or very close in hue. If you set a high tolerance with this slider, PhotoSuite fills the pixels that are similar but not exactly the same in the area you click.

After making your modifications to the Flood Fill settings, you can fill sections of the photo by clicking the paint bucket mouse pointer on the area you want filled. Which pixels are filled with the selected color, using the designated fill style in the area you click, depends upon the tolerance you use. If you want to fill more areas than the current tolerance allows, you can drag the paint bucket mouse pointer around the area to be filled. If PhotoSuite ends up filling more of the photo that you wanted, click the Undo button on the Canvas toolbar to remove it.

Bring on the clones

The Clone Brush dialog box opens by clicking the Clone Brush link in the Tools pane on the Common or All tab, and contains the controls for sampling an area of the photo and then painting another area with the same pixels. This feature is great for repairing damaged or washed out areas of a photo by taking a part of the nearby background and using it to fill in the missing or damaged places.

To use the Clone Brush to repair an area of your photo, you follow these steps:

1. **(Optional) Click the Zoom In button and drag the horizontal and vertical scroll bars until both the damaged area and the area whose pixels you want to clone are prominently displayed in the PhotoSuite window.**

2. **Position the mouse pointer (which assumes a circular shape with a crosshair in the middle) over one edge of the undamaged area whose pixels you want to paint with.**

   Next you may need to adjust the Size, Transparency, and Edge Fading settings with their respective sliders. Use the Size slider to adjust the size of the circular mouse pointer, keeping in mind that its diameter becomes the size of both the source brush you use to sample the pixels you want to clone and the destination brush you use to paint the damaged area with the cloned pixels. Use the Transparency slider to determine the intensity of cloned pixels: drag to the right for a lighter effect and to the left for a more opaque effect. Use the Edge Fading slider to increase or decrease the amount of fading around the edge of the destination brush (that is, the one you paint the damaged area of the photo with).

2. **(Optional) Manipulate the Size, Transparency, and Edge Fading sliders until you've got the settings you think you want to use in cloning.**

   Now you're ready to establish the starting point for the cloned pixels by clicking the mouse pointer. This establishes the starting point for the source brush that clones whatever pixels it passes over.

3. **Click the mouse pointer to establish the starting point for the source brush, which clones the pixels it passes over.**

All that's left to do now is paint with the mouse pointer over the damaged or washed out portion of the photo using the pixels in the area around the cloning start point.

4. **Drag the mouse pointer over the damaged or washed out area of the photo, replacing its pixels with those passed over by the source brush.**

When painting the damaged or washed out area, be aware of the strokes of your destination brush that's repairing the damaged area, and also keep your eye on the strokes of your source brush picking up the pixels you're painting with. If the strokes of your source brush go outside of the area you want cloned in the damaged area, you start painting with part of the image that you don't want copied to the damaged area. If this happens, click the Undo button on the Canvas pane's toolbar until the cloned pixels that don't belong are removed from the photo.

If you find that you keep painting with an unwanted part of the picture, try resetting the start point of the source brush at a place where there are more pixels you want to use. To do this, click the Reset Start Point button near the top of the Clone dialog box and then click the mouse pointer at a new, safer starting point for the source brush before dragging the mouse pointer to paint with the destination brush.

When you've repaired all the damaged or washed out areas in the photo, click the Close button in the Clone Brush dialog box.

Now, cut that out!

The Mask and Cutout feature enables you to separate an area of special interest in a photo from its background by cutting that area out so that you can manipulate it independently of the rest of the photo (such as apply a special effect to that area alone or save it in it own graphics file). When defining the object or area in a photo to cut out, you can either enclose the area in a wide variety of predefined shapes or you can select the area by tracing it or having PhotoSuite automatically attempt to trace the area by its edges or its color.

To create a cutout using a predefined shape, you follow these steps:

1. **Open the Mask/Cutout by Shape dialog box by clicking the Mask/Cutout by Shape link in the Tools pane on the All tab.**

   The Mask/Cutout by Shape dialog box is shown in Figure 6-10.

2. **Click the shape that you want to use in defining the cutout in the list box and then click the Add Selected Shape button.**

   When you click the Add Selected Shape button, PhotoSuite inserts that shape in your photo surrounded by rotation and sizing handles.

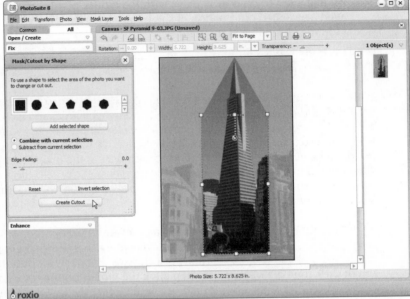

Figure 6-10:
Making
a cutout
for the
Transameric
a Pyramid
using rec-
tangular and
triangular
shapes.

3. **Move, size, and rotate the shape as required so that it encloses the area to be included in the cutout.**

   When enclosing the cutout area with preset shapes, you can use more than one shape (Figure 6-10 shows an example of this where I combined a triangle and rectangle to enclose the Transamerica Pyramid building in downtown San Francisco). When the Combine with Current Selection option button is selected (as it is by default), PhotoSuite adds each new shape to the cutout. When you click the Subtract From Current Selection option button, each new shape reduces the cutout area (depending on how you make them overlap the original cutout shape, you can end up with very interesting effects). PhotoSuite differentiates between the shape enclosing the cutout and that outside of the cutout by displaying the cutout area normally and the area beyond the cutout as transparent.

   If you're happy with the cutout selection and are ready to save it in a new file or make it into a new graphics object, proceed to Step 6. If, however, you want to cut out everything but what's in the shape(s) you've set in the photo, you need to follow Step 5 first.

4. **(Optional) If you want to make the cutout everything in the photo except what's enclosed within the preset shapes, click the Invert Selection button.**

Now you're ready to proceed to area 4 where you follow the last steps in the process.

5. **Click the Create Cutout button to open the Create Cutout From Mask dialog box.**

   This dialog box contains four options buttons from which you can choose:

   - **Cut It Out** to replace the existing image in the Canvas pane with the masked area (which you can then enhance and save as a new file using File⇨Save As)

   - **Create a New Object** (the default) to create a new independent object from the masked area that appears in the Objects pane without disturbing the original photo (good when you want to create a duplicate of an image in the photo)

   - **Cookie-cut It Out** to create a new independent object from the masked area that appears in the Objects pane by removing it from the rest of the photo (so that when you move it around there's a gap in the rest of the image where the cutout once was)

   - **Save Masked Area to a File** to save the masked area in its own PNG (Portable Network Graphics) file

6. **Select the type of cutout you want to create by selecting the Cut It Out, Create a New Object, Cookie-cut It Out, or Save Masked Area to a File option button and then click OK to close the Mask/Cutout by Shape dialog box.**

As soon as the Mask/Cutout by Shape dialog box closes, PhotoSuite displays the new cutout (except in the case of Save Masked Area to a File — the Save to File dialog box opens where you assign the filename and location of the new PNG file).

If you selected the Cut It Out option, only the image in the cutout remains displayed in the Canvas pane (be sure to save this image with a new filename using File⇨Save As) if you don't intend to replace the original photo with its cutout.

If you selected the Create a New Object option, the cutout is selected in the photo and you can then reposition it and enhance only its image as you see fit (for example, you can change its transparency with the Transparency slider on the Canvas pane's Options bar). Figure 6-11 shows the photo originally seen in Figure 6-10 after moving the cutout created with the default Create New Object option to create a duplicate Transamerica Pyramid building. Note that if I had created this cutout using the Cookie-cut It Out option, instead of a duplicate Transamerica Pyramid building, you would see a big blank white space in the middle of the photo where the building used to be.

Figure 6-11:
Photo with
duplicate
Transameric
a Pyramid
buildings
after moving
the new
cutout to
the left.

Cutouts using predefined shapes are great for giving whimsical or meaningful shapes to the parts of photos that you intend to put into a collage project (see "Playing with PhotoSuite Projects" later in this chapter). For example, you can cut out heart-shaped figures in photos intended for Valentine's or wedding collages and cards or starburst-shaped ones for graduation albums.

The procedure for creating a cutout by freehand tracing, picking colors, or edge tracing is similar in every way except for the process of actually selecting the cutout area. In the Tools pane on the All tab under the Mask/Cutout by Shape link, you have the following choices for creating a cutout:

✔ **Freehand Mask/Cutout:** choose this link to manually designate the cutout area by clicking a starting point (which appears as a white circle) and then tracing all around the area until you meet back with and connect the selection by clicking on the starting point (as you trace, you can click to establish intermediary points that enable you to turn corners and change direction)

✔ **Mask/Cutout by Color:** choose this link to select the cutout area simply by clicking on its color in the photo with the magic wand mouse pointer (you can use the Tolerance slider to determine how much the hues can differ when making the selection)

✔ **Mask/Cutout Edge Tracing:** choose this link to manually designate the cutout area by clicking a starting point (which appears as a white circle) and then clicking all around the area until you close the selection by clicking on the start point and then clicking the Create Cutout button in the Mask/Cutout Edge Tracing dialog box

After selecting the cutout area using any of these three methods, the rest of the steps outlined for creating cutouts from predefined shapes apply (that is, from Step 4 on in the step-by-step procedure that appears earlier in this section).

Mask that effect!

The Mask/Cutout features enable you to apply a special effect to just a particular area in your photo by masking out and thereby protecting all the other areas in the picture. The procedure for actually creating the mask (which, remember, defines the area that you can then apply special effects to) is identical to that for creating cutouts: you can either create a mask using any of the preset shapes or by freehand tracing, picking colors, or edge tracing, (see the section, "Now, cut that out!" for details).

After you define the mask, you are ready to use it when applying special effects in the Special Effects dialog box (opened by clicking Special Effects in the Enhance pane on the Common and All tabs — see "Dazzling special effects for every mood" earlier in this chapter for details).

Figure 6-12 illustrates how this masking concept works. For this photo, I created a mask that included only the blue sky above the buildings on Columbus Street in San Francisco. I then applied the Magenta special effect to the photo. Because of the mask, only the sky is given this wild color, leaving the buildings their original colors (a fact that you surely can't appreciate seeing the photo only in black-and-white).

Figure 6-12: When you apply a special effect to a masked photo, only the areas within the mask are modified.

Adding More Images and Clip Art to a Photo

PhotoSuite's Insert Photos & Cutouts link in the Open/Create pane on the Common and All tabs makes it easy to combine photos by superimposing one on top of the other. This feature makes it easy to put together a photo montage that combines different images into one. In addition, the Clip Art link in the Enhance pane on the Common and All tabs also lets you add stock images along the line of Windows clipart (but a great deal classier) to your photos.

To superimpose a photo on top of the photo you're currently editing, you follow these steps:

1. **Click the Add Photos & Cutouts link in the Open/Create pane of the Common or All tab to open the Add dialog box.**

   The Add dialog box (which works just like the Open dialog box) is where you select the Smart View, album, or folder containing the photo or the cutouts (see "Now, cut that out!" earlier in this chapter) you want to add and then click the photo's filename before clicking the Add button.

2. **Open the Smart View, album, or file folder that contains the file with the photo or cutout you want to add, then click the graphic file's icon before you click the Add button.**

   When the Add dialog box closes, the added photo or cutout appears selected (indicated by its sizing and rotation handles) in the center of the photo you're currently editing. Next, you can reposition and, if necessary, resize and rotate the added photo.

3. **Resize and rotate the added image and then drag it to its final position on the background photo.**

   You can also edit this added photo with any of the features available on the Common and All tabs of the Task pane.

4. **(Optional) Make any needed editing changes to the added photo, including improving its overall quality, removing red eye and dust, adding special effects, changing the transparency, or adding a shadow.**

   Now you're ready to save your changes either in the original graphics file, or, more likely in a new graphics file.

5. **Choose File⇨Save on the PhotoSuite menu bar to save your combined photos in the original photo's file or choose File⇨Save As and modify the folder location and/or filename before you click the Save button in the Save As dialog box to save your photo montage in a new graphics file.**

When you add one photo to another, a thumbnail of the newly added photo appears in the Objects pane along with that of the original photo. You can use this pane to easily select the photo you want to edit: simply double-click its thumbnail in the Objects pane. PhotoSuite shows you that the photo you click is now selected in the work area by enclosing the photo in dashed lines and adding sizing and rotation handles to it.

As I mention at the beginning of this section, instead of superimposing just photos on top of the photo you're editing, you can also add Clip Art.

To superimpose a piece of PhotoSuite Clip Art to the photo you're currently editing, you follow these steps:

1. **Click the Clip Art link in the Enhance pane on the Common or All tab of the Task pane to open the Clip Art dialog box.**

   The Clip Art dialog box arranges the different types of Clip Art images that it offers into albums whose icons appear in its list box.

2. **Click the drop-down button in the Clip Art dialog box and then click the icon of the album with the type of images you want to use or double-click its icon in the list box.**

   Note that if you open the All album at the very top of the drop-down list, PhotoSuite displays thumbnails of all its Clip Art in the list box.

3. **Double-click the thumbnail of the Clip Art you want to add or drag it over to the photo in the work area and drop it anywhere.**

   PhotoSuite superimposes a copy of the Clip Art prop in the exact center of the background photo. Now you're ready to resize it and put the prop in its proper position (I dare you to say that twenty times really fast).

4. **If needed, resize the Clip Art and rotate it before you drag it to the desired position in relation to the background photo.**

   To see how your Clip Art image fits in with the background, you may want to select it (especially if you reduced its size) to remove all the selection hash marks and sizing and rotation handles. You can do this by clicking the background photo anywhere outside of the Clip Art or by double-clicking the thumbnail image of the background photo in the Objects pane.

5. **Click the Close button in the Clip Art dialog box and then save the changes to the file in the All Edit Features task pane with File⇨Save or in a new file with File⇨Save As.**

Bring on the Borders

PhotoSuite's Borders feature enables you to give your photos a finished look by surrounding them with some sort of decorative border. In the Enhance pane on the All tab of the Task pane you can choose between these three links:

- ✔ **Frame** to surround the photo in any of a wide variety of frame-type graphics
- ✔ **Mat** to mat the photo either with a solid color or colored texture
- ✔ **Edge** to select a type of edging that you then combine with a mat color or pattern

When you select the Frame link, PhotoSuite opens the Frame dialog box containing a number of albums (All, Beveled Wood, Classic Black, and Metal) and then lets you choose a particular frame style. After you find the frame to add in the album of your choice, double-click its frame icon to add it to the photo in the Canvas pane.

PhotoSuite then lets you move and, if necessary, resize the photo in the frame. To help you in moving and resizing the photo in its frame, PhotoSuite indicates the edges of the image by showing its perimeter as a dotted line with round sizing handles at the corners and midpoints. Most often these edges of the image extend beyond the cutout portion of the frame. Moving and/or resizing the photo in the frame therefore displays different parts of the image in the cutout region (the frame actually ends up cropping parts of the image). Be careful when manipulating the image in the frame that you don't expose the white background behind the photo or crop a part of the image that you want displayed.

When you select the Mat link in the Enhance pane, PhotoSuite opens the Mat dialog box (similar to the one shown in Figure 6-13). This dialog box contains three albums (All, Colors, and Textures) that you can use to select the proper mat with the proper color and texture. If none of these mats will do, you can click the Use My Own Photo button to select a photo to use as a textured mat. After applying the colored or textured mat to your photo (by double-clicking its mat icon), you then can adjust the width of the mat as well as control whether or not to display beveling on the mat's edges and include v-groove (and adjust its offset from the inside of the mat) by using its sliders.

When you select the Edge link in the Enhance pane, PhotoSuite opens the Edge dialog box that enables you to select an edging style to use with the matting. The Edge dialog box (shown in Figure 6-14) contains a Select an Edge list box containing albums with different types of edging patterns (All, Brush, Digital, and Torn). Below this you find a Select a Mat Category list box that contains the same albums as the Mat dialog box (All, Colors, and Textures).

Figure 6-13:
The Mat dialog box enables you to select the color, text, width, and bevel for a mat for your photo.

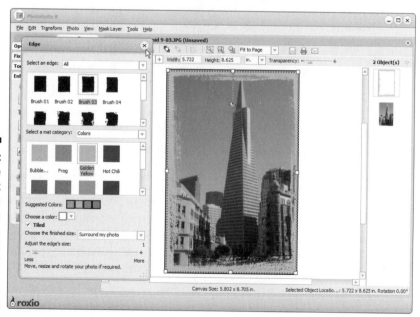

Figure 6-14:
The Edge dialog box enables you to select the color, text, width, and bevel for a mat for your photo.

Select an edge style in one of the albums in the Select an Edge list box and then apply it to your photo by double-clicking its icon. Then, apply the color or text that you want to use with that style by double-clicking its icon after opening the Colors or Textures album in the Select a Mat Category list box.

After selecting the edge style and mat color or texture, you can then adjust the width of the edging if you want by using its size slider before clicking the Close button in the Edge dialog box.

Playing with PhotoSuite Projects

Roxio Creator 8 contains a Photo Project Assistant that makes it really easy to use your digital photos to create fun and interesting photo projects. This Assistant supports a wide variety of project types that run the gamut from the ever-popular photo collage to posters. All are based on adding your own digital photos to project templates that give you ready-made background and, in many cases, stock text that you can adapt to your own needs.

To launch the Photo Project Assistant, you can either click the Photo Projects link in the Open/Create pane on the Common or All tab within PhotoSuite, or you can click the More Projects link on the Photo tab of the Project List in the Roxio Creator 8 Home window.

When the Photo Project Assistant window first opens (as shown in Figure 6-15), you can choose from the following project types:

- ✔ **Albums** to put your photos into the pages of photo albums using pre-designed pages dedicated to subjects such as the new baby, your wedding, the latest vacation, and the like

- ✔ **Calendars** to make calendars with your own photos using any of a wide variety of different calendar designs

- ✔ **Cards** to make greeting cards with your own photos for almost all the major holidays and occasions (including birthdays, anniversaries, graduation, and so on)

- ✔ **Collage** to make a collage with your photos using either a blank collage background or any of a number of pre-designed backgrounds including those for the new baby, birthdays, Christmas, weddings, and so on

- ✔ **Gift Tags** to make gift tags carrying your photos for decorating anniversary, birthday, and Christmas presents

- ✔ **Posters** to make a poster using your own photos for events such as a book club, concert, birthday, and so on

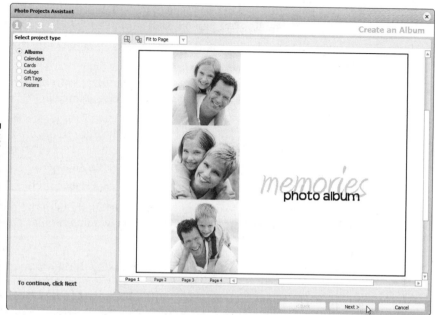

Figure 6-15:
When you first open the Photo Projects Assistant, you can choose from among several types of projects.

For all the project types, PhotoSuite makes it as easy as possible to create your new photo project by walking you through the steps. In most cases, all you have to do is select the project template you want to use, choose the photos you want to add to that template, and then make a few changes to modify the arrangement of the photos and customize the stock text.

Stitching It All Together

PhotoSuite's Panorama Assistant makes it possible to create a single photo with a sweeping panorama from sequential and overlapping individual photos that you take of the same view. This feature is great provided that you've done your homework and the photos that you're trying to stitch together match up and overlap correctly. Accordingly, Roxio has set up some important guidelines for you to follow before attempting to stitch together your favorite photos of the Grand Canyon:

✔ Use a tripod when taking the photos to stitch together (if you don't have a tripod, try to keep the camera level and in the same position when taking the pictures by rotating your body around the camera rather than rotating the camera around your body)

✔ Overlap each photo that you take in the sequence (Roxio recommends between 20% to 40% overlap on each shot)

✔ Don't change any of the settings on your camera between the shots you take

✔ Use only optical zoom when taking the picture: if your camera has a digital zoom, don't use it in shooting the photo sequence

✔ Take your photos in sequence from left to right or if you're scanning in developed photos, scan them in left-to-right order to ensure that their filenames appear in order

✔ Do not edit your photos in PhotoSuite before you stitch them together: instead, edit the final panorama produced by Photo Stitch

✔ Rotate your camera 90 degrees to take portrait shots of the panorama: doing this requires more shots but results in a much taller panorama with more detail

In addition to following these guidelines when taking the shots you would later like to stitch together, you must have one more piece of information at your fingertips when using Photo Stitch and that is the *focal length* used in taking the photos. Focal length, as any photographer will tell you, is the distance between the film (or CCD in a digital camera) and the optical center of the lens when the lens is set on infinity (this distance is usually given in millimeters and marked on the side of the fixed lenses on a standard 35mm camera).

Trying to determine the focal length for digital cameras, even real fancy ones like my Sony that are equipped with an optical zoom lens, can be difficult. Determining this information is complicated by the fact that the actual focal length for digital cameras is much less than for a standard 35mm camera because their CCDs are much smaller than 35mm film.

If your digital camera has an optical zoom lens, check and see if the camera records the focal length at the time you take your photos. If your camera doesn't record this information (I know that mine doesn't), check your camera manual. If you can't find that or it doesn't give you a clue as to the focal length of your lens when set at infinity, you'll just have to guess when it comes time to give Photo Stitch that information.

The procedure for stitching two or more sequential photos together to create a single panoramic photo is as follows:

1. **After clicking Applications on the Home tab to launch the Panorama Assistant, click the Create Panoramas link under Utilities in the Applications Project window of the Roxio Creator 8 Home window.**

   The first Panorama Assistant window, Add Photos, is the place where you select the photos to be used in the panorama. Here, you must select a minimum of two photos, although most panoramas (especially those taken in portrait mode) require more.

2. **Click the Add Photos button to open the Add Photos dialog box and then select all the photos you want to stitch together before you click the Add Photos button.**

   You now need to make any adjustments to the rotation or order of the photos you added to the work area of the first Create Panorama window. If they're not in order, you need to drag them into order (don't forget to select the Fit to Page setting at the very bottom of the Select Zoom Level drop-down list box to display all the photos together in the work area).

3. **Make any necessary adjustments to the orientation or order of the photos so that they're all in portrait or landscape mode and are in left-to-right order for stitching and then click the Next> button.**

   The second Panorama Assistant window, Adjust, appears and attempts to automatically determine the focal length of your photos. If it can't determine this value (which is true for most of the digital photos you take), you need to select this value by dragging the Focal Length slider until the correct number (in millimeters) appears immediately above the right end of the Focal Length slider.

4. **(Optional) If Photo Stitch can't automatically determine the focal length for your photos, select the correct length (or your best guess) with the Focal Length slider.**

   Now you're ready to have Photo Stitch do its magic.

5. **Click the Auto Align button.**

   The Panorama Assistant stitches together your photos, showing you a preview of the new panorama in the work area. If you notice some problems, try clicking the Fine Tuning button to see if the Assistant can detect and fix the problem. If this doesn't do it, click and manually drag the photos into final position (remember that you can use the arrow keys to nudge the selected photo into place).

6. **If necessary, fine-tune the positioning of the photos and then click the Next> button.**

   The Panorama Assistant shows you the final product ready for you to save or print. Be sure to save your photo after you click the Done button in the Create Panorama dialog box asking you if you want to save the panorama.

7. **Click Done in the Panorama Assistant and then click Yes in the Create Panorama dialog box. Then, replace the temporary filename, Stitch.jpg, with the filename of your choosing before you click the Save As button in the Save As dialog box.**

After saving your panorama, you can edit its JPEG graphics file in PhotoSuite as you would any other digital photo that you had at your disposal. That is the place to improve any exposure or color balance problems.

Group Editing

The Multi Photo Enhance feature enables you to do group editing to a bunch of photos that all need the same kind of modifications or enhancements. It's a real timesaver when you have a lot of photos that all need the same kind of changes made to them. You open this application by clicking the Multi Photo Enhance link under Utilities in the Applications Project window of the Roxio Creator 8 window after you click Applications on the Home tab of the Project List pane.

The Photos to Enhance dialog box that opens when you click Multi Photo Enhance contains an Add Files button that you use to select all the photos that require the same kind of editing. The modifications and enhancements that you can perform at one time on a group of photos that you've selected include:

- **Fix** to take care of any of the exposure, color saturation, sharpness, or red eye problems in the group (you can even use AutoFix on them)

- **Transform** to rotate, flip, or resize all the photos in the group in the same way

- **Special Effects** to apply the Black and White, Invert, or Sepia special effects to all the photos in the group

- **Convert/Rename** to use Rename to give new filenames made up of a keyword and a sequential number (such as Newbaby00, Newbaby01, Newbaby02, and so on), or Convert to convert the group from one type of graphics file to another (such as DMSP to JPEG for use on the Internet)

Among the most important and unique modifications that you can perform with the Multi Photo Enhance feature are surely the Rename and Convert options. The Rename option enables you to name of group of related photo files so that they all show up together in a preset order in any file listing you do. The Convert option enables you to move a batch of photos from one file format to another in a fraction of the time it would take to convert them individually.

Printing Your Photos

Printing your photos with PhotoSuite is a straightforward process. Simply click the Print button on the Canvas pane's toolbar to open the Print window (similar to the one shown in Figure 6-16). The Print dialog box contains controls at the top that enable you to select the printer to use and the size of the paper. The Layout section of the Print window gives you the following printing options:

- ✔ **One Photo per Page** to print each of the selected photos on a separate sheet of paper

- ✔ **Multiple Photos per Page** to choose between a wide variety of layouts using different readily-available paper, card, and label stock for printing more than one photo per page

- ✔ **As a Contact Sheet** to print all the selected photos sequentially as thumbnails along with their filenames for easy identification

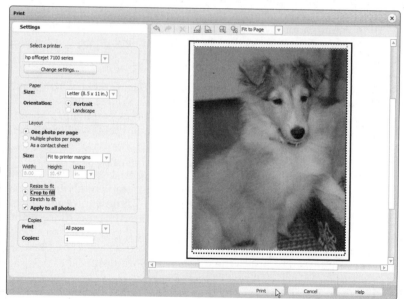

Figure 6-16: Getting ready to print a single photo after editing in PhotoSuite.

After you select one of these three basic Layout options, the Layout section of the Print window gives you different sizing options based on the type of layout you've chosen. When you select the One Photo per Page Layout printing option, PhotoSuite gives you a choice among three different sizing options:

- ✔ **Resize to Fit** (the default) to reduce photos to the size required for them to print within the margins for the specified paper size
- ✔ **Crop to Fill** to crop the photos as required for them to fill the page and still print within the margins for the specified paper size
- ✔ **Stretch to Fit** to stretch the photos as required for them to fill the page and still print within the margins for the specified paper size

When specifying the photo layout for the Multiple Photos per Page printing option, PhotoSuite lets you decide between printing the same photo as many times on the same page as your selected photo size allows (with the default Fill Each Page with Same Photo option button) and printing each of the selected photos only once per page with the Repeat Each Photo option button. Note that when you select the Repeat Each Photo option button, the Times text box (with 1 as the default value) becomes available. If you want to have each of the multiple photos that you've selected printed a set number of times (using as many pages as the photo size and layout require), you enter that number in this text box.

When specifying the photo layout for the As a Contact Sheet printing option, PhotoSuite lets you specify the number of columns and rows (with 4 columns in 5 rows being the default) and the spacing between them. You can also choose not to print the filenames beneath each thumbnail by clicking the Print Titles check box to remove its checkmark.

After specifying your print settings, be sure that you've loaded your printer with the right type of paper and that the printer is ready to go before you click the Print button at the bottom of the Print window to begin. During the brief moments that PhotoSuite takes to send your photo(s) to the printer, you can click the OK button in the Cancel dialog box if you decide to stop the printing. After PhotoSuite finishes printing your photo(s), click the Close button in the Print window to return to the PhotoSuite 8 window.

The Print dialog box opened from within PhotoSuite allows you to print only one photo at a time so that even if you select the Multiple Photos Per Page or As a Contact Sheet Layout option, you only get multiple printouts of the same photo on each page. If you want to print more than one photo on a single page or a bunch of different photos as a contact sheet, you need to open a slightly different version of the Print dialog box by clicking the Print Photos link on the Photo tab of the Project List pane in the Roxio Creator 8 Home window.

To add all the photos you want, click the Add Photos button (the one with an album icon at the top of the pane on the right that says No Photos Selected) and select them in the Add Photos dialog box. After adding your photos, click the Multiple Photos Per Page button and the Repeat Each Photo option button once you've selected the proper paper size and orientation. To print the photos you've added as a contact sheet, simply click the As a Contact Sheet option button instead.

E-mailing Your Photos

PhotoSuite also makes it easy to e-mail your edited photos to friends and family. All you have to do is follow these steps:

1. **Click the E-mail button (the one with envelope) on the Canvas pane's toolbar.**

   PhotoSuite opens the E-mail Assistant window (shown in Figure 6-17) containing the photo currently open in PhotoSuite's Canvas pane. If you want, you can select additional photos to send.

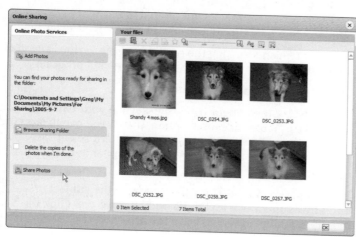

Figure 6-17: E-mailing an edited photo with the E-mail Assistant.

2. **(Optional) Click the Add Files button and then select all the additional photos to send in the Add Files dialog box before clicking OK.**

   By default, the E-mail Assistant uses your normal e-mail program (usually Microsoft Outlook or Outlook Express) and formats your photos as HTML in the new message.

3. **(Optional) Click the Other (e.g. Yahoo!, webmail) option button if you don't want the E-mail Assistant to use your default e-mail program.**

   Note that if you select the Other (e.g. Yahoo!, webmail) option button, the Just Send the Files with No Conversion Options button becomes available. Click this button if you don't want your photos to be compressed using one of the JPEG compression options listed under the Convert Photos to JPEG option.

   By default, the E-mail Assistant converts your photos to JPEG graphics files using the Medium (800) pixel compression setting. If you want you can modify the amount of compression or select no compression.

4. **(Optional) Select a new compression setting, Small (640) or Large (1024) or, if you don't want the photo(s) compressed at all, click the Original Size option button.**

   Instead of sending your photos as individual images embedded in a new e-mail message, you can have PhotoSuite package them into a slideshow complete with music that is sent as a file attachment in an e-mail message. When recipients receive the message, they can then play this slideshow with the Windows Media Player on their computers.

5. **(Optional) Click the Make a Slideshow option button to have the E-mail Assistant group your selected photos into a WMV slideshow file that is attached to a new e-mail message in your e-mail program.**

   When you finish selecting the photos and the various e-mail options, you are ready to open a new message in your e-mail program.

6. **Click OK in the E-mail Assistant window.**

   The Assistant then opens a new message in your e-mail program. If you selected the Make Slideshow option, the slideshow file appears as an attachment to the new message. If you did not select this option, all the photos selected in the E-mail Assistant appear in the body of the new e-mail message.

7. **Indicate the recipient(s) for the message, the subject of the message, and any explanatory text to its body before you click the Send button in your e-mail program to send the attached slideshow file or the embedded photos.**

After your e-mail program closes, you are automatically returned to the PhotoSuite 8 window where you can continue working.

Putting Your Photos Online

PhotoSuite not only lets your friends and family enjoy your digital photos via an e-mail message but also enables you to upload your images to online photo albums that they can visit any time using their Web browsers.

To upload photos, you follow these steps:

1. **Choose File⇨Online Sharing on the PhotoSuite menu bar.**

   PhotoSuite opens the Online Sharing window (similar to the one shown in Figure 6-18) where you select the photos you want included in the online album.

2. **Click the Add Photos button.**

   The Add Files dialog box opens where you can select the Smart View, album, or folder containing the photos to use.

3. **Select the Smart View, album, or folder with the photos and then select the thumbnails for all the photos you want to share online before you click the Add Files button.**

   PhotoSuite closes the Add Files dialog box and adds thumbnails for all the selected photos to the Your Files pane in the Online Sharing window.

   Before uploading the selected photos to your online photo album on the Internet, PhotoSuite copies them to a sharing folder on your hard disk. The folder name where these photos are copied along with its path name is displayed in bold in the Online Sharing window's Task pane. If you want, you can select a different folder into which to copy these photos.

4. **(Optional) Click the Browse Sharing Folder button and then select a new browse location in the Select a Folder for Sharing Files dialog box and then click OK.**

   If you want, you can have PhotoSuite delete the copies it makes of your photos after they have been uploaded to your online photo album.

5. **(Optional) Click the Delete the Copies of the Photos When I'm Done check box to remove its check mark.**

6. **Click the Share Photos button.**

   The Share Photos dialog box appears telling you what location the original photos have been copied to. To browse the contents of this folder, click the View Folder in Windows Explorer button. To copy the location of this folder to the Windows Clipboard (so that you can later paste it into another document), click the Copy Location to Clipboard button.

7. **Click the Launch Browser button in the Share Photos dialog box.**

   PhotoSuite launches your Web browser program (usually Microsoft Internet Explorer), which connects you to the Internet and opens the Roxio Online Shopping page. Here you must either sign up for a new account, or if you already have a Snapfish account, log in.

   To sign up for a new Roxio Photo Center password-protected account (which is free), click the Sign Up Free button and then fill out the new account form. After filling in your name, e-mail and physical address and picking a new password, you submit the account form by clicking the Get Started button. After submitting your account form, you can then start using the Online Photo Services (run by an outfit called Snapfish) by clicking the Start Using Snapfish button.

8. **Click the Sign Up Free button and create your new account or, if you already have an account, click the Login button and then enter your e-mail address and your password before you click Login.**

   Your Web browser opens the Snapfish: Home page.

9. **Click the Upload Photos link in the Snapfish: Home page.**

   Your Web browser opens the Snapfish: Upload page.

10. **Enter a name for your album (replacing the temporary album name with the current date) underneath New Album and then click the Upload to This Album button.**

    Your Web browser opens the Snapfish: Upload Pictures page.

11. **Click the Select Photos button.**

    The Snapfish Upload – Select Photos dialog box opens.

12. **Select the sharing folder on your hard disk that contains the photos you want in the online photo album in the Look In drop-down list box, and then select the thumbnails of all the photos to upload before you click the Upload Selected Photos button.**

    Snapfish then displays thumbnails of each of the photos you've selected with progress bars keeping you abreast of how the uploading process is proceeding.

13. **When all the photos are uploaded, click the View Entire Album button.**

    Your Web browser opens the Snapfish: Photo Album page. Here you can click the Play Slideshow button to view them in sequence.

14. **Click the Share link to display the Share This Album and Share a Photo links and then click the Share This Album link.**

    Your Web browser opens the Snapfish: Share Invitation page. This page enables you to specify the e-mail addresses of all the people who you want to invite to visit your online photo album. It also lets you modify the stock subject lines and message text. In addition, you can specify Full Access (the default), which enables your visitors to copy the photos to their computers as well as to view them and order prints online. To prevent your visitors from copying the photos, click the Restricted Access option button.

15. **Specify the recipients and how the photos are to be shared and then click the Share Album button.**

    Your Web browser returns you to the Snapfish: Share page, informing you that your photos have been shared.

16. **Click the Close button in your Web browser's window to return to PhotoSuite.**

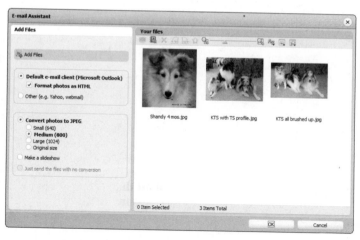

Figure 6-18: Selecting the photos to share and the Sharing Folder into which they are copied before uploading.

Keep in mind that you can use the Roxio Online Shopping Web page to get high-quality prints of your favorite digital photos, develop and digitize rolls of standard photo film, and to upload and store your digital photos online for sharing on the Internet.

Chapter 7

Burning Audio CDs, MP3, and DVD Music Discs

In This Chapter

▶ Creating and burning a new Audio CD project

▶ Creating a MP3/WMA Disc project

▶ Creating a DVD Music Disc project

▶ Creating an Enhanced CD with audio and data

▶ Creating a Mixed-Mode CD with audio and data

The Music Disc Creator application makes it easy for you to compile your favorite tunes and burn them onto CDs for playing on standalone audio CD players (such as the one in your car and the Walkman-variety you listen to at the gym) as well as on the CD-ROM drive in your computer. The audio CDs that you burn can be composed of music tracks that you've downloaded and purchased from online music stores such as Napster or Rhapsody, recorded from analog recordings (such as LPs and audio cassettes) with the Sound Editor (see Chapter 5), or ones that you rip from audio CDs that you already own.

As you find out in this chapter, with the Music Disc Creator you can create not only standard audio CDs but MP3/WMA discs, DVD Music Discs, Enhanced CDs, and Mixed-mode CDs as well. MP3/WMA discs are audio CDs whose tracks are saved in the MP3 (MPEG3) or WMA (Windows Media Audio) compressed file formats. These file format enables you to fit many more tracks on the CD than is possible on a standard CD-R disc (hundreds of tracks in MP3 versus about 20 maximum in the CD-R's normal WAVE format, which aren't compressed at all). Besides being able to play the MP3/WMA discs that you burn in the Music Disc Creator application of the Roxio Creator 8 suite on your computer's CD-ROM drive, however, you can only play MP3/WMA discs on standalone players that support either the MP3 or WMA file format. Fortunately, many of today's audio CD players, including the ever-popular Walkman-type, support the MP3 file format and newer players support WMA as well so that this limitation may be no problem at all.

DVD Music Discs are audio DVDs that contain 4.7 or 8.5 gigabits worth of tunes (and that's a lot of tracks!) that you can then play on standalone DVD players or with the DVD player in your computer. Because of the enormous size of DVD discs, you can use DVD music discs to quickly back up your entire CD collection (no matter how many CDs you happen to own).

Enhanced and Mixed-mode CDs are CDs that mix computer data and audio files together. Enhanced CDs are multi-session CDs with the first session containing the audio tracks that can be played by any standard audio CD player and CD-ROM drive and the second session containing the data files that can be played only on the computer's CD-ROM drive. Mixed-mode CDs are also CDs that mix computer data and audio files. However, unlike the Enhanced CD which separates music tracks from data files in separate sessions, the Mixed-mode CD contains only one session with both the data and music (the data is laid down in the first track of the CD and all the audio tracks follow). This means that a Mixed-mode CD can only be played by your computer's CD-ROM drive (regular audio CD players like the one in your car can't play this kind of CD at all).

Creating an Audio CD Project

Music Disc Creator is the Roxio Creator 8 suite application that you use for compiling and burning all your audio CDs. To launch Music Disc Creator from the Roxio Creator 8 Home window, click the Music Disc Creator link in the Applications Project Window after clicking Applications on the Home tab of the Project List.

When you first launch the program, the Music Disc Creator window with a new untitled Audio Project shown in Figure 7-1 appears. This window contains three panes: Project Type and Add to Project in the Task pane on the left and the Audio CD pane that shows the project name along with the discs and tracks added to it.

Adding audio tracks to your project

After starting a new Audio CD project, you are ready to start adding tracks to it. These tracks can those saved on your computer's hard disk or ones on audio CDs that you own. When adding your tracks to the Audio CD project, you follow these simple steps:

1. **To add audio files saved somewhere on your computer, click the Add Audio Tracks link in the Add to Project pane. To rip tracks from an audio CD or DVD and add them to the project, click the Import from CD/DVD link instead. To record your own audio files and add them to the project, click the Record Audio link.**

If you click the Add Audio Tracks link, the Media Selector dialog box shown in Figure 7-2 appears. Here, you select the media containing the audio files you want to add to the project:

- If you've already copied the tracks you want to add to your computer's hard disk, these tracks are probably located in the My Music folder on your computer.

- If the audio files are stored in Smart Views or albums (see Chapter 4) on your computer, select the view or album after clicking the Smart Views or My Albums button.

- If you're copying tracks from an audio CD in your computer's CD-ROM drive, select that drive's letter to display the tracks.

If you select tracks on a commercially produced CD in your computer's CD-ROM drive in the Media Selector after clicking the Import from CD/DVD link, Music Disc Creator attempts to obtain the track names and other album information of the CD it contains from the online Gracenote CD database. When this information is found, the track numbers and the names of the individual tracks appear in the list box on the right side of the Media Selector.

If you click the Record Audio link, the Record Audio dialog box appears where you can record your new audio file (see Chapter 5 for details).

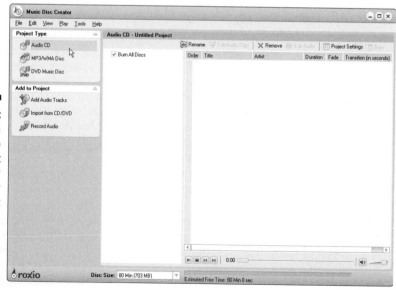

Figure 7-1:
Starting a new Audio CD project in Music Disc Creator is the first step in creating your audio CD.

My Albums

Folders

Smart
Views

My MediaSpace (UPnP)

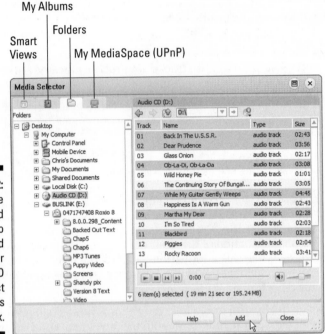

Figure 7-2:
Select the
media and
the audio
files to add
to your
Audio CD
project
in this
dialog box.

2. **Select the names of the audio files and track(s) you want to add in the Media Selector and then click the Add button.**

The Adding to Project dialog box appears. If you are ripping tracks from a CD, the Save Audio Tracks to File dialog box appears where you need to select the type of audio file format to use in Output Settings drop-down list box and use the Browse button to select the location in which to save the tracks in the Save To list box. After designating these settings and clicking the Save button in the Save Audio Tracks to File dialog box, the Copying Track dialog box appears displaying the progress of the ripping process plus an Audio alert dialog box for each track you rip indicating the filename of the track and its location by means of its path name.

After the new recording or track ripping is complete or you click the Add button in the Media Selector after selecting all the audio files saved on your computer you wanted added, the Adding to Project dialog box replaces the Copying Track dialog box. This dialog box displays the overall progress of adding each of ripped or selected tracks to the new Audio

CD project, and it too displays an Audio alert dialog box for each track with its file and path name. When the tracks have all been added to your Audio CD project, you are returned to the Media Selector dialog box.

If you try to add a track that you've downloaded to your computer's hard disk for playback but for which you don't have permission to copy by burning to disc, the Error alert dialog box appears. If this Error dialog box appears for a track that you've downloaded from an online music store without actually purchasing, you can rectify this situation by going back to the store and buying the track. When you purchase a music track from most online music centers such as Napster or Rhapsody, you obtain both the play and burn rights to the song (although the burn rights may not enable you to make unlimited copies — you need to check this with the particular store).

3. **After you finish adding tracks to your new Audio CD project, click the Close button in the Media Selector dialog box.**

   Music Disc Creator adds an icon for each disc needed to accommodate the number of tracks you added to the project. These icon(s) have generic numbered names (Disc 1, Disc 2, and so on) which you can change. To the right of the disc icon(s) you see the names of all the selected tracks that will be burned onto it. Their names appear in the Title column in this part of the Audio CD Project pane along with their total estimated playing time in the Duration column. To the right of the Duration column, you find a Fade and to the right of that a Transition column where you can assign a fade-in and fade-out effect as well as designate a gap or overlap transition. At the bottom of the Music Disc Creator window appears the relative track size and the estimated amount of total free playing time still left on the disc selected in the project.

   If you find that you've added a track that you don't really want to include on the final CD, click the track and then press the Delete key or click the Remove button on the Audio CD Project pane's toolbar.

   If you want, you can add descriptive names to the Discs listed in your Audio Project.

4. **(Optional) Click the icon for the disc you want to rename and then press F2 (or right-click it and then select Rename on its shortcut menu).**

   You can adjust how a particular track fades in and/or fades out. To add a fade-in effect, click the Fade In button (the one with the upper-left corner bracket) in the Fade column of that track and then click one of the options on its pop-up palette as identified in Figure 7-3.

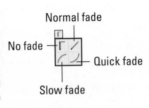

Figure 7-3:
Select the
fade-in
option you
want to
assign a
track from
its pop-up
palette.

To add a fade-out effect, click the Fade Out button (the one with the upper-right corner bracket) in the Fade column of that track and then click one of the options on the pop-up palette as identified in Figure 7-4.

Figure 7-4:
Select the
fade-out
option you
want to
assign a
track from
its pop-up
palette.

5. **(Optional) In the Fade column of the Track list, select the fade-in and/or fade-out effect you want to assign on the option pop-up menu opened by clicking its Fade In or Fade Out button. To assign the same fade-in or fade-out effect to several tracks, select the tracks prior to clicking these buttons.**

You can add a transition between tracks, choosing a gap transition that creates a silence between two tracks or an overlapping transition that starts playing the first part of the next track before the current track is finished playing. You can then set the duration for either of these types of transition effects.

By default, the Music Disc Creator selects a gap of 0.0 seconds (in other words, one track leads directly to another). To set a gap between tracks, you enter the number of seconds for that gap in the Transition (In Seconds) column to the immediate right of the Transition icon. To set an overlap, you click the Transition button and then click the Overlap button on the pop-up menu (the second one at the bottom of the pop-up menu that shows one tracking extending into another) before you set its duration.

6. **(Optional) Select the track beneath the one you want to set a transition for and then replace 0.0 with the number of seconds in the Transition (In Seconds) column to the right of the Transition icon. If you want the tracks to overlap rather than a silence, click the Transition button and then click the Overlap button on its pop-up menu before setting its duration.**

   You can also edit a track after adding it to your Audio CD project in the Quick Sound Editor. This is a mini-version of the Sound Editor application (see Chapter 5) that enables you to trim the length of the audio, add fade-in and fade-out effects to it, and to enhance it with some of the more commonly used special effects.

7. **(Optional) To edit a track by trimming or assigning different effects to its audio in the Quick Sound Editor, click the track to select it and then click the Edit Audio button on the toolbar above the track list. When you finish editing the track, click the Done button to return to the Music Disc Creator.**

   Now it's time to save the Audio CD project before you burn it to disc.

8. **Choose File⇨Save Project on the Music Disc Creator menu bar and then enter the filename and select the location for the .dmsa file (Music Disc Creator Project File) before you click the Save button.**

Tagging the tracks in the project

If the disc information including the album title, artist's name, and track titles for a particular audio CD doesn't show up in the Track list of the Music Disc Creator window after adding the tracks, you can try to have this information located and downloaded from the online Gracenote CDDB (CD Database). The Gracenote CDDB is the world's largest online database of music information (listing about two and a half million CDs with just a little over 55 million songs!).

To get the vital statistics on the tracks, follow these steps:

1. **Select all the tracks you want information on in the Track list and then click the Edit Audio Tags button on the toolbar at the top of the list.**

   Music Disc Creator opens an Edit Audio Tags dialog box album similar to the one shown in Figure 7-5.

2. **Click the Music ID button near the bottom of Audio Tags pane in the Edit Audio Tags dialog box.**

   Music Disc Creator then connects you to the Internet and the Gracenote CDDB to look for the CD's ISRC (International Standard Code) number in this humongous database. When it finds a match to a track's IRSC number in the Gracenote CDDB, it then downloads the information and replaces the To Be Done indicators in the MusicID Status column of the Select One or More Tracks pane on the left side of the Edit Audio Tags dialog box.

Sometimes, multiple matches are found for a track in which case, you need to click the Multiple Matches link and then select the information you want to use.

3. **Click the Use MusicID Tags check box to use the information returned from the database in your project.**

   In addition to using the information in your audio project, you can also have save the track information with the audio file, if the particular audio file format used by the track supports this option.

4. **(Optional) Click the Embed or Replace Tags Inside the Audio Files (If Supported by the Audio Format).**

5. **Click the Done button to close the Edit Audio Tags dialog box and return to the Music Disc Creator window.**

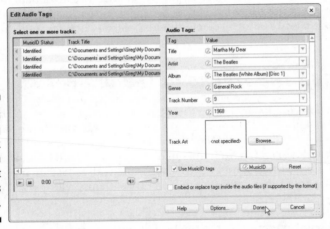

Figure 7-5: Identifying the track information in the Edit Audio Tags dialog box.

A music track's ISRC number serves as the recording's international identifier for the purposes of rights management. In other words, an ISRC number indicates who's entitled to the royalty payments for the distribution of that recording. If you're making a CD of your own music for distribution to various record companies and radio stations, you will definitely want to obtain ISRC numbers from an approved ISRC Agency and encode the tracks of the CD you're burning with Creator Classic for any type of distribution with those numbers.

Rearranging tracks

When you add individual tracks from various sources that you copied on your computer's hard disk to your Audio CD Project (as opposed to a block of audio tracks from a single source such as a CD in your CD or DVD drive), Music Disc Creator automatically lists these tracks alphabetically by track title in the Project pane. You will not, however, always want to burn your audio CD with its tracks in this type of alphabetical order. More often than not, you'll end up arranging the tracks in the order in which you think you'd most prefer to listen to them (regardless of what havoc that inflicts on the alphabetical track name order).

To modify the track order prior to burning the final audio CD, you need to drag the tracks in the Audio CD project to their desired positions. To do this, click the track that you want to move to select it and then drag up or down to reposition it. As you drag, a dashed line appears right above the mouse pointer indicating where the track you're moving will be inserted when you release mouse button. Once you've positioned this dashed line in between the tracks in the Project pane where you want it to appear, release the mouse button to move the selected track to that new position in the list. As soon as you release the mouse button, Music Disc Creator renumbers all the tracks to suit the new track order.

Although it is a little tedious to have to reposition each track in this manner, it is the only method that Music Disc Creator supports for rearranging the tracks you add so that they don't appear in alphabetical order by track name on the new CD.

Renaming tracks

Music Disc Creator enables you to rename the tracks that you add to your audio CD project. You might need to do this when Gracenote can't return the correct track name or when you're dealing with tracks that aren't registered with this database (as in the case of original music).

To rename one of the tracks, click its name in the Track list in the Audio CD Project pane and press F2 (you can also do this by right-clicking the track name and then clicking the Rename item on the track's shortcut menu). Music Disc Creator then selects the track name within a text box waiting for you to make your changes to the name. To replace the name entirely, just start typing the new track name.

To edit the track name by inserting text, you can just click the Insertion point at the place in the track name where you need to start inserting characters. To delete just some of the characters in the name, drag through them with the arrowhead mouse pointer to select them and then press the Delete key. When you finish editing or replacing the track name, press the Enter key or click the mouse anywhere outside of the of the track name's text box.

Inserting a disc break

Music Disc Creator automatically adds a new disc to the audio project when the combined size of the tracks you've added exceeds the total capacity of the CD disc media currently selected in the Disc Size drop-down list at the bottom of the Music Disc Creator window.

You can, if you want, ensure that certain tracks in the project are burned to the same disc by inserting a custom disc break. To do this, select the track in the Track list above which the disc break is to occur and then choose Edit⇨Insert/Remove Custom Disc Break on the Music Disc Creator menu bar. Music Disc Creator then inserts a new numbered disc icon in the Project pane along with a disc break that is clearly marked as a custom disc break in the Track list. You can then rename the new disc by clicking its icon and then pressing F2.

To move a custom disc break, drag its indicator in the Track list up or down as required. To remove a custom disc break, right-click it in the Track list and then press the Delete key or click Remove Custom Disc Break from its shortcut menu.

Changing the Project Settings

Prior to burning the tracks that you've added to the Track List in the Audio CD Project pane, you can check and, if necessary, change the properties for the CD project. To do this, you open the Project Properties dialog box shown in Figure 7-6 by clicking the Project Settings button on the Audio CD Project pane's toolbar, or by pressing Crl+R. A Project Properties dialog box appears.

The Audio CD Properties dialog box contains a Disc Name and Artist Name text box where you can modify the name of the Disc currently selected in the audio project. It also contains an Add CD-Text check box (selected by default). When this box is checked, Music Disc Creator saves the artist, album name, and track names on your hard disk after burning the CD so that the next time you put the disc into your computer's CD or DVD drive to play it, these vital statistics will be available to the program you use to play the disc (such as the Windows Media Player or iTunes).

Below the Add CD-Text box, you find a Maximize Volume of Each Track (Will Require Extra Time to Output) check box (which is not automatically selected). Click this check box when you've added audio tracks from different sources and want to have Music Disc Creator maximize their volume at the time that the tracks are burned onto the CD.

Beneath these two check boxes, a UPC text box appears where you can enter the CD's 12-digit Universal Product Code if you've obtained one for your CD or are copying a CD and happen to know it.

Figure 7-6:
Changing
the settings
for the
project in
the Audio
CD Project
Settings
dialog box.

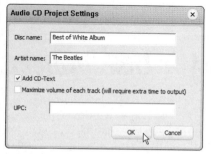

Burning the CD

After you've added all the tracks you want to your audio CD project and made any necessary adjustments to the tracks, including merging, audio transitions, track ISRC information, project settings, and the like, you're ready to burn the CD. Prior to starting the burn process, you should make sure that you've saved all your changes in the .dmsa project file (Ctrl+S or choose File⇨Save Project).

To burn the audio project to CD, you then click the Burn button on the far right side of the Audio CD Project pane's toolbar or choose File⇨Burn on the Music Disc Creator menu bar. Music Disc Creator then opens the Audio CD – Burn Setup dialog box. To expand the dialog box so that it displays all of your options for burning the CD, you need to click the expand button (+) in front of Burn Options at the bottom of the dialog box. The expanded form of the Burn Setup dialog box contains two sections: General Options (already fully displayed) and Advanced Options which you can display by clicking its expand button (see Chapter 3 for details on using these options).

After making changes to any of these options in the Burn Setup dialog box, click the OK button to open the Audio CD – Progress Information dialog box. This dialog box shows its progress in writing the tracks to the new audio CD.

After Music Disc Creator finishes writing the tracks to the last CD disc required for all the tracks in the project, the program automatically ejects the disc. To have the Audio CD – Progress Information dialog box automatically close when this process is complete, click the Close This Dialog Box When Finished Successfully check box. To launch the Label Creator application for creating a custom label for your new audio CD after its recording is completed, click the Create a Label (see Chapter 9 for details).

If you don't want to make a label for your new audio CD after all the tracks are burned onto it and Music Disc Creator ejects the disc, simply click the Close button to close the Audio CD – Progress Information dialog box and return to the Music Disc Creator window.

Creating an MP3/WMA Disc Project

If you have a standalone or portable CD or DVD player capable of playing audio files saved in the MP3 (MPEG3) or WMA (Windows Media Audio), instead of using Music Disc Creator to start an audio CD Project for burning standard audio CDs, you can start an MP3/WMA Disc project and burn an MP3 audio disc. The benefit of creating an MP3 audio disc instead of a standard CD is clear: because MP3/WMA discs are composed only of audio files saved in the MP3 or WMA compressed file formats, you can fit many, many more song tracks on your average MP3 or WMA disc than you ever can on a standard audio CD composed of tracks saved in the uncompressed WAVE file formats.

To start a new MP3/WMA Disc Project from the Music Disc Creator window, click the MP3/WMA Disc link in the Project Type pane. Music Disc Creator then starts a new untitled MP3/WMA Disc Project that contains a default disc/MP3 player icon called Untitled (see Figure 7-7).

After starting a new MP3/WMA Disc Project, you can edit the name of the disc/MP3 player icon. Either click the icon in the Folder Navigation Tree in the MP3/WMA Disc Project pane and then press F2 before you replace Untitled and press Enter or click the Project Settings button on the toolbar and then enter a new name in the Disc Name text box before you click OK.

TECHNICAL STUFF

What's up with WMA?

The WMA (Windows Media Audio) file format is Microsoft's response to the MP3 file format. Like MP3s, WMA files are compressed and are perfect for streaming audio from the Internet. In addition, Microsoft's audio format restricts the copying of copyright-protected songs for which you do not possess the proper digital rights. This may be one of the reasons that WMA has found favor over MP3 with many professional music- and movie-producing companies.

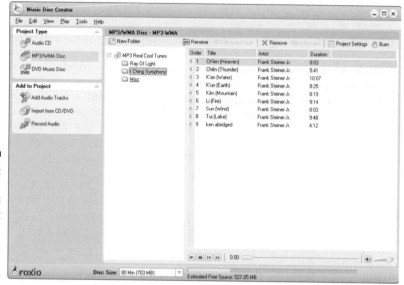

Figure 7-7:
Starting a
new MP3
Disc project
in the Music
Disc
Creator.

Adding audio files to a new MP3/WMA Disc Project is essentially the same process as adding tracks to an Audio CD Project: Click the Add Audio Tracks link in the Add to Project pane when you want to add audio files saved on your computer, click the Import from CD/DVD link when you want to rip tracks from other audio CD or DVD discs, and click the Record Audio link when you want to record new audio for the disc.

The big difference is that instead of just adding individual songs as you do with an Audio CD Project, you can add entire folders of audio files to the disc. To add a folder along with all its files, simply click the Folder tab in the Media Selector dialog box and then click the icon of the folder that you want to add before clicking the Add button.

Keep in mind that MP3/WMA Disc projects will accept any type of audio file that you care to add to the project. This is because, by default, the Project Settings for any new MP3/WMA Disc project are set to automatically convert all audio formats using the MP3 (Good Quality) setting. If you want to convert the files in your MP3/WMA Disc project using another setting, open the MP3/WMA Disc Project Settings dialog box by clicking the Project Settings button on the toolbar and then selecting the format and quality you want used in the Convert All To drop-down list box before clicking OK. To convert the audio files to WMA to play in a standalone player that reads this file format, you need to select either the WMA (Good Quality) or WMA (Low Quality) settings on this drop-down list.

Note that when adding individual audio files to the MP3/WMA Disc Project pane, you can create a new folder in which to add them. To create a new folder in the MP3/WMA Disc Project pane, click the disc/MP3 player icon or folder icon in the Navigation Tree in which you want the new folder and then click the New Folder button above it on the toolbar. Music Disc Creator adds a new folder named Untitled which you can then rename by typing in the new name and then pressing Enter. You can then add audio files to the new folder by clicking its icon in the Navigation Tree before you click one of the Add to Project links. To move audio files that you've already added to the MP3/WMA Disc project, drag them from the Track list and then drop them on top of the new folder icon in the Navigation tree.

Keep in mind that many simple MP3 disc players can't play tracks that you put into folders. When in doubt, keep all the tracks in the MP3 project in the root directory under Untitled and don't add them to folders beneath this root level.

As you add MP3 files to your MP3 disc project, Music Disc Creator displays their order in Track list. Before burning the MP3/WMA disc, you can change the order of its folders or of the tracks with the folders. To move a folder up or down on the disc, drag its folder icon to the desired position in the Navigation tree. To move a track up or down in its folder, drag its track to the new position.

You can use the controls in the Playlist Editor to arrange the order in which the MP3 normally plays in the final MP3 disc you burn. If you want a truly random order for the songs, simply click the Random button. If you want to manually determine where a particular song appears in the playlist, you can either drag its filename up or down the list or click the song filename and then click the Promote button (the one with triangle pointing upward) or Demote button (the one with the triangle pointing downward) to move the song up or down to the desired position.

After adding all the audio files that you want (or can fit) onto a new CD and arranging them in the order in which you want them to normally play, you're ready to burn the CD. To do this, you click the Burn button on the right side of the MP3/WMA Disc Project pane's toolbar (see "Burning the CD" earlier in this chapter for details on the process of burning a new CD).

Creating a DVD Music Disc

A DVD Music Disc is special kind of DVD that contains tons of audio files that are arranged in menus or tracklists. You can play DVD Music Discs on a DVD set-top player or on your computer using a software program such as Windows Media Player.

The main difference between DVD Music Discs and other types of audio discs you create with Music Disc Creator is not only that they accommodate so many more tracks — remember we're talking about 4.7GB or 8.5GB (with the new DVD discs) of space as opposed to 740MB) — but also that you can create menus or playlists that enable you to quickly and easily select the music you want to listen to on the disc. In addition, because DVDs are also visual players, you can display track screens while a track is playing: this track screen can be an image you want displayed or album information.

DVD Music Discs support three types of menus:

✔ **Top menu** that is displayed when you play the DVD disc. The top menu can include the following buttons:

 • **Play All** to play all the tracks in order starting with the first track in the Track list

 • **Track Lists** with a link to Track List menus (see below) that arrange the tracks in groups of 10 (according to the order in which the tracks are added to the project) as well as alphabetically from A to Z

 • **Smart Menus** with a list of all the Smart Menus used in the disc (see the upcoming bullet on Smart Menus)

✔ **Track List menus** that contain a list of all the tracks or links to other track lists are created as you add tracks or that you set up yourself

✔ **Smart Menus** that are created automatically as you add tracks to your DVD Music Disc project using the audio tag information associated with each track

Music Disc Creator imposes a limit of 99 menus total in the project. If you exceed this limit, you will not be able to burn the DVD Music Disc. Should this ever happen, you will have to remove Track List menus or deselect some of the Smart Menus criteria until you are within this limit.

Creating a new Music DVD Disc project

To create a new DVD Music Disc project, click the DVD Music Disc link in the Project Type pane of the Music Disc Creator window. Music Disc Creator then opens a new untitled DVD Music Disc in the project pane on the right, while at the same time adding a DVD Music Disc pane below the regular Project Type and Add to Project panes on the left. Immediately below the DVD Music Disc pane, you see a thumbnail of the main or top menu of the disc (see Figure 7-8).

Figure 7-8:
Creating a
DVD Music
Disc in the
Music Disc
Creator.

You can display a larger (and somewhat more legible) version of the main menu screen at the bottom of the DVD Music Disc project pane immediately beneath the Track List by clicking the faint button centered immediately above the playback controls with a triangle pointing upward at the bottom of this pane. When you click this button, the main menu screen preview disappears from the Task pane and appears instead at least twice as large in the lower half of the project pane. To hide this larger preview of the main menu screen and restore the Track List, click the button centered at the top of this main menu screen image with a downward pointing triangle.

The Navigation pane of a Music DVD Disc project contains an icon at the top representing the disc (and given the temporary name, Untitled) followed by a section with the Track Lists and below that, Smart Menus.

The process for adding music tracks to a DVD Music Disc is the same as when creating Audio CD or MP3/WMA Disc projects. Click the Add Audio Tracks link in the Add to Project pane to add audio files already saved on your computer system. Click the Import from CD/DVD to rip tracks from discs you put on your computer's CD/DVD drive. Click the Record Audio link to record new audio for the project (see "Adding audio tracks to your project" earlier in the chapter for details).

To name the Untitled DVD disc, click the Project Settings button on the Project pane toolbar and then enter a new name in the Disc Name before you click OK. Note that you can click the Auto-play (Starts Playing the First Track When Disc

Is Inserted) check box to put a check mark in it in this dialog box to have the first tune automatically play as soon as the standalone DVD player starts reading the disc (and before anyone can make a menu selection).

You can also select a new background style for the main or top menu of your Music DVD Disc project. Click the Styles link in the DVD Music Disc pane and then click the thumbnail of the style you want to use. If you want all the submenus and track screens on the disc to match the style you selected for the main menu screen, click the Apply to Menus and Track Screens Below check box before you click OK in the Styles dialog box.

Working with track lists

When you first start a new DVD Music Disc project, the Music Disc Creator adds a single Untitled track list (which is automatically selected). This Untitled track list displays all the tracks in order as you added them to the project, although you can modify this order easily by clicking the column heading at the top of the list to sort the list alphabetically or numerically (in the case of the Order and Duration columns). The first time you click the column heading, Music Disc Creator sorts the tracks in ascending order (A to Z and smaller to larger). The second time you click the column heading, the program sorts the tracks in descending order (Z to A and larger to smaller).

To name this original track list, press F2 while it's still selected in the Navigation pane (indicated by the highlighting of its name) and then replace Untitled with a name of your own before pressing Enter.

If you want to add your own track lists under the original Untitled (parent) track list automatically created by Music Disc Creator, click the New Track List button on the toolbar at the top of the DVD Music Disc project pane. The program then adds another numbered Untitled track list (as in Untitled 2, Untitled 3, and so on) as a subordinate list (indicated by its indentation in the Navigation tree).

You rename these new untitled track lists by typing your own descriptive names and pressing Enter. To add tracks that you want to appear in them, click the main track list icon (the original Untitled track list) to display all your tracks, and then sort them if necessary to put like tracks together (by Title or Artist). Select all the tracks you want to appear in the new track list you created and then drag them to the track list in the Navigation tree (as shown in Figure 7-9).

You can end up completely emptying the parent track list if you create subordinate track lists for all the different kinds of music tracks and then add the related tracks to these lists.

After adding all your tracks to the subordinate track lists you want on the Music DVD Disc, you can arrange the tracks within their respective lists. To do this, click the track list icon in the Navigation pane to display all its tracks in the Track List. You can then sort the tracks in ascending or descending on a column (Order, Title, Artist, or Duration) by clicking its headings at the top of the Track List (once for ascending and twice for descending).

Figure 7-9:
Adding selected tracks to the Real Country track list by dragging them from the Track List and dropping them on it.

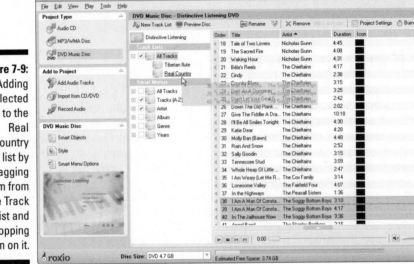

You can also have Music Disc Creator automatically arrange the tracks in a particular track list into subordinate lists using the smart tag information associated with them. To do this, right-click the name of the track list and then position the mouse over Arrange By on the shortcut menu before you click one of the following options on the Arrange By submenu:

- ✔ **All Tracks** to create subordinate track lists with groups of 10 tracks (0-10, 11-20, 21-30, and so on)

- ✔ **Tracks (A-Z)** to create subordinate tracks lists for each letter of the alphabet (A, B, C, D, and so forth)

- ✔ **Artist** to create subordinate tracks lists with the names of all the identified artists in alphabetical order

- ✔ **Album** to create subordinate tracks lists with the names of all the identified albums in alphabetical order

- ✔ **Genre** to create subordinate tracks lists with the names of all the identified music genres in alphabetical order

- ✔ **Years** to create subordinate tracks lists with the years of all the identified release years in numerical order

Working with Smart Menus

Smart Menus use the information in the audio tags identified for each track (see "Tagging the tracks in the project" earlier in this chapter for details) to group the music tracks that you add to the DVD Music Disc project into sub-menus that you can access from the main or top menu screen.

When you start a new DVD Music Disc project, Music Disc Creator adds two Smart Menus, Tracks (A-Z) and Artist (indicated by the check marks in front of their respective icons). This means that in addition to a Track Lists link (that takes you to a screen with links to all the track lists you add to the project as described in the preceding section), the main menu screen contains a Tracks (A-Z) link (that takes you to a screen with alphabetical links, A through Z, that lead to screens whose titles begin with that letter) and an Artist link (that takes you screens with links to the various artists on the DVD arranged in alphabetical order).

If you want to add other Smart Menus to the project, simply click the check box in front of their name:

- ✔ **All Tracks** to create menus and associated screen for groups of ten tracks on the DVD

- ✔ **Album** to create menus and associated screens for each album identi-fied in the tracks on the DVD

- ✔ **Genre** to create menus and associated screens for each music genre identified in the tracks on the DVD

- ✔ **Years** to create menus and associated screens for each release year identified in the tracks on the DVD

When using Smart Menus, you can easily modify how the tracks are grouped on the various submenus and associated screens. Right-click the name of the Smart Menu whose grouping you want to change and then click Smart Menu Options on the shortcut menu. Doing this opens the associated Smart Menu Options dialog box where you can modify the track order by selecting new options in the three Order By drop-down list boxes in conjunction with the related Ascending or Descending option buttons.

For example, you could use this dialog box to customize the Years Smart Menu by ordering it first by Year released in Descending order (from most recent to least recent), then by Album Name, and then by Artist, both in Ascending order.

To remove a Smart Menu from the project (thereby removing all links and associated screens), simply click the check box in front of a selected Smart Menu name to remove its check mark.

Customizing the menus and track screens

Smart Menu options are not the only things you can customize in your Music DVD Disc project. You can also customize its menu and track screens. To customize the screens for a Smart Menu or track list add to your project, you need to right-click its icon in the Navigation pane and then Smart Objects at the bottom of its shortcut menu.

Music Disc Creator opens a Smart Objects dialog box similar to the one in Figure 7-10. You then can select from the drop-down list whether to apply the changes to the Smart Objects options to just the currently selected menu or track screen only (This Menu), to the menus and track screens below it as well (This Menu and Below or Track Screens Below), or to all the menus or track screens in the project (All Menus, All Track Screens, or All Menus and Track Screens).

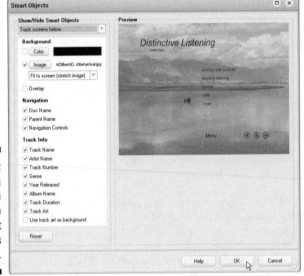

Figure 7-10: Customizing a menu screen in the Smart Objects dialog box.

After designating which menu(s) and track screens to customize, you can then select a new background color and/or background image. When you click the Color button, a color palette appears where you can click a predefined color or define custom colors of your own. When you click the Image button, a Media Selector dialog box appears where you can select the photo or graphics file to use (be sure that the image you select is not so dark as to obscure the text on its menu or screen).

When you select an image, Music Disc Creator automatically selects the Fit to Screen (Stretch Image) setting so that the graphic image fills the entire screen. If you find that the image is distorted, select the Fit to Screen (Keep Aspect

Ratio) option in the drop-down list box underneath the Image button. If your image is smaller than the screen, you can select among these other sizing options on the drop-down list:

- ✔ **Center (100% Scale)** to center the image in the center of the screen at actual size

- ✔ **Fill Screen (Keep Aspect Ratio)** to enlarge the image so it fills the screen while retaining the original aspect ratio to keep it from being distorted

- ✔ **Tile** to fill the screen by replicating the image as required

Note that if you select the Center (100% Scale) and assign a background color, this color will appear in the areas of the screen not filled by the image.

In addition to customizing the background color and image, you can also remove the options listed in the Navigation area of the Smart Objects dialog box to remove certain items from the designated menus and/or track lists (the particular options listed in this area vary depending upon what areas you've selected for customization in the drop-down list box at the top of the dialog box). To remove the display of a particular screen item, click its check box in the list to remove its check mark.

Previewing and burning a Music DVD Disc

As you build your Music Disc Creator project, you can use Preview Disc button on the DVD Music Disc pane's toolbar to test out the menus and preview the display of its various screens. When you click this button, a Preview DVD Music Disc window opens with simulated DVD controls on the left side and the preview of the currently selected menu or track screen displayed on the right (see Figure 7-11).

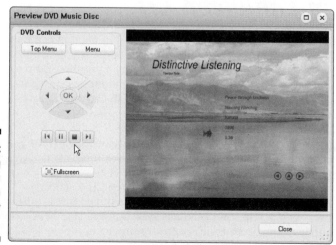

Figure 7-11: Previewing a Music DVD Disc in the Preview window.

To display the main menu screen, click the Top Menu button in the DVD Controls area. Then click the up and down buttons (the ones with the triangles pointing upward and downward) on the virtual controller to simulate selecting the various menu items and buttons on each screen (the text of the selected menu item or onscreen button appears in red). To follow a selected menu link, click the OK button in the center of the simulated DVD controls.

To play a track listed on one of the track list or Smart Menus, select it by clicking the up and down buttons on the virtual controller and then click OK. The track screen appears in the preview area for the music track you selected. To simulate returning to the top menu after exploring the projects various menu and track screens, use the virtual controller to select the Menu option at the bottom of the screen and then click OK.

Click the Fullscreen button below the virtual controller and playback controls make the preview area full screen as it would be when playing the disc on a standalone DVD player. Just keep in mind that when previewing the project full screen, you no longer have access to the virtual DVD controller. To select and activate menu items and buttons in full-screen mode, you must click them with the mouse. When you finish previewing the project in full-screen mode, press the Esc button to redisplay the regular Preview DVD Music Disc window.

When you are finished previewing the DVD Music Disc, click the Close button in the Preview DVD Music Disc window to close it and return to the Music Disc Creator window. When you are satisfied that your project has all the tracks on the DVD arranged as you want them, save the project by choosing File➪Save Project on the Music Disc Creator menu bar and then insert a blank DVD in your DVD burner drive and click the Burn button at the very end of the toolbar to burn your new DVD disc (see "Burning the CD" earlier in this chapter for details on the burning process).

Creating an Enhanced CD

An Enhanced CD is a type of multi-session CD that combines data and audio together. The first session on the CD contains audio tracks (such as you add to a standard Audio CD Project — see "Creating an Audio CD Project" earlier in this chapter for details). The second session contains the data file such as you might add to a standard Data Disc Project in Creator Classic — see Chapter 3 for details.

When you play an Enhanced CD disc in a standalone CD player (such as the one in your car or a Walkman-type portable unit), the player plays the music session so that you can listen to its music tracks as you would any other audio CD. When, however, you play an Enhanced CD disc in your computer's CD-ROM or DVD drive, you cannot only play its music tracks with a software program such as the Windows Media Player, but you also have access to its data portion with the appropriate software program.

Enhanced CDs are a perfect solution when you've created an MTV-type music video that you want to package along with a bunch of music tracks. You can then add the music tracks to the first audio session and the music video file to the second data session of the Enhanced CD Project and then burn them together on a CD disc for distribution to friends, family, and, yes, that MTV producer who's about to discover you.

To start a new Enhanced CD Project, open the Roxio CD Extra Disc Creator by clicking the CD Extra Disc Creator link in the Roxio Creator Application window (opened by clicking the Creator Classic link on the Data tab of the Project List pane in the in the Roxio Creator 8 Home window) Then, when the Roxio CD Extra Disc Creator window opens, click the Enhanced CD link at the top of the Projects pane.

CD Extra Disc Creator opens a new untitled Enhanced CD Project in the project pane area. The Navigation tree in Enhanced CD Project pane contains two icons: an Audio Project icon and a Data Disc icon (indicated by the numeric volume name) appear immediately below the Enhanced CD icon in the Navigation Tree. You add your audio tracks to the Audio Project portion of this tree (see "Adding audio tracks to your project" earlier in this chapter) and you then add your folders and data files to the Data Disc portion of the tree below (see Chapter 3).

After you finish adding your music tracks and data files to your Enhanced CD Project, you can save the project with the File➪Save command and then burn the CD by clicking the Burn button on the Enhanced CD Project pane's toolbar (see "Burning the CD" earlier in this chapter for details on the burn process).

Creating a Mixed-Mode CD

Like an Enhanced CD, a Mixed-mode CD also combines data files and music tracks on the same CD disc. Unlike the Enhanced CD, however, the Mixed-mode CD records both the computer data and music tracks in a single session and therefore can only be played back in your computer's CD or DVD drive using the appropriate software such as the Windows Media Player. Mixed-mode CDs are typically used to create multimedia projects for learning or entertainment (game) purposes that you can enjoy exclusively on the computer.

To start a new Mixed-Mode CD Project, launch Roxio CD Extra Disc Creator, as described in the preceding section; then click the click the Mixed-Mode CD link in the Advanced Projects area. The program then opens a new untitled Mixed-Mode CD Project in the project pane. The Navigation tree in the Mixed-Mode CD Project pane contains two icons: a Data Disc icon (indicated by the numeric volume name) and an Audio Project icon appear immediately below the Mixed-Mode CD icon in the Navigation Tree. You add your folders and data files to the Data Disc portion of the tree (see Chapter 3) and then add your audio tracks to the Audio Project portion below (see "Adding audio tracks to your project" earlier in this chapter).

After you finish adding your data files and your music tracks to your Mixed-Mode CD Project, you can save the project with the File⇨Save command and then burn the CD by clicking the Burn button on the Mixed-Mode CD Project pane's toolbar (see "Burning the CD" earlier in this chapter for details on the burn process).

Chapter 8

Creating Disc Labels and Case Inserts

. . . .

In This Chapter

▶ Getting comfortable with the Roxio Label Creator window

▶ Using Express Labeler to quickly and easily create your disc label and inserts

▶ Editing the image, graphic, and text objects in your label project

▶ Printing disc labels and case inserts

▶ Applying adhesive labels properly so you don't ruin your discs

. . . .

*T*he Roxio Label Creator program in the Roxio Creator 8 Suite makes it a snap to create professional-looking disc labels, covers, booklet inserts, and jewel case inserts for the audio CDs, MP3/WMA discs, and DVD discs that you burn with various Roxio Creator programs including Drag-to-Disc, Disc Copier, Creator Classic, Music Disc Creator, and MyDVD. And for you serious CD/DVD producers, it also works with LightScribe recorders that burn labels directly onto discs.

As you find out in this chapter, Roxio Label Creator makes the job of creating disc labels so easy through the combination of its predefined layouts and styles, Smart Objects, and Auto-Fill features that automate the filling in of vital information on the contents of your disc. This contents information can come either directly from the Gracenote CDDB in the case of audio CDs or from the Creator Classic, Music Disc Creator, and MyDVD projects (see Chapters 3, 7, 8, and 12), which you use in burning the discs in the case of both audio CDs and Music DVDs and video CDs and DVD discs.

This chapter also covers how Roxio Label Creator can make short work of designing CD and DVD case covers, booklet inserts, and jewel case inserts. When designing these types of case inserts, you can make use the Smart Objects and Auto-Fill features you use to fill in disc label content as well as apply the same or new graphic themes. Finally, you find out how to print the labels and case inserts you create with Roxio Label Creator and how to properly apply the labels you print to the CD and DVD discs you burn.

Getting Familiar with the Roxio Label Creator Window

You can launch the Roxio Label Creator tool from Roxio Creator 8 Home window by clicking the Label Creator link in the Applications Projects Window after selecting Applications on the Home tab of the Project List. Figure 8-1 shows the Roxio Label Creator window that then opens. As you can see in this figure, this window is made up of the follow areas:

✔ The **Add Object** pane contains tools for adding existing images, predefined shapes, drawing lines, adding text, and scanning new images for the layout you're editing.

✔ The **Edit Layout** pane contains options for applying a style for all the layouts in your label project, selecting new Smart Objects to include in the project, adding track list and other disc information from an existing disc, and selecting a new background for the project.

Figure 8-1:
The Roxio Label Creator window contains the design tools you need and a preview of the label or insert you're editing.

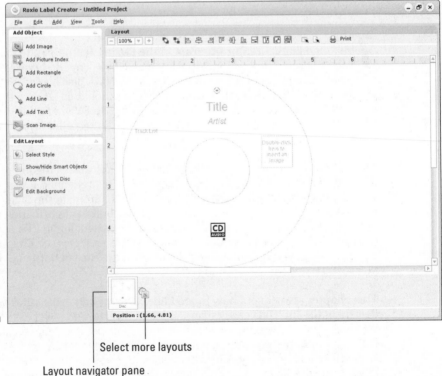

Select more layouts

Layout navigator pane

✔ The **Layout** pane contains a toolbar with a print button along with various zoom and alignment buttons and a preview of the label or insert currently selected for editing.

✔ The **Layout Navigator** pane (on the right side immediately below the Layout pane) shows which one of the layouts (label and insert) in your label project is selected (with a rectangle around its thumbnail) and contains a Select More Styles button that opens the Show/Hide Objects dialog box where you can select which layouts to include in the project.

The Add Object pane

The Add Object pane (shown in Figure 8-1) contains the seven tools that you can use when you need to add images to or draw specific shapes in the disc labels or case inserts in the label you're creating. Roxio Label Creator recognizes three different types of objects that you can add to and manipulate in the labels and case inserts you're designing:

✔ **Image objects,** which are graphics or photo images stored in separate files that you can bring into the label project

✔ **Graphic objects,** which are rectangular or oval shapes or straight lines that you can size and place in the label project

✔ **Text objects,** which are blocks of text inside text boxes that you can size and position on the label project

The Add Object pane contains the following links for adding image, graphic, or text objects to your label project:

✔ **Add an Image** to open the Add dialog box where you can select the Smart View, album, folder, or MediaSpace containing the graphic or photo image you want to add to the layout you're editing

✔ **Add Picture Index** to open the Picture Index Properties dialog box where you can assemble a grid of tiny thumbnails of pictures that is so many rows wide by so many columns long as a graphic object for use in the layout you're editing

✔ **Add Rectangle** to add a new rectangular graphic object to the layout you're editing

✔ **Add Circle** to add a new circular graphic object to the layout you're editing

✔ **Add Line** to add a straight line as a new graphic object to the layout you're editing

✔ **Add Text** to add a text object to the layout you're editing where you can enter text that you want to appear on the label or insert

✔ **Scan Image** link to launch the Roxio Media Import application (see Chapter 9), where you can use your scanner to scan in a new image for the layout you're editing (if you get an error message when you click the Scan Image link, choose File➪Select Scanner on the Roxio Label Creator menu bar and make sure that your scanner is selected in the Select Source dialog box before you click this link again)

The Edit Layout pane

As you can see in Figure 8-1, the Edit Layout pane consists of the following links that you can click to perform common tasks for designing your disc labels and case inserts:

✔ **Select Style** to open the Select Style dialog box where you can select the type of layout including background, object placement, and typestyle to use the label project you're creating

✔ **Show/Hide Smart Objects** to display and hide the Select/Edit Content dialog box where you can select the type of label project (Audio, Data, or Video) as well as select what type of information (such as Title, Track List, Disc Type, and so on) to include on the disc label on case inserts in the label project

✔ **Auto-Fill from Disc** to add the name of the album, artist, and track list for the CD that you're burning or you have inserted into your computer's CD-ROM or DVD drive

✔ **Edit Background** to open the Background Properties dialog box where you can select an image or a color to use for the background of the label or case inserts you're currently designing in Roxio Label Creator

The Layout toolbar

The Layout toolbar at the top of the Layout pane contains a whole cartload of useful stacking and alignment tools (see Figure 8-2) that you can use to control which image, graphic, or text objects are front and which are behind the others as well as how selected objects are aligned on the disc label or case insert layout you're editing. The controls on this toolbar include:

✔ **Zoom In** and **Zoom Out** buttons to zoom in or out on the displayed layout by selecting one of the predefined zoom percentages (50%, 75%, 100%, 150%, or 200%)

✔ **Zoom** drop-down list box to select a new, predefined zoom percentage (50%, 75%, 100%, 150%, or 200%) on its drop-down list

✔ **Bring Object to Front** button to bring the object you select in front all of the other objects that cover it in some way

✔ **Send Object to Back** button to place the object you select in back all of the other objects that its covers in some way

✔ **Align Selected Objects Left** button to left-align all the selected objects with the object you last select

✔ **Center Selected Objects Vertically** button to center all the selected objects on the vertical centerline of the disc label or case insert you're currently designing

✔ **Align Selected Objects Right** button to right-align all the selected objects with the object you last select

✔ **Align Selected Objects Top** button to align all the tops of the selected objects with the top of the object you last select

✔ **Center Selected Objects Horizontally** button to center all the selected objects on the horizontal centerline of the disc label or case insert you're currently designing

✔ **Align Selected Objects Bottom** button to align all the bottoms of the selected objects with the bottom of the object you last select

✔ **Match Object Width** button to match the width of all the selected objects to that of the object you last select

✔ **Match Object Height** button to match the height of all the selected objects to that of the object you last select

✔ **Match Object Width and Height** button to match the width and height of all the selected objects to that of the object you last select

✔ **Size to Text** button to resize the text box of a text graphic object so that all of its text is displayed

✔ **Select Object** button to open the Select Object dialog box where you can designate the object in your layout project that you want selected

✔ **Select Paper Stock** button to open the Page Setup dialog box where you can select the type of paper and size to use if you're printing your label project on a standard laser or inkjet printer or indicate that you are printing to disc if you're using a fancy LightScribe recorder

✔ **Print** button to open the Print dialog box where you can calibrate and preview your project before you send it to the printer or LightScribe recorder

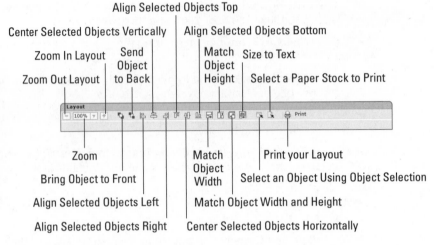

Figure 8-2:
The toolbar
at the top of
the Layout
pane
contains a
number of
zoom and
alignment
options
buttons.

Align Selected Objects Top

Center Selected Objects Vertically   Align Selected Objects Bottom

Zoom In Layout   Send   Match   Size to Text
                  Object   Object
Zoom Out Layout   to Back Height   Select a Paper Stock to Print

Zoom   Match   Print your Layout
        Object
Bring Object to Front   Width   Select an Object Using Object Selection

Align Selected Objects Left   Match Object Width and Height

Align Selected Objects Right   Center Selected Objects Horizontally

The Object Properties toolbars

The Layout toolbar is not the only toolbar that you will see at the top of the Layout pane as you edit your label project. When you add or select a rectangular or circular graphic or photo in the current layout, an Object Properties toolbar immediately below the Layout toolbar (see Figure 8-3). This toolbar contains the following controls:

✔ **Fill Color** button to select a new fill color for the selected object along with a Transparency drop-down button that when clicked displays a transparency slider you can use to set its opacity

✔ **Line Color** button to select a new outline color for the selected object along with a Transparency drop-down button that when clicked displays a transparency slider you can use to set its opacity and a Thickness pop-up palette to reset the line thickness

Note when you add or select a line graphic object in the current layout, only the line-related controls. (Line-Color button and Transparency and Thickness buttons appear on the second toolbar at the top of the Layout pane. Also, keep in mind that Fill-Color and Line-Color controls have no effect on any text objects that are selected in the layout at the time you change their settings.)

When you add or select a text box in your current layout, a much more extensive Object Properties toolbar appears immediately below the Layout toolbar atop the Layout pane (see Figure 8-4). The text controls on this version of the Object Properties toolbar include:

✔ **Font** drop-down button to select a new font for the text in the selected text object

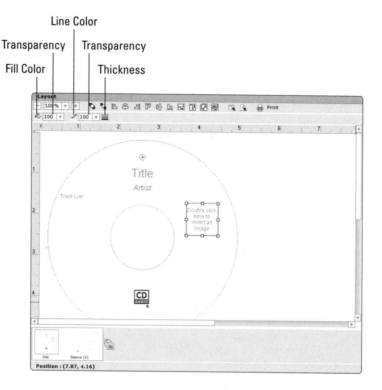

Line Color

Transparency Transparency

Fill Color Thickness

Figure 8-3:
These tools
appear on a
second
toolbar in
the Layout
pane when
you select a
rectangular
or circular
graphic
object or
photo
image.

✔ **Font Size** drop-down button to select a new font size for the text in the selected text object

✔ **Bold** button to bold the text in the selected text object

✔ **Italic** button to italicize the text in the selected text object

✔ **Underline** button to underline the text in the selected text object

✔ **Shadow Text** button to add a shadow effect to the text in the selected text object

✔ **Text Color** button to open the Select Color dialog box to select a new color for the text in the selected text object

✔ **Fill Color** button to open the Select Color dialog box to select a new color for the text object's text box

✔ **Transparency** button to open a transparency slider to modify the opacity of the text in the selected text object

✔ **Straighten Text** button to straighten text in a text object that you've curve with the Curve Text button

✔ **Curve Text** button to curve text in a text object so that is bends with the curve of a disc label

✔ **Flow Text** button to reflow the text in a text object that you've curved with the Curve Text button

✔ **Left Align** button to left-align the text in the selected text object

✔ **Center** button to center the text in the select text object

✔ **Right Align** button to right-align text in the selected text object

✔ **Text Object Properties** to open the Text Properties dialog box for the selected text object where you can edits its text and select new attributes for it

Figure 8-4:
These tools
appear on a
second
toolbar in
the Layout
pane when
you select a
text object
or photo
image.

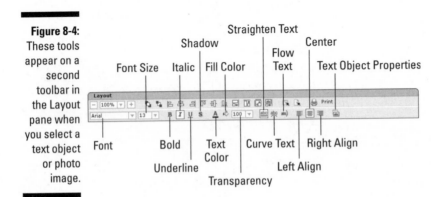

Express Disc Labels and Case Inserts

Roxio Label Creator 8 supports a three-step Express Labeler assistant that enables you to whip up new disc labels, case inserts, and booklets in a jiff. You can access the Express Labeler by clicking the Create Label button in any Progress Information dialog box or by choosing Tools➪Express Labeler from the Roxio Label Creator menu bar within the Roxio Label Creator window itself.

Roxio Label Creator responds by displaying the first Express Labeler – Untitled Project window shown in Figure 8-5. Here, you select the type of layout(s) that you want to create by clicking the appropriate check box or boxes:

✔ **Disc** to create a standard CD or DVD disc label (the default already checked whenever you open the initial Express Labeler window)

✔ **Front** to design the front cover insert for a CD jewel case

✔ **Booklet** to create the front and back of a booklet insert for a CD jewel case

✔ **Back** to create to the back cover insert for a CD jewel case

✔ **Mini Disc** to create a disc label for the smaller 3-inch diameter mini-CD (sometimes called a micro-CD)

✔ **DVD Case** to create a front, back, and spine cover insert for a DVD case

✔ **DVD Booklet** to create the front and back of a booklet insert for a DVD case

✔ **Slim Case Insert** to create the front cover insert for a slim CD jewel case

✔ **Core** to create a CD or DVD core label

✔ **Disc Sleeve** to create a prefolded printed page with a tab that you can use in filing that keeps a record of the information in your label project

✔ **Disc Sleeve (Double-Sided)** to create a double-sided version of a disc sleeve

✔ **Binder Page** to create an 8.5 x10 inch page (that works with letter-size or A4 paper) with thumbnails organized a picture index that you can use as record of your digital photos and keep in a binder

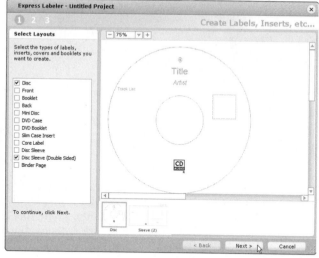

Figure 8-5:
Selecting the layouts to create in the initial window of the Express Labeler.

After you select all the check boxes for the layouts you want to include in the new label project and click the Next> button, the second Express Labeler window similar to the one shown in Figure 8-6 appears. Here, you can customize the label project by doing any of the following:

▌ ✔ **Select a Project Type:** Choose between Audio Project (default) for an Audio Project, Data Project, or Video Project.

✔ **Select Style:** Click the Select Style button to open the Select Style dialog box where you can select a style that determines the background art, placement of the information on the label and inserts, and font to use.

✔ **Edit Content:** Click the Edit Content button to open the Smart Object Editor dialog box where you select what smart object information to include on the label and inserts in the label project and edit the actual contents of the selected smart objects by clicking them.

✔ **Auto-Fill from Disc:** Click the Auto-Fill from Disc button to have Express Labeler fill in the title, artist, and track list information (provided that their smart objects are selected) on the label and inserts from the audio CD or DVD that you have inserted into your computer's CD/DVD drive.

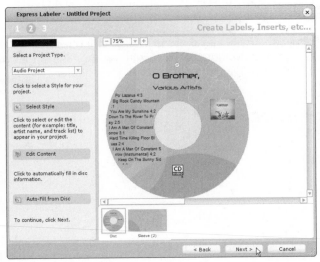

Figure 8-6:
The second window of the Express Labeler enables you customize the style and contents of your label project.

If the layout you're using for the disc label contains a disc type icon, you can select the proper icon in the Smart Object Editor dialog box by clicking the Disc Type Icon Smart Object in the list on the left side. Doing this displays a list box on the right side of the dialog box with every conceivable disc type (from cDVD Video to VCD Video RW).

If you selected more than one layout check box in the initial Express Labeler window, you can select any of those layouts in the Layout Navigation pane at the bottom of the Customize Express Labeler window. You can then modify the style for that particular layout or edit a particular Smart Object that the layout uses.

When you finish editing the elements for the different layouts in your label project in the second, Customize, window of Express Labeler, click the Next> button to proceed to the third and final, Complete the Project window (see Figure 8-7). Here, you have a choice between three actions before finishing the project and closing the Express Labeler:

- ✔ **Print** to open the Print dialog box where you select the printer, paper, and other settings before sending the project to be printed

- ✔ **Save** to open the Save As Project dialog box where you can save the project as a .jwl project file so that you can reuse it if you later make more copies of the same CD or DVD disc

- ✔ **Edit in Label Creator** to close the Express Labeler and open the project up in Roxio Label Creator for further refinement and editing

After saving and/or printing the label project, click the Finish button to close the Express Labeler (this happens automatically if you click the Edit in Label Creator button).

Figure 8-7:
The third window of the Express Labeler enables you print and save the project as well as continue to edit it in Label Creator.

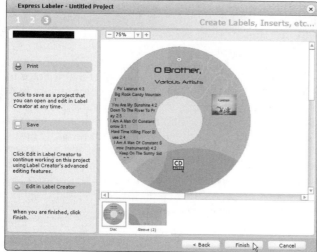

Editing Elements of the Label Project

Many times even after editing the contents of the layouts you select in the second, Customize, window of the Express Labeler, you will still want to make some modifications to the layouts of the disc label and case inserts in Roxio

Label Creator. To open the project for further editing in Roxio Label Creator, you click the Edit in Label Creator button in the third, Complete the Project window in Express Labeler.

When the label project is loaded into Roxio Label Creator, you can select the layout to edit in the Navigation pane (clicking its thumbnail) and then use the buttons that appear on the toolbars at the top of the Layout pane to make changes to particular objects.

Editing the text objects in your layouts

When you click a text object box in one of your layouts, the text-related buttons appear on the Object Properties toolbar (see Figure 8-4). Most of its tools are the standard ones you're probably familiar with from using them in your word processing program. For example, you use the Font drop-down list box to select a new font for the selected text objects and the Font Size drop-down list box to select a new font size. So too, you click the Bold Text button to add or remove the boldface enhancement in the selected text objects, the Italicize Text button to add or remove italics, the Underline Text to add or remove underlining, and the Shadow Text to add or remove the shadow text enhancement (note that you can only apply the shadow enhancement to certain fonts).

The Change Text Color button enables you to select a new color for the text in the text objects you've selected by clicking its color square in the Select Color dialog box that appears when you click the button (you can also create new colors for the text by clicking its Create Colors button and then using the Eyedropper tool, the Hue and/or Shades mixing boxes, or by entering new Red, Green, and Blue values or new Hue, Saturation, and Value percentages). You can use the Left Align Text, Center Text, and Right Align Text buttons to modify the text alignment within the text boxes of the selected text objects. Note that Center Text option is the default for all new text objects and that Roxio Label Creator automatically adjusts the text using whatever alignment option you select when you modify the size and shape of text object's text box.

The only two buttons that are definitely not standard in word processing programs are the Straighten Text and Curve Text buttons. These buttons are great, however, when editing the layout for your disc labels. Because of the round nature of disc labels, it often makes sense to put text like the album and artist's name on a curve rather than on a straight line.

To curve a particular text object in the Disc Label Layout, click the text object or objects (Ctrl+Click to select more than one) and then click the Curve Text button. After curving the text box of a particular text object, you can then rotate that text box around the disc label (Label Creator will modify the text to suit the new orientation on the disc). If you decide that a particular text object doesn't look so hot on the curve, you can convert it back to a standard text box with straight text by clicking the Straighten Text button.

When it comes to the text objects that contain track lists (automatically generated by clicking the Auto-Fill from Disc button in the Express Labeler or by choosing Tools⇨Auto-Fill Smart Objects from Disc on the Roxio Label Creator menu bar), Label Creator automatically left-aligns their text in their text boxes. Further, in the layout of the disc label the program also automatically indents the list to fit the curve of the label (both the curve of the inside hole and that of the outer diameter) when you position this list on the left or right side of the disc label.

Figure 8-8 shows my edited disc label after making modifications to all of its text objects. In this example, I used the Curve Text button to put both the album and artist name on the bias at the top of the label (I also used the Bold button to boldface their text and the Font drop-down list box to change the font from Neuropol to Arial). For the text object containing the track list, I manually resized its text box after clicking the Flow Text button and selecting Arial Narrow in the Font drop-down list and reducing the font from 9 to 7 points by selecting 7 in the Font Size drop-down list. Then I dragged this text object to its final position on the right side of the label, making sure that all of the track list information was now displayed.

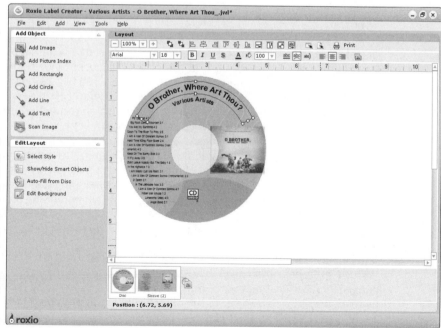

Figure 8-8:
The layout of the disc label after editing its text objects with the tools at the top of the Layout pane.

Remember that instead of having to manually resize each text box to suit a font or font size change, you can have Roxio Label Creator automatically do this for you by clicking the Size to Text button on the Layout toolbar (see Figure 8-2).

Editing the image and graphic objects in your layouts

When editing the layouts for the disc label and case inserts in your label project, you may well have to edit their image and graphic objects. Remember that image objects contain any graphics files that you add to the layouts, whereas graphic objects are composed of the rectangles, circular shapes, and straight lines that you insert with the Add Rectangle, Add Circle, and Add Line links on the Add Object pane.

When you click an image or graphic object in the layout, Roxio Label Creator indicates that it is selected by placing sizing handles around the perimeter of the object. You can then drag these sizing handles to make the selected image or graphic object larger or smaller.

To reposition the image or graphic object that you've selected, position the mouse pointer in the middle of the selected image or graphic and then use the hand pointer to drag the object to the desired position in the current layout.

The sizing and moving of line graphic objects present a little different story from all the rest. To select a line graphic for resizing, click one of its two ends to add a gray resizing handle. Then position the arrowhead mouse pointer over that sizing handle and drag the mouse (the pointer then becomes a hand) until the line is longer or shorter (you can also rotate the line around the opposite, unselected end which remains stationary).

To reposition a line graphic, drag the mouse to draw a bounding box around the line to select both ends. One end of the line then displays a gray sizing handle, while the other end displays a white repositioning handle. You position the arrowhead mouse pointer over the white repositioning handle and then drag the mouse (the pointer then becomes a hand) to move the entire line graphic object to the desired position in the current layout.

You can also delete and cut or copy a selected image or graphic object to the Windows Clipboard. To delete the object, press the Delete key. To cut the image (for later pasting in other layout), press Ctrl+X. To copy the object instead, press Ctrl+C. To paste the object you've cut or copied to the

Clipboard in a new part of the layout (or another layout that you've selected by clicking its tab button on the top row of the Roxio Label Creator window, press Ctrl+V.

Keep in mind when editing the images and graphics in a particular layout that you can also select a new background image or color to use in that layout by clicking the Edit Background link in the Edit Layout pane. Label Creator then opens the Background Properties dialog box with the current background object selected (any color or image you select in this dialog box overrides any background graphic supplied to the current layout by the style you've applied to the entire label project).

To add a new background color, click the color in the color palette or click the More Colors button and create a custom color in the Select Color dialog box. To add a new background image instead, make sure that Use the Following Image as Background Image check box is selected and then click the Browse or Scan button. When you click Browse, Label Creator opens the Add dialog box where you can select the graphics file with the image you want displayed as the background of the layout you're editing. When you click Scan, Roxio Label Creator launches the Roxio Media Import application (see Chapter 9) where you can scan the image to be used.

Figure 8-9 shows you my sleeve for audio CD label in the Label Creator's Layout pane after resizing the scanned album cover image and repositioning the album title and artist information.

Figure 8-9:
Sample sleeve in the Layout pane after resizing and repositioning its album cover image.

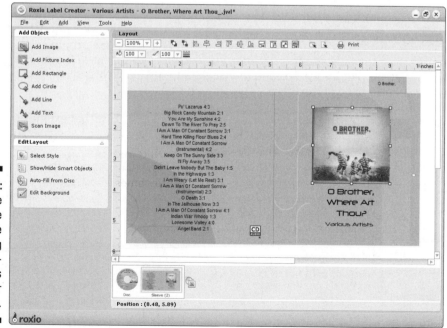

If you decide that you want to replace a particular image object in the layout, double-click the object. Doing this causes Label Creator to open the appropriate dialog box for selecting a replacement graphic.

Printing Disc Labels and Case Inserts

After you have all the layouts in your label project edited the way you want them, you're ready to print the project (after you saved your changes with Ctrl+S, of course).

Because you want to use special paper in printing the different layouts in a typical label project (high-gloss adhesive label paper for labels and matte finish perforated paper for case inserts), you often need to change the page settings before printing each layout in the project separately, each time putting the right paper into your printer as well as making sure that you've put the paper in the right way (some printers want the glossy side of the label paper facing down, while others want it facing up).

Open the Page Setup dialog box by choosing File⇒Page Setup on the Roxio Label Creator menu bar (shown in Figure 8-10) where you can select the Media to use in printing. By default, Standard Paper is selected as the media to use. To select a different paper type besides the default Letter (8.5 x 11 inches), click the Paper Type drop-down list button and then select the type and size of paper you'll be using.

If you are printing on special label paper, you need to select Commercial Paper in the Media drop-down list and then select the appropriate brand and size in the Paper Type drop-down list box. If you are printing direct to disc with a LightScribe recorder, you need to select Print to Disc in the Media drop-down list box and then make sure that your brand of LightScribe is selected in the Paper Type drop-down list box.

If you want Label Creator to print any image or text that extends into the center of the disc label, click the Printer Center/Core Label check box before closing the Page Setup dialog box.

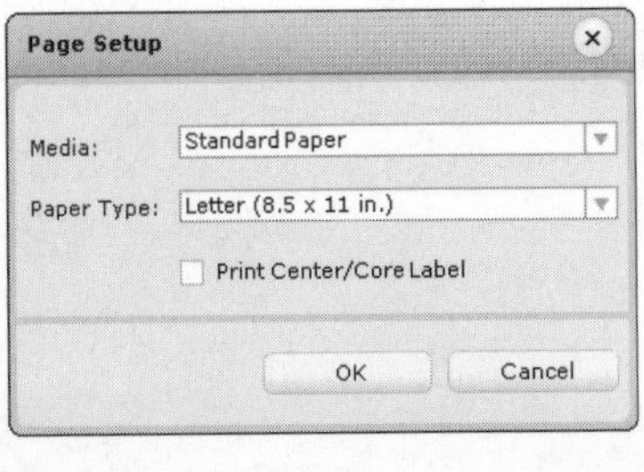

Figure 8-10:
Selecting
the Media
and Paper
Type to use
the Page
Setup dialog
box.

Page Setup	✕
Media:	Standard Paper ▼
Paper Type:	Letter (8.5 x 11 in.) ▼
	☐ Print Center/Core Label
	OK Cancel

After you finish selecting the media and paper type for your label project, you're ready to print it. To do this, close the Page Setup dialog box by clicking OK and then click the Print button on the Layout toolbar or choose File⇨Print or press Ctrl+P to open the Print dialog box like the one shown in Figure 8-11.

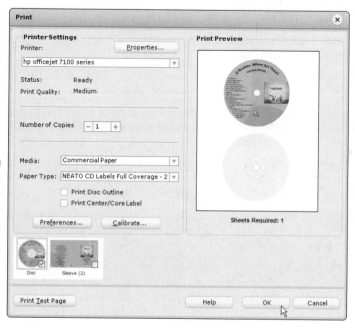

Figure 8-11: Getting ready to print the first layout in the label project in the Print dialog box.

To check the layouts in the Print dialog box, click the thumbnail of the layout in the Layout Navigator at the bottom and then inspect the image shown in the Print Preview section on the right side of this dialog box.

If you find some details that need changing, modify the necessary print options before actually sending the print job to the printer by clicking the OK button:

- ✔ **Printer** drop-down list box to select a different printer installed on your computer system to use in printing the label project

- ✔ **Properties** button to open the Properties dialog box for the type of printer currently selected where you can change certain advanced settings (which are entirely printer dependent) such as the paper orientation (Portrait or Landscape), the page order in printing, the paper source, and the printer quality, among other things

- ✔ **Status** displays the current printing status of the printer selected in the Printer drop-down list box

✔ **Print Quality** displays the quality (Best, Normal, or Draft) for the printer selected in the Printer drop-down list box (to change this setting, click the Properties button)

✔ **Number of Copies** text box to indicate the number of copies to print of the selected layout

✔ **Media** drop-down list box to change the media (Standard Paper, Commercial Paper, or Print to Disc) to use

✔ **Paper Type** drop-down list box to select the appropriate page size, brand name or Light

✔ **Print Disc Outline** check box to print the outline of the disc label (when Disc layout is selected in the Layout Navigator)

✔ **Printer Center/Core Label** check box to print any information or image that bleeds into the center of the disc label (when Disc layout is selected in the Layout Navigator)

✔ **Preferences** button to open the Print Preference dialog box where you can manually adjust where the printer starts printing by changing the OverPrint/Bleeding and Fine Tuning settings

✔ **Calibrate** button to open the Printer Calibration dialog box where you can have Label Creator calibrate the print alignment for your printer using test pages

✔ **Print Test Page** button to obtain a quick and dirty printout just showing part of the outline of the disc label or case insert you're printing; you can then use this test page to compare with the outlines of the labels on the actual label paper or perforations of the case inserts on the actual insert paper to see if you need to make any adjustments to where the printing starts before actually returning to the Print dialog box and printing the real disc labels and case inserts

After you finish modifying the necessary print settings in the Print dialog box, you can start the printing by clicking the OK button to send the print job to the printer. If your printer requires manual feeding of the type of paper you selected for printing one or more of the selected layouts, you will be prompted to insert the paper before the printing actually begins.

Applying Labels to Discs

Applying the disc label to the actual CD or DVD disc is, perhaps, one of the most daunting tasks that a body can perform because if you mess up and get any wrinkles or bubbles in the label, you might as well toss the CD or DVD disc in the trash, 'cause it'll never play properly (if at all).

So too, you must never, never, ever try to remove and reapply a disc label that you've only got partially applied to a disc, as the adhesive in the label will undoubtedly rip off part of the coating on the top of the disc (the one that's not read by the laser) and as a result the disc is dead meat and will never play again.

In other words, the application of disc labels to your CD or DVD discs is a one-shot deal during which you cannot afford any flub-ups (enough to make you sweat bullets). In fact, because it's such a delicate practice that I've screwed up plenty in my time, I won't even attempt to apply a disc label without the aid of one of the those applicators which consists of a spindle for centering the disc and label and a base for holding the label (adhesive side up and printed side down) with a spring-loaded plunger-type spindle in the middle, with the button in the middle for pushing down the disc (with the top, coated side facing down and the shiny, data side that you never touch facing up) to meet and bond with the adhesive on the label. (The particular model I favor is a sweet Italian number by Neato that has a felt pad on the bottom of the base so it won't slide during the crucial punch-down phase where the top, coated side of the CD or DVD disc meets the adhesive of the disc label.) You can also find other models by manufacturers such as DYMO and USDM that you can use to do the same thing.

Part IV
Creating Projects for DVDs

The 5th Wave   By Rich Tennant

Dating requirements have definitely changed. Today you've got to have a good job, a nice car, and at least one CD/DVD burner.

In this part . . .

*I*t seems to me that the heart of the Roxio Creator 8 suite lies in its two major applications for video productions: VideoWave 8, which provides you with an easy-to-use but robust video editor; and MyDVD 8, which provides you with both an easy-to-use DVD project builder and Roxio's great burn engine for burning both your video and DVD projects to disc. Part IV not only covers the complete use of these two applications but also covers, Roxio Media Import, a program that you'll come to rely on heavily for acquiring the various types of digital media you use in your projects destined for DVD.

Chapter 9

Acquiring Digital Media

. . . .

In This Chapter

▶ Launching the Roxio Media Import and selecting the type of media to acquire and the devices with the media

▶ Scanning photos or copying them directly from your digital camera

▶ Capturing live video or video clips from your Web camera or digital camcorder

▶ Capturing live audio and copying tracks from an Audio CD or Music DVD Disc

▶ Copying movie titles from unencrypted DVD discs to your computer's hard disk

. . . .

*B*efore you can get down to making your own videos and movies with either the Roxio Creator's VideoWave program or MyDVD, you have to acquire the digital media files that you need in putting together your final multimedia productions. These media files can include video clips taken from your digital camcorder, still images from your digital camera and scanner, audio files recorded with your computer's microphone or taken through a line into your computer from an analog device like an LP record player or audio cassette as well as audio tracks from an audio CD and, if all that's not enough for you, DVD movie titles that you've saved on your computer's hard disk as well.

This chapter gives you the lowdown on how to use Roxio Media Import to acquire all these different types of digital media for your video and DVD movie productions. You can import the media to folders on your hard disk that you can then organize into media albums (see Chapter 4) for use when you go on to make your multimedia productions with VideoWave (see Chapter 11) and the MyDVD (see Chapter 12).

Using Roxio Media Import

In acquiring media for your video and DVD movie productions, you will come to rely heavily on the Roxio Media Import application. To launch Roxio Media Import from the Roxio Creator 8 Home window, click the Media Import link in Utilities column in the Applications Project Window after selecting Applications on the Home tab.

Roxio Media Import is also supposed to automatically launch whenever you use Windows XP's plug-and-play feature to an external digital device such as a scanner, digital camera, or digital camcorder to your computer using the cable and port appropriate to that device. Note, however, that this feature may not work if you've installed another graphics or video editing program after installing the Roxio Creator 8 suite on your computer. In such a case, you have to manually launch Media Import after connecting the device.

The Welcome to Roxio Media Import window appears. This window contains a Photo, Video, and Audio button that enables you to select the type of media you're importing. When you click one of these buttons, a Device drop-down list box (initially called Select Device or Source to Import From) appears. This is where you can select the actual device or disc that contains the media you want to use (note that specific items listed on these drop-down lists vary according to the type of media selected and the devices actually connected to your computer).

Figure 9-1 shows the Device drop-down list box for my computer system in the Roxio Media Import window after clicking the Photo button to import digital photos.

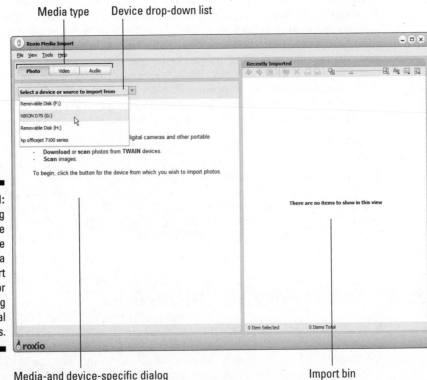

Figure 9-1:
Selecting
the device
to use in the
Media
Import
window for
importing
digital
photos.

Connecting digital devices to use in Media Import

Before an external device such as your scanner, digital camera, or camcorder will appear in the Device drop-down list pane of the Media Import window, you must have it properly installed and connected to your computer. Note that most digital devices such as digital cameras and scanners connect to your computer through an available USB (Universal Serial Bus) port using a special USB cable. Others devices such as digital video cameras (also known as camcorders) usually connect to your computer via the faster, IEEE1394 FireWire connection necessary to handle streaming video (note, however, that some of the newer digital cameras that take video as well as still pictures also support FireWire).

When dealing with external digital devices such as scanners and digital still cameras, there are two standards (both of which are supported by Media Import) for acquiring still images and streaming video: the so-called TWAIN (as in Kipling's "Never the twain shall meet . . .") standard and Microsoft's WIA (Windows Image Acquisition) standard developed for Windows XP. In order for Media Import to recognize your TWAIN or WIA device, you must have installed the TWAIN or WIA device drivers on your computer (these drivers are supplied on the CDs that come with your devices — if you don't have the CD readily available, check the manufacturer's Web site for them).

To install the drivers for a new digital device, you may need to open the Scanners and Cameras control panel dialog box (do this by clicking the Control Panel item on the Windows Start menu, the Printers and Other Hardware link in the Pick a Category area of the Control Panel dialog box, and then clicking Scanners and Cameras link in the Or Pick a Control Panel Icon area of the Printers and Other Hardware dialog box). In the Scanners and Cameras dialog box, click the Add an Imaging Device link in Imaging Tasks pane on the left and then follow the steps in the Scanner and Camera Installation Wizard that appears. When prompted for the name of the scanner or camera you want to install, either select the name of the manufacturer and model in the Manufacturer and Model list boxes or click the Have Disk button and then select the letter of your computer's CD drive in the Copy Manufacturer's Files From drop-down list box before you click the OK button.

After Windows finishes copying the device drivers from the manufacturer's CD, an icon with the name of the new digital scanner or camera appears in the Scanners and Cameras dialog box. If you close this dialog box and then launch Media Import, the name of the scanner or camera you just installed with the Windows Scanner and Camera Installation Wizard appears in the Device drop-down list when you select the Photo as the type of media to import. This happens as soon as you connect the scanner or camera to your computer with the proper USB or IEEE1394 FireWire cable and turn the device on (the name of the device appears behind a WIA or TWAIN icon depending upon which type of driver it uses). You can then start acquiring images from these digital devices in Media Import after selecting them in the Device drop-down list.

Customizing the Media Import options

Before you start working with Media Import to acquire your favorite media files, you may want to modify the default locations where the program automatically saves different types of media files in the Options dialog box. To do this, choose Tools➪Options to open the Options dialog box similar to the one shown in Figure 9-2. As you can see in this figure, this dialog box contains two tabs: File Locations where you can change where Media Import automatically saves a particular media type and TWAIN Options where you can change what method Media Import uses to transfer data from TWAIN devices.

Figure 9-2: Modify the location where different types of media files are automatically saved in the Options dialog box.

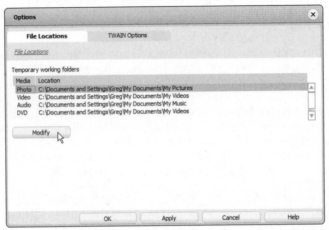

To change any of these default folder locations on the File Locations tab, click the type of media and its pathname in this list box and then click the Modify button (that becomes active only after you click one of the media types in the Temporary Working Folders list box). The Browse Location dialog box then appears with a list box containing a Navigation Tree that shows the selected media type's current default folder location. Use the Navigation Tree in this list box to select a new folder location (you can also use the Create Folder button at the bottom of the Browse Location dialog box to create a new folder to use) and then click the OK button.

The TWAIN Options tab contains three option buttons, File (Recommended), Memory, and Native, which determine how devices using the TWAIN-type drivers transfer their files. The File (Recommended) option button is the default and the Roxio people highly advocate leaving this option selected. Should you connect a TWAIN device that can't use the File transfer option, Media Import is programmed to talk to the device and automatically select either the Memory or Native transfer option. You would manually change to one of these two other options only if Media Import proved unable to automatically detect which of these two other transfer methods to use.

Acquiring Digital Photos

Most of the time, you will acquire the digital photos that you use in your various photo and DVD productions either from your scanner or directly from your digital camera. You use the scanner to acquire and simultaneously convert developed photos into digital media. Photos taken with a digital camera, of course, require no analog-to-digital conversion and don't have to be acquired through Media Import (you may prefer to acquire digital photos from your camera and save them on your computer using the software that came with the camera or using Windows Scanner and Camera Wizard).

The next two sections cover how to use Media Import to acquire digital photos from these two types of devices. First, you find out how to acquire photos that you scan via Media Import and then you find out how to acquire photos when your digital camera is connected to your computer using either a TWAIN or WIA device driver.

Scanning images into Media Import

To scan a photo into Media Import, you follow these steps:

1. **Launch Media Import and then connect the scanner to your computer and turn it on if you haven't already done so.**

   Place the photo that you want to acquire in Media Import in the proper position on the scanner's glass plate. If you're using a scanner in which you feed the sheet, get the paper ready to feed. If you're using a hand-held scanner, position the scanner at the top of the sheet.

2. **Click the Photo button in the Welcome to Roxio Media Import window.**

3. **Select the name of your scanner in the Device drop-down list box.**

   Media Import opens a Media Import window that contains two panes. On the left, you find a Preview pane with the name the scanner, a pre-view area, the capture settings, and save to location. On the right, you see the Import Bin within the Recently Imported pane that shows all the media you've imported during the current work session (this will be empty, if this is the first time you've imported digital media).

4. **Click the Preview Scan button to have the scanner preview the photo you're scanning.**

   After the scanner finishes previewing the image you're scanning, its preview appears in the left pane. You can then adjust the scan rectangle so that it surrounds only the photo or the part of the photo you want scanned. To adjust the scanning area, you drag the sizing handles on the scan rectangle until it encloses just the area you want included (see Figure 9-3).

5. **Drag the sizing handles in the scan preview until this rectangle encloses the area of the photo you want scanned.**

   You can adjust the scan quality by selecting among the Good (100 dpi), Better (150 dpi), Best (300 dpi), and Custom options on the Capture Settings drop-down list. When you select Custom, you can also choose between 600 x 600 dpi (dots per inch) and 1200 x 1200 dpi, assuming that your scanner supports these very high resolution settings. To do this, click the Options button and select it in the Resolution drop-down list box of the Scanner Options dialog box. Of course, the higher the scan resolution, the more detail you get and the larger the resulting graphics file.

   Note that you can also select save the scanned image either the PNG or BMG instead of the default JPEG graphics format. To do this, click the Options button and then select PNG (*.png) or BMP (*.bmp, *.rle, *.dib) from the Final File Format drop-down list in the Scanner Options dialog box.

6. **(Optional) Select the desired scan quality option in the Capture Settings drop-down list box.**

   Media Import saves the scanned image in the default location designated for photos.

7. **(Optional) To save the photo in a folder other than default folder for Photo media, click the Browse Folders button (the one with the three dots) and then select the desired destination folder using the Navigation Tree in the Browse Location dialog box.**

   By default, Media Import names file that holds the scanned image by appending a sequential number to the text, Scanned Photos, shown in the Prefix text box as in Scanned Photos 00000.jpg, Scanned Photos 00001.jpg, and so on. If you wish, you can change this prefix text or eliminate it altogether.

8. **(Optional) Click Scanned Photos in the Prefix text box and replace it with a more appropriate descriptive name or delete it altogether before pressing Enter.**

   After you've made all your desired changes to the settings in the Media Import window, you're ready to have Media Import actually scan the photo and save it on your hard drive.

9. **Click the Import Now button at the bottom of the Media Import window to scan the photo.**

   After Media Import finishes scanning your photo, a thumbnail of the image appears in the Import Bin on the right side of the Roxio Media Import dialog box (see Figure 9-3).

10. **Click the Close button in the upper-right corner of the Media Import dialog box to close it.**

Figure 9-3: The Media Import window after successfully scanning a photo onto my computer's hard drive.

Prefix text box

Copying photos directly from your camera

The procedure for capturing photos directly from a digital camera that you've connected to your computer is very similar to that for capturing scanned images. The big difference between the two procedures is the amount of photos that you capture: normally, when you use Media Import to copy photos from your digital camera, you import a whole bunch of photos at one time rather than copying just a single image as when capturing from your scanner.

The general steps for copying the photos on your digital camera onto your hard disk are as follows:

1. **Launch Media Import and then connect the digital camera to your computer and turn it on if you haven't already done so.**

   Note that connecting your camera may cause the Windows XP Photo Wizard or some other photo editing software that came with your camera to automatically start up. If that happens, click the program's close box to return to the Media Import program.

2. **Click the Photo button in the Welcome to Roxio Media Import window.**

3. **Select the name of your camera in the Device drop-down list box.**

   Media Import opens a window which contains two panes: a pane with a list of the photos currently on your camera's memory card on the left and an empty Import Bin within the Recently Captured pane on the right.

   Depending on the make of your camera, the left pane may contain more than one folder from which you can import files (this is especially true in the case of digital cameras that take video as well as still images). By default, all the thumbnails in this folder are selected for importing.

4. **Select the folder in the pane on the left that contains the images you want to import. If you don't want all the images in a folder, click somewhere outside the thumbnails and then Ctrl+click the thumbnails of the images you do want to copy.**

   By default, Media Import saves all the selected files to default location for Photo media on your computer's hard disk. You can change this location if need be.

5. **(Optional) To save the photos in a folder other than the default folder for Photo media, click the Browse Location button (the one with the three dots) and then select the desired destination folder using the Navigation Tree in the Browse Location dialog box.**

   By default, Media Import renames all the photos your camera (which themselves use non-descriptive sequentially numbered temporary names) by prefacing the numeric part of the filename with the text, Imported Photos, shown in the Prefix text box. You can modify this prefix text used in renaming the imported photo files or eliminate it altogether.

6. **(Optional) Click Imported Photos in the Prefix text box and replace it with another modifier to use in renaming the photos or delete it entirely before pressing Enter.**

   You may burn the photos you're importing to a new CD or DVD disc as well (or instead of) copying them to your computer's hard disk.

7. **(Optional) Click the Burn to Disc check box to have Media Import burn the photos you're importing to a CD or DVD disc at the same time it copies them to your hard disk. If you want Media Import to only burn the photos on a CD or DVD, click the Hard Drive check box to remove its check mark.**

You may want to have Media Import remove the selected photos from the camera after copying them to your hard disk.

8. **(Optional) Click the Delete Photos from Device After Transfer check box if you want Media Import to remove the selected photos from the camera's storage after it copies them onto your hard disk.**

Now you're ready to have Media Import import the selected photos to the destination folder that you've specified.

9. **Click the Import Now button at the bottom of the Roxio Media Import dialog box to import the selected photos.**

As Media Import transfers the selected photos from your camera, thumbnails of their images appear in the Import Bin on the right side of the Roxio Media Import dialog box (see Figure 9-4).

10. **Click the Close button in the upper-right corner of the Media Import dialog box to close it.**

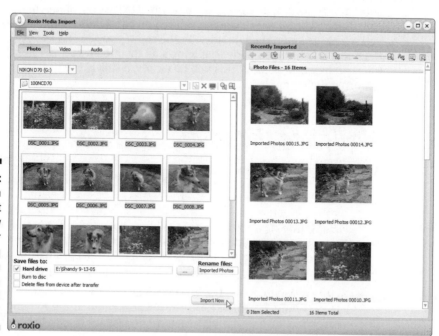

Figure 9-4:
The Media Import window after importing photos from my Nikon D70 Digital Camera.

Acquiring Digital Video

Media Import is perhaps most useful when you use it to capture digital video that you've taken with your DV (digital video) camera (also known affectionately as a camcorder). Note that although you will mostly use capture to import video clips from footage that you've already taken, you can also use Media Import to capture live video taken with your camcorder (which, of course, must remain connected to your computer throughout the shoot) or with a Web camera.

When importing previously recorded video clips from your DV camera, you can choose between importing the video in Normal or SmartScan mode. When you capture clips in Normal mode (the only one available when you're capturing live footage with your DV or Web camera), you decide which video to capture by manually operating a Capture Now and Stop button. When you capture clips with SmartScan Media Import, Media Import scans the entire video tape, using the time-code information stored on the tape to automatically divide it into discrete scenes which you can then import.

Figure 9-5 shows the type of Media Import window that appears after you connect your camera to you computer, turn the camera on in Video mode (sometimes abbreviated VTR) and then click the Video button and select your DV Camera in the Device drop-down list. This DV Media Import window contains a Capture preview pane where you can see the video footage that you're capturing on the left side. On the right, you see the Import Bin within the Recently Imported pane that shows all the media you've imported during the current work session (this will be empty, if this is the first time you've imported digital media).

Modifying the capture settings

Beneath the name of your camcorder in the Preview Pane, you see the following controls that enable you to select the Media Import settings that you now want to use in capturing your video:

- ✔ **Normal** drop-down list box that enables you to choose between manually capturing the video in Normal mode with the Capture and Stop buttons and SmartScan to have the Media Import program scan the video tape and divide it up into scenes that you can then import

- ✔ **Quality** drop-down list box that enables you to choose between the default DV mode, which captures full-size video in the AVI uncompressed file format that eats up hard disk space like nobody's business, and MPEG-2 mode, which captures full-size video using the MPEG-2 compressed file format (which still gives you good quality video along with smaller files sizes)

Figure 9-5:
Selecting
the Media
Import
settings you
want to use
in importing
video from
your digital
video
camera.

✔ **Save Files To** text box to change the location where the video clips are saved (to change this location, click the Browse button and then select the drive and folder in the Browse Location dialog box)

✔ **Rename Files Prefix** text box to change what text, if any, precedes the numeric part of the filename automatically assigned to the clips generated during the capture session (Media Import automatically uses Captured Videos as in Captured Videos 00000, Captured Videos 00001, and so on)

✔ **Capture Now** button to start capturing video from the current frame in the preview area until you click the Stop button (which replaces Capture Now)

✔ **Capture Entire Tape** button to have Media Import capture all the footage on your current DV tape (provided that the drive designated in the Save Files To text box has sufficient available space)

Capturing recorded video in SmartScan mode

When you select SmartScan on the drop-down list box immediately below the one showing the name of your DV camera and then click the Start Scan button that appears immediately above the Capture preview window, Media Import scans your entire tape for scenes.

As Media Import fast forwards through the video, scanning its time code, the program displays thumbnails of all the scenes it locates in the SmartScan to the immediate right of the Capture preview window (see Figure 9-6). Note that these scene thumbnails display the first frame in the scene and are sequentially numbered (Scene 1, Scene 2, and so on) with the timecode of the frame (as in 0 – 00:00:00, 1 – 00:00:25, 2 – 00:00:45 and so forth).

After the scanning is complete, you need to select the scenes you want to capture by clicking their thumbnails (hold down Ctrl as you click to select several or press Ctrl+A to select all the scenes).

After you've selected the scenes to capture and specified the capture settings you want to use (see "Modifying the capture settings" in the section immediately preceding), you're ready to have Media Import capture them. All you have to do is click the Capture Now button and then sit back and wait for the program to finishing capturing and saving the clips.

Capturing recorded video in Normal mode

Instead of having Media Import decide where the scenes are in your video tape, you can identify the scenes yourself and determine what video you want to import using the Normal mode. To manually capture video, make sure that Normal mode is selected in the drop-down list box right below the one showing the name of your video device.

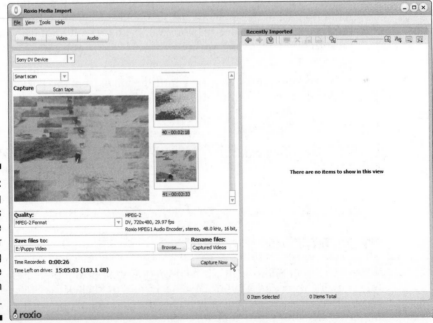

Figure 9-6:
Selecting the scenes to capture after scanning the tape with SmartScan.

To capture a video clip, select all the necessary capture settings (quality, location to save files, and filename preface as outlined in earlier in the section, "Modifying the capture settings") and then use the standard playback controls beneath the Capture preview window to locate the place in the tape where you want to begin recording the clip. Next, click the Capture Now button to begin recording a new scene.

When you reach the place in the tape where you want to stop the recording, click the Stop button (which replaces the Capture Now button the moment you click it). Note that Media Import may automatically divide your video clip into sequentially numbered scenes starting with Scene_000000 depending on the Limit Media Import setting in effect for your video camera before you actually click the Stop Capturing button.

If you want to record all the video on the tape, simply click the Media Import Capture Entire Tape button. Media Import then rewinds the tape and records all its video from beginning to end.

As soon as you click the Stop button, Media Import saves your new clip in the selected location, giving it the automatic filename that incorporates the stock text and the next available sequential number (such as Captured Videos 00026) and the thumbnail of the new clip appears in the Import Bin on the right side of the Roxio Media Import window.

To playback the new clip in the Import Bin inside the Recently Imported pane, click the Play button at the bottom of its thumbnail. To pause the video clip playback, click the Pause button (which replaces Play). To open thumbnails for all the individual scenes within the clip, click the button with the bent arrow point down point down ninety degrees to the right. Then, to return to the clip thumbnail, click the Up One Level button on the toolbar at the top of the Recently Imported pane.

Recording live video with Manual Media Import

Instead of importing video clips from the video you've already recorded on tape, you can use Media Import's Normal import mode to import live video as you're actually recording it. To record live video in Media Import, you have to make sure that you switch your DV camera to Camera or Record mode rather than Video mode before you select the DV camera in the Device drop-down list box on the Video tab.

The Media Import Capture preview window now shows you what your video camera's lens is actually seeing at the time rather than a key frame recorded on the tape. To start capturing what the camera is seeing (even if the video camera is in standby mode), click the Capture Now button in the Media Import window. Media Import then records what the camera sees in real time. To get the shot you want, you can then pan the camera and use its zoom lens to zoom in and out on objects around you. When you're finished recording a clip in real time, click the Stop button (which replaces the Capture Now button as soon as you click it).

Acquiring Audio Files

Media Import enables you not only to import images (both still and video) for use in other Roxio Creator 8 projects but your audio as well. When using Media Import to import audio, you have a choice between recording the audio live, that is, capturing it in real time as the audio is playing or copying audio tracks from a pre-recorded audio CD or DVD.

To acquire live audio, you can use your computer's built-in microphone or some analog audio device such as an amplifier with a record player playing an LP or audio cassette that you connect to your computer's line-in connection (see Chapter 5 for details).

To acquire audio tracks from a CD or DVD, you insert the disc in your computer's CD/DVD drive and then select that drive in the Device drop-down list box on the Audio tab of the Roxio Media Import window. This audio CD can be one that you've purchased or one that you've burned with the Music Disc Creator program. The DVD can be a Music DVD Disc that you've burned with it (see Chapter 8 for details).

Capturing live audio

To record an audio file with Media Import, connect the external analog audio device to your computer (usually through its external microphone jack). Turn on the analog audio device and cue up the LP record or audio cassette you want to record. Then launch Media Import, click the Audio button, and then select the name of your computer's sound card on the Device drop-down list.

Media Import then opens a Media Import window similar to the one shown in Figure 9-7. This window is divided into two panes: one on the left that is almost identical to the Record Audio dialog box (see Chapter 5) where you select the audio capture settings and start and stop the recording and an empty Import Bin inside the Recently Imported pane on the right where icons for the files you record appear.

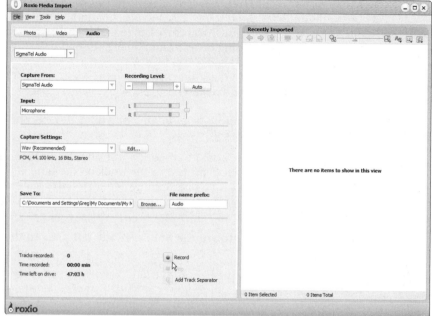

Figure 9-7:
Selecting
the
recording
settings for
recording
live audio
with Media
Import.

The top section of the left pane contains controls that enable you to select the recording level, input device along with peak meters that let you monitor the decibel levels during recording.

In the section below you find the Capture Settings dialog box, which enables you to select the audio file format and compression you want to use in recording. By default, WAV (Recommended) is selected to save the new audio file in the uncompressed WAV audio file format. You can also select these settings on the Capture Settings drop-down list:

- **Custom,** which enables you to select the file format and compression settings on the File Format tab of the Advanced Options dialog box opened by clicking the Edit button

- **MP3 (Good Quality)** for MPEG3 at 192 Kbps

- **MP3 (Low Quality)** for MPEG3 at 96 Kbps

- **WMA (Good Quality)** for Windows Media Audio at 128 Kbps

- **WMA (Low Quality)** for Windows Media Audio at 64 Kbps

By default, Media Import selects the folder designated for Audio as the place to save the audio files you record. If you want to record the files in a different folder, click the Browse button to open the Media Selector where you select the folder to use.

Media Import also automatically prefixes the names of the audio files you record with Audio followed the next available sequential number (as in Audio_1, Audio_2, and so on). You can change this prefix by clicking the File Name Prefix text box, editing the current name, and then pressing Enter.

After selecting the desired recording settings in the Media Import window, you're ready to record the live audio by following these steps:

1. **If the source of the audio is an analog playback device, cue up the track on that device.**

   For example, if you're about to record a track on the audio cassette, you need to find the silence right before the track on the tape. If you're recording live audio with a microphone connected to your computer, you need to make sure that the mike is on and positioned correctly for recording the sound.

2. **Click the Record button at the bottom of the left pane in the Media Import window.**

   Right after you click the Record button, you need to start the playback of the analog recording that you're saving. If you're recording live audio through a microphone, you don't perform Step 2 until the live audio you want to record starts playing.

3. **If the source of the audio is an analog playback device, start playing the recording that you want to capture with that device.**

   As soon as Media Import starts recording the live audio, the Play button changes to Pause and the peak meters monitor the left and right decibel levels and the Recorded Length indicator keeps you informed of how long the you've been recording.

   To temporarily pause the recording, click the Pause button (whose name then becomes Continue). To resume recording, click the Continue button (which then changes back to Pause).

   To insert a track separator at the end of the recording, click the Add Track Separator button.

4. **When the audio source stops playing or you finish recording, click the Stop button.**

As soon as you click the Stop button, Media Import adds the thumbnail for the recorded audio file using the prefix and the next available sequential number to the Import Bin on the right. To playback this recording, clicks its Play button.

Remember that you can edit the audio files that you record in Media Import with Roxio Creator's Sound Editor tool where you can use its many features to enhance the raw audio that you've captured (see Chapter 5 for details).

Copying tracks from an audio CD

To copy tracks from an audio CD or Music DVD disc, insert the disc in your computer's CD/DVD drive and then click the Audio button in Roxio Media Import window before you select the drive on the Device drop-down list.

Media Import then opens a Media Import window similar to the one shown in Figure 9-8. This window is divided into two panes. On the left, you find a list box with the disc name and the tracks on the disc above the Capture Settings and Save To drop-down list boxes. On the right, you see the Import Bin within the Recently Imported pane that shows all the media you've imported during the current work session (this will be empty, if this is the first time you've imported digital media).

After you specify the capture settings (see "Capturing live audio" immediately preceding this section) and the location where you want the copied track(s) to be saved, you are ready to select them in the Select Tracks list box.

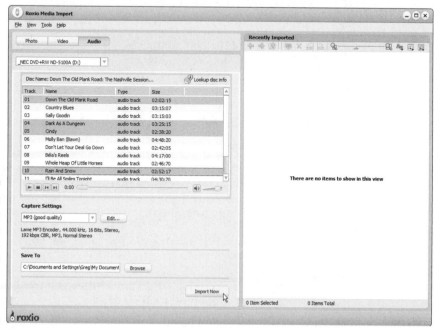

Figure 9-8: Specifying the settings for copying tracks from an audio CD with Media Import.

If you're copying tracks from a CD or DVD that contains commercially-produced music tracks but which are not currently named, you can have Media Import try to replace the track numbers with the appropriate track names by clicking the Lookup Disc Info button to the immediate right of the Disc Name at the top of the Select Tracks list box. Media Import then connects to the Gracenote CDDB Web site from which it attempts to obtain the track information. If the program finds this information online, Media Import then replaces the track numbers in the Select Tracks list box with their corresponding names and playing time.

If you want to listen to a particular track on the disc before selecting it for copying in the Select Tracks list box, click its track number or name in this list box. Then, click the Play button in the playback controls that appear at the bottom of the Select Tracks list box (these controls only appear when one track is selected in this list box). When you finish listening to the track, click the square Stop button in the playback controls (which replaces the Play button as soon as you click it).

To select only certain tracks from the list in the Select Tracks list box, hold down the Ctrl key as you click it. To select all the tracks in the list, click the first one at the top of the box; then drag the scroll button down and hold down the Shift key as you click the final track.

Once you've selected the tracks that you want Media Import to copy to your hard disk in the Select Tracks list box, click the Import Now button at the bottom of the Media Import window. Media Import displays the Copying Audio Tracks dialog box that shows you the progress of the track copying. When Media Import finishes copying the selected tracks, this dialog box disappears and thumbnails of the copied track(s) appear in the Import Bin on the right side of the Media Import window.

Importing Movies from DVDs

If you've created DVD discs with the Roxio Creator's VideoWave or MyDVD applications, you can use Media Import to copy particular movie titles from the disc to your computer's hard disk (note that you can't use Media Import to copy movie titles from professionally recorded DVDs that you rent or purchase, as these discs are copy protected).

To copy movie titles from a DVD disc that you've prepared, you follow these steps:

1. **Place the DVD disc that contains the movie titles you want to copy to your hard disk in your computer's DVD drive.**

   Now you're ready to launch the Media Import tool.

2. **Launch Media Import and then click the Video button before selecting the DVD drive in the Device drop-down list.**

   A Media Import window appears showing a list of the movies on the DVD disc along with Capture Settings, Save To, and Prefix controls on the left (see Figure 9-9). On the right, you see the Import Bin within the Recently Imported pane that shows all the media you've imported during the current work session (this will be empty, if this is the first time you've imported digital media).

3. **Click the movies you want to copy in the list.**

   If a movie has chapters and you only want to copy some of its chapters, click the Chapters expand button (the one with the downward pointing triangle) and then Ctrl+click the chapters to use.

   If you want to play a movie from the disc, click its name in the list box and then click the button named Play to the right of the disc name at the top of the list box.

   By default, Media Import saves the copied movies using the Standard DivX (DivX) video file format. You can if you wish select between the MPEG compressed video and the standard Windows Movie Video file format.

4. **(Optional) Click the Captured Settings drop-down list box and then select a new video file format, MPEG (MPEG) or Standard WMV (WMV), for the copied movies.**

   By default, Media Import saves the copied movie files in the Video folder specified on the File Locations tab of the Options dialog box and prefixes the filenames with DVDBUILDER followed by Movie and the next available sequential number (starting with 00000).

   To save your copied movie files in another location or using another filename prefix, follow Step 5.

5. **(Optional) Make any necessary changes to the destination folder in the Save To drop-down list box using the Browse button and edit the filename prefix in the Prefix text box.**

   Now you're ready to have Media Import copy the selected movie titles to your hard disk.

6. **Click the Import Now button at the bottom of the Media Import window to begin copying the selected movies and chapters.**

Media Imports displays the Progress Information dialog box that keeps you informed of the progress in copying the selected movie titles. When Media Import finishes making the copies, the dialog box closes and thumbnails of the copied movie files appear in the Import Bin. To play a movie, click its Play button below its thumbnail.

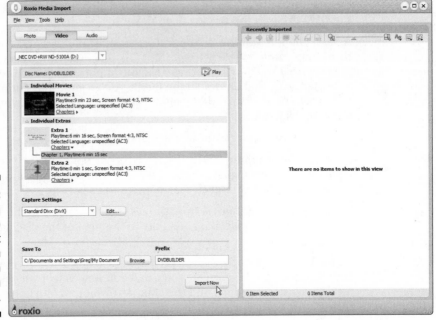

Getting
ready to
import
movies from
a DVD with
Media
Import.

Chapter 10

Creating and Editing Video Productions

* *

In This Chapter

▶ Getting familiar and comfortable with the VideoWave window and components

▶ Using CineMagic to quickly turn your video clips into music videos

▶ Using SlideShow Assistant to turn groups of digital photos into slideshows you can edit in VideoWave

▶ Assembling and editing videos using the VideoWave Production Editor

▶ Adding audio, transitions, and special effects to your video

▶ Outputting your finished video in various file formats or burning it to a DVD

* *

*V*ideoWave is a powerful video editing program that enables you to quickly assemble your digital video clips, audio tracks, and photo images (which you can capture with the Roxio Media Import as described in Chapter 9) into professional-looking finished video productions. You can then output the finished VideoWave video productions into a variety of file formats or burn the video onto a DVD for distribution to your friends and family. You can also use your VideoWave video productions as movie titles in the next DVD project that you create with Roxio Creator's MyDVD application (see Chapter 11).

This chapter covers all the major aspects of using VideoWave to create a wide variety of video productions. It begins by familiarizing you with the features and components of the VideoWave window, and then goes on to introduce you the use of the program's new CineMagic component, a nifty little feature for turning your favorite video clips into instant music videos using music of your own choice. Next, the chapter covers the use of the SlideShow Assistant, a Wizard-like utility that enables you to whip up slideshows using your favorite digital photos, background music, and transitions with almost no effort at all.

If CineMagic and SlideShow Assistant aren't enough for your video needs, the chapter then introduces you to the use of VideoWave's full-featured Production Editor. Here, you discover how to edit your videos in both the standard storyline and the more advanced timeline view. As part of this process, you also find out how to add audio to your video and apply any of a variety of scene transitions and special video effects.

The chapter concludes with information on your options for outputting your final video productions into a variety of different formats. These include formats for playback on your computer with programs like Windows Media Player or playback on your TV or camcorder, as well as for uploading to the Web or e-mailing to your friends and family. You also find out how to burn your final video productions to DVD disc for playback on your computer's DVD drive and standalone DVD players.

Getting Cozy with VideoWave

You can launch VideoWave from the Roxio Creator 8 Home window by clicking the VideoWave link in the Applications Project window opened by clicking Application on the Home tab of the Project List pane. You can also launch the program by clicking the Edit Video link on the DVD & Video tab of the Project List pane.

When you first launch VideoWave, a Welcome to VideoWave dialog box opens where you can choose between starting a new video production and editing an existing one. When you click OK in this dialog box with the Create a New Production option button selected, a window called VideoWave 8 – Production 1 appears (see Figure 10-1). This window is divided into three panes:

- ✔ The **Tasks** pane in the upper left divided into Add Content and Tools areas with the links you can use to add content and formatting to your video production

- ✔ The **Preview** pane in the upper right where you can preview the video clips, transitions, and special effects you add to your video production

- ✔ The **Production Editor** pane in Storyline view in the lower third of the VideoWave 8 window where you can add and edit video clips, background audio or narration, scene transitions, and special effects for your video production

The Preview pane

The Production Preview pane enables you to review your video at any stage as you build and edit its content. Figures 10-2 and 10-3 show you the Preview pane at two different times in the production: Figure 10-2 shows the pane with the very first slide selected at the very beginning of the production (time code 00:00:00). Figure 10-3 shows the pane when the very first video clip is selected five seconds into the production (time code 00:05:00).

Tasks pane

Preview

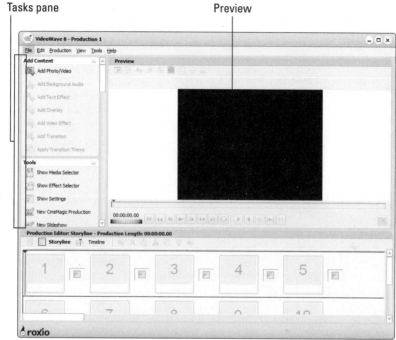

Figure 10-1:
The Video-
Wave
window
when you
start a new
video
production.

Align

Delete

Show/hide TV safe zone

Add text

Save as custom object

Edit internal tracks or
entire production

Output as

Show/hide task

Burn with my DVD express

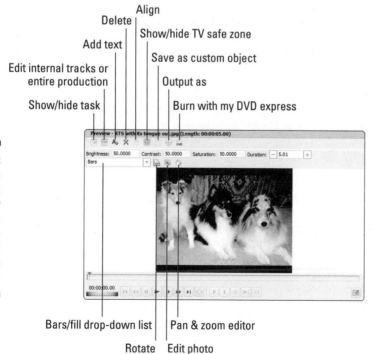

Figure 10-2:
The
Production
Preview
pane when
initial slide
is selected
in the
production.

Bars/fill drop-down list | Pan & zoom editor

Rotate   Edit photo

Figure 10-3:
The
Production
Preview
pane when
initial video
clip is
selected
in the
production.

Adjust duration

Volume

More setttings

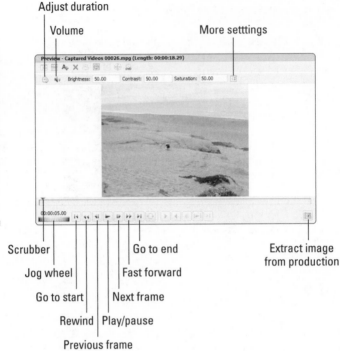

Scrubber

Jog wheel

Go to start

Rewind

Previous frame

Go to end

Fast forward

Next frame

Play/pause

Extract image
from production

To the immediate right of the current time code, the Preview pane displays playback buttons and controls that you find on your standard DVD controller. To advance to the first frame of the video, you click the Go to Start button. To then play the video, you click the Play button (which immediately changes to a Pause button).

To advance through the video quickly to find a particular frame to review, you click the Fast Forward button. So too, if you want to go back through the video to find an earlier frame, you click the Rewind button. If you're reviewing a really long video and you want to increase the fast forward or rewind speed, you simply click the Fast Forward or Rewind button again.

To manually advance forward or backward in the video to find a particular frame, you drag the Scrubber button right or left along the bottom of the Production Preview pane. If you want to move forward or backward through the frames in equal increments to find a specific place, drag the Jog Wheel control to the right or left instead.

The Production Editor pane

The Production Editor pane (shown in Figures 10-4 and 10-5) is the area where all the VideoWave designing action takes place. This is the spot where you add and sequence the video clips, audio track, still photos and other graphics that you want played in your finished movie production. When designing and sequencing a movie in the Production Editor pane, you can work in one of two modes:

- ✔ **Storyline** mode (the default), which presents the movie in storyboard fashion by showing the sequence of video clips and still images that you add to the movie in the order in which they play, along with all the scene transitions you add to take you from one video or still image to another (see "Working in Storyline mode" later in this chapter for details)

- ✔ **Timeline** mode, which presents the movie as individual video, audio, effects, text, and overlay tracks along a time line that indicates when particular elements on each track play in the movie (see "Working in Timeline mode" later in this chapter for details)

Most of the time, you want to construct the basic elements for your new movie in Storyline mode, including the video clips, still images, and the transitions you want between them. Then, if you add background audio or narration, or any text, overlays, and special effects to your production, you will want to switch over to Timeline mode so that you can check up and adjust their timing in relation to the movie's video.

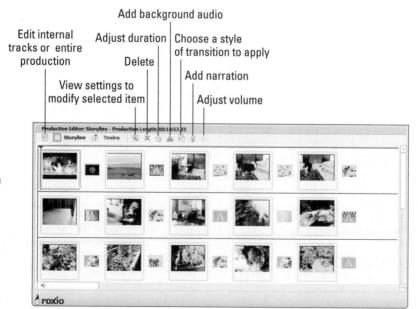

Edit internal tracks or entire production

Adjust duration

Add background audio

Choose a style of transition to apply

View settings to modify selected item

Delete

Add narration

Adjust volume

Figure 10-4:
The Production Editor in default Storyline mode.

Snap to objects

Edit volume envelope for Audio object | Zoom in/out slider

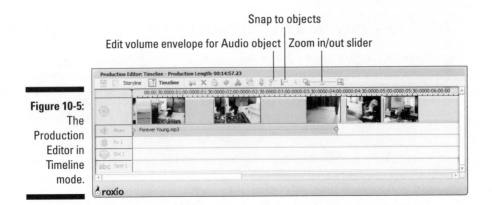

Figure 10-5:
The
Production
Editor in
Timeline
mode.

Instant Music Videos with CineMagic

CineMagic is a nifty feature of VideoWave 8 for creating videos that have no other sound than the music track that you choose to play (the wizard automatically suppresses the audio track recorded by your camcorder). CineMagic automatically edits your video productions, adding transitions and trimming your stills or video clips to suit the background music you select.

The best way to understand how easy it is to create a new music video with CineMagic is to follow along with the steps for creating one. For this example, I'm creating a music video using vacation video of my recent trip to India with background music provided by Budhaditya Mukherijee's *Raga Deshmalhar (Gat in Ektal)* from his album, *Magic Moments*.

To begin the new CineMagic music video production, I begin by launching the Roxio Creator 8 Home window and then clicking its Auto Edit Video with CineMagic link on the DVD & Video tab in the Project List pane (you can also launch it from within VideoWave by clicking New CineMagic Production link in the Tools area of the Tasks pane). The initial, Add Content, CineMagic Assistant window opens similar to the one shown in Figure 10-6.

To use the CineMagic Assistant to create a new video production, you then follow these steps:

1. **Click the Add Video/Photos link to open the Add Video/Photo dialog box where you select all the video and graphics files you want in the production before clicking the Add Video/Photo button.**

   When creating a video production with CineMagic, you have a choice between having your media played in the order they appear in the Add Content list box or randomly. If you intend to have the media played sequentially, you may want to rearrange the video clips and photos in this list.

Figure 10-6:
The initial
CineMagic
Assistant
window
where you
add the
content for
your new
music video
production.

To rearrange media, you drag their video clip or photo thumbnails and drop them in the desired position in the Add Content list box, keeping in mind that the media is played from left to right across each row and as you move down the rows. To display more thumbnails in the list box, drag the Zoom slider to the left.

2. **(Optional) If your video production is to be played sequentially, use drag-and-drop to rearrange the media icons in the Add Content list box so that they appear in the order (left to right and down the rows) you want followed in the final production.**

   Now you're ready to add the background music for the video production. In doing this, you can add as many tracks (provided that you have the digital rights to use them) as fit in the duration of the video clips and still images.

   If the audio file you select as the background music is too short for the duration of the video portion, you can have CineMagic loop the music until the production ends by clicking the Loop Soundtrack If Too Short check box.

   If you add multiple tracks for the background music, you can have CineMagic apply a crossfade effect (whereby the volume of the current track fades as the volume of the next track comes up) with an overlap of your choice. To do this, click the Crossfade Tracks check box and then enter the number of seconds for the effect in the Sec. Overlap text box.

3. **Click the Add Background Audio button, and then click the Add Audio Track button in the Background Audio dialog box and select the track(s) to use in the Add Audio dialog box. After you click the Add Audio button, select the Loop Soundtrack If Too Short or the Crossfade Tracks check boxes if applicable before you click OK.**

   By default, the CineMagic Assistant selects the Normal 4:3 screen aspect ratio. If you plan to play your final video production on a really large TV or monitor and are dealing with really panoramic images and video, you may select the Widescreen (16:9) for your video production.

4. **(Optional) Click the Normal (4:3) drop-down list box and then click the Widescreen (16:9) option in the drop-down list to modify the aspect ratio for the production.**

5. **When you finish adding and arranging the video clips and still images for your production and assigning the background music, click the Next> button to advance to the second, Customize, CineMagic Assistant window.**

   The Customize CineMagic window (shown in Figure 10-7) is where you select a style for your new music video. Each style uses slightly different cuts, transitions, and backgrounds. In deciding which style to select, click the name in the Style list box and then read the description of that style beneath the list box. For my India video, I naturally selected the Travel style described as being "suitable for movies which emphasize outdoor scenes and wide open spaces."

Figure 10-7: The second Customize, CineMagic Assistant window where you designate the style of the production and its duration and order.

6. **Click the name of the style of video production you want to create in the Styles list box.**

   If your video production uses slides, you can set how long they remain on screen by selecting a new value in the Set Duration of Photos in Production text box (five seconds is the default). If you wish, you can set the duration of the entire production by entering the number of total seconds in the Set the Production Duration text box. If you want the production to be timed to the running time of the background music, click the Fit to Audio check box.

7. **Set your slide and production duration values or click the Fit to Audio check box to make the production last only as long as the background music.**

   By default, the CineMagic Assistant displays the video clips and slides you add to the production in the order they appear in the Add Content list box. To have CineMagic randomize the order in which the media play in the production, follow Step 8.

8. **(Optional) Click the Random Order option button to randomize the order of the media in the production.**

9. **Click the Next> button to advance to the third and final, Output, CineMagic Assistant window.**

   The Output CineMagic Assistant window (shown in Figure 10-8) contains options for saving the video project, burning it to CD or DVD disc, creating a movie file for playback on your computer, digital video camera, TV or VCR, or to e-mail, or editing it further in VideoWave 8.

Figure 10-8: The third Output, CineMagic Assistant window where you indicate how you want to output the production.

Before you select one of the output options, you may want preview your production.

10. **(Optional) Click the Preview button to have CineMagic Assistant play back your video and music with all its transitions and cuts in a preview window.**

If you click the Save This Project link, CineMagic opens a Save Slideshow dialog box where you designate the filename and location for the DMSM file before clicking the Save button (DMSM is the file format created and recognized by VideoWave so that you can do further editing on it in the VideoWave application).

If you click Burn to Disc link, the MyDVD Express program opens and automatically adds your movie to the main menu level (see Chapter 11). You can then modify the menu settings and burn the DVD production to a DVD disc before returning to the CineMagic Assistant.

If you click the Create Video File link, CineMagic opens the Make Movie dialog box where you indicate the ultimate destination of the movie as well as its video quality before rendering it and saving it on your hard disk. After the movie is rendered and saved, click the Done button to return to the CineMagic Assistant.

If you click the Edit in VideoWave link, you bypass entirely Step 11 for the CineMagic Assistant automatically closes as your video production opens up in the VideoWave application. Once in VideoWave, you can make any editing changes you want to the project (including enhancing it with text, video, and overlay effects) as well as saving it as a DMSM file, outputting it into a commonly used video format, and burning it onto DVD disc.

11. **Select the appropriate output link (Save This Project, Burn to Disc, and/or Create a Video File) and then when you return to the CineMagic Assistant, click the Finish button or click the Edit in VideoWave link to open the production in this program.**

Instant Slideshows with SlideShow Assistant

Slideshow Assistant is the fastest and easiest way to put together slideshows from the digital images you take and edit in the Roxio PhotoSuite application (see Chapter 6). Using the Slideshow Assistant to create your slideshow is very much like using the CineMagic Assistant (described in detail in the preceding section). In fact, the only significant difference (other than the fact you're restricted to selecting photos in the first, Add Content, Slideshow Assistant window) occurs in the second, Customize Your Slideshow, Slideshow Assistant window where you select a transition style and whether or not to apply a pan-and-zoom effect to your slides (see Figure 10-9).

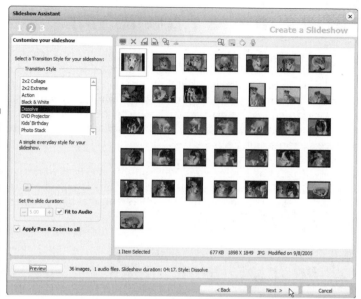

Figure 10-9:
The second
Customize
Your
Slideshow
window
enables you
to select a
transition
style for the
show.

When selecting the type of transitions to use when going from one slide to the next in your show in the Transition Style list box, be aware that some transitions do not support the use of the apply pan-and-zoom effect (in which case, the Apply Pan & Zoom to All check box is grayed out). Also, some transition styles such as Vintage Album and Black & White actually change the appearance of the photos by applying filters to them (a sepia toned filter in the case of Vintage and black-and-white in the case of Black & White).

Your best bet when selecting a transition style with which you are unfamiliar is to click the Preview button at the bottom of the Customize Your Slideshow Slideshow Assistant window to see how the style affects the appearance of your photos and the overall flow of the slideshow.

After you have the transition style, duration, and pan and zoom options selected in the Customize Your Slideshow Slideshow Assistant window, click the Next> button to advance to the third and final, Output, Slideshow Assistant window. This window contains the very same Save This Project, Burn to Disc, Create Video File, and Edit in VideoWave options as the third and last, Output, CineMagic Assistant window (see Steps 10 and 11 in the steps in the preceding section).

The only difference is that when you click the Save This Project link, a Save Slideshow dialog box appears where you can save your slideshow project in a DMSS file format (which is one that VideoWave also knows and supports).

Video Editing in the Production Editor

As great as CineMagic and Slideshow Assistant are for quickly putting together finished video and slideshow productions, by their very automation of common video tasks they can put a damper on your own creativity. If you want to be free to make your own decisions when it comes to what goes into a particular scene, how long a scene lasts, or what transition to use when going on to the next scene, you need to be familiar and comfortable using VideoWave's Production Editor.

Fortunately, Roxio has made using the Production Editor to design your own video movies as easy as pie. Both its Storyline and Timeline modes are intuitive and take very little getting used to make you feel like you're ready for video editing with the "big boys."

Working in Storyline mode

In the Production Editor pane in the VideoWave window, individual scenes are represented by panels that are sequentially numbered and arranged in rows as a kind of digital storyboarding (see Figure 10-4). Each scene panel can contain a particular photo, video clip, or color panel that you add.

In between each scene panel, you find a transition panel that you can use to add a particular scene transition, determining how one scene leads into the next. VideoWave gives you a choice among hundreds of different transitions, the most widely used one being the Dissolve transition whereby the last frames of the current scene literally dissolve into the first frames of the next scene (the duration of the Dissolve transition being the determining factor in how much information from the current scene remains visible as the beginning of the next scene takes over).

Note that you don't have to add any transition between scene panels in your video production, but keep in mind that if you don't use add transitions, your finished movie will have a jumpy feel to it if it contains multiple video clips and still images. This is because the moment one scene ends, the next one abruptly starts up. Depending on how different the visual information at the end of one clip is from that of the beginning of the next, the effect can be jarring to the eye and disrupting to the flow of your story. Therefore, I highly recommend the use of transitions to smooth the changeover from one scene to the next, while at the same time, I caution against using a whole bunch of different transitions in the same movie. Be careful with your transition selections because using a variety of different transitions to make scene changes can be almost as distracting as using none.

The Storyline Playback Head keeps your place in the Production Editor as you preview the video production using the playback controls at the bottom of the Production Preview pane. As you review your video production, the Storyline Playback Head moves through the scene and transition panels in the Production Editor pane, keeping track of your present position in the current video clip, still image, or transition as its images appear in the Production Preview pane above. Note that you can't move the Storyline Playback Head directly in the Production Editor: to move it to a new place in this pane, you need to use the playback controls in the Production Preview pane. For example, to find the place in the movie where you want to start playing back the production, you drag the Scrubber button or the Jog Wheel to advance to frame in the video production where you want the playback to begin and then click the Play button to start the playback from that position.

The different kinds of files you can add to your movie

Most of the movies that you'll make with VideoWave will consist of video clips that you've acquired with the Roxio Media Import application (see Chapter 9 for details). Some of the movies you make may also include digital still photos that you've acquired with the Media Import program and then edited with the PhotoSuite application (as described in Chapter 7).

In addition to standard video clips and still photos, you may also want to add color panels to the first and last scenes of the movie. These color panels, usually in black, enable you to transition from a black matte screen into the first frames of the initial video clip and then from last frames of the final video clip to another black matt (when you use the Dissolve transition between the final video clip and the final black matt, in Hollywood lingo, your movie is said to fade to black).

Note that you can also add finished movies created with VideoWave and output to the MPG file format to scene panels in a new VideoWave video production. When you add a finished movie to a panel, VideoWave then plays that movie (with all of its scenes, transitions, audio, and so on) as soon as the Storyline Playback Head reaches it during playback.

Don't forget that you can use VideoWave to make a really effective slideshow out of your digital photos. All you have to do is add your digital photos to the sequential scene panels in the Production Editor pane in the order you want them to appear in the slideshow, add the type of transition you want between each photo, and then add any background audio or narration that you want your audience to hear.

Table 10-1 shows a list of all the files types that you can add to your video production. Note that the graphic file formats supported include the BMP, JPEG, and PNG graphics file formats. Bitmap graphics are most often used for storing simple images such as Clip Art. The JPEG graphics format is most often used for storing digital still photos as well as more complex graphic images. The PNG graphics file format is mostly used for Web graphics where it's attempting to replace the older, GIF (Graphics Information File) format.

The video and audio file formats supported by VideoWave include all the major formats that you're likely to run into. In terms of the video file formats, the Easy Media Creator applications are only able to save its video productions in the MPEG2 and WMV compressed video formats. The Windows AVI and MOV video files that you use in your VideoWave productions must be produced in programs not part of the Easy Media Creator suite and then imported into VideoWave.

Table 10-1 File Formats Supported in VideoWave Video Productions

Category	File type (file extension)	Description
Graphics files	BMP (.bmp, .rle, .dib)	Bitmap graphics
	TIF (.tif, .tiff)	Tagged Information Graphics
	PNG (.png)	Portable Network Graphics
	JPEG (.jpg, .jpeg, .jpe)	Joint Photographic Experts Group
Video files	MPEG (.mpg, .mpeg, .m2s)	Moving Pictures Experts Group
	AVI (.avi)	Audio Video Interleave
	MOV (.mov)	QuickTime Movie
	WMV (.wmv)	Windows Media Video
Audio files	WAV (.wav)	WAVE or PCM (Pulse Code Modulation) files
	MP3 (.mp3)	MPEG Layer 3
	WMA (.wma)	Windows Media Audio

In addition to the standard graphics, video, and audio file formats listed in Table 10-1, VideoWave lets you add Roxio project files created with the PhotoSuite application and saved in its native file format to a new video production. These project files carry the .dmsp filename extension. Note, however, that you cannot add VideoWave project files (that carry the .dmsm filename extension) directly to a new VideoWave video production. Before you can add movies that you create with VideoWave to new VideoWave video productions, you must first output them and save them as MPG files (see "Outputting the Video Production" later in this chapter for details).

Adding color panels and text to your movie

As stated earlier, you can add black color panels to the beginning and end of your movies and then with the help of the Dissolve transition start the video production by fading in from black and then end it by fading to black. Because you can add text to your color panels, you can also use them to introduce new scenes in the movie, to create general introductions to the movie as well as to provide the credits for production (with you, of course, as the director).

You follow these two steps to create a new color panel in your video production:

1. **Right-click the scene panel in the Production Editor pane where the color panel is to appear and then click Insert Color Panel on the shortcut menu.**

   The More Colors dialog box appears where you select the color for the new panel. If none of the pre-defined colors will do, click the Create Colors >> button to expand the dialog box. Here, you can create a new color by dragging through the Hues and Shades boxes, clicking the Eyedropper mouse pointer on some color in the Production Preview pane, or entering new values in the Hue, Saturation, and Values or the Red, Green, and Blue text boxes.

2. **Select the color for the new color panel in the More Colors dialog box and then click the OK button.**

   VideoWave inserts a panel in the color you selected in the More Colors dialog box in the scene panel you right-clicked. If the panel already contained a video clip or still image, its media is shifted one panel to the right to make room for the new color panel.

After inserting a color panel in your video production, you can, if you want, add text to the panel that explains the upcoming scene in the vein of those old silent movies or gives your audience some important information about the video clip that they're about to witness. To add text to a color panel you added, you follow these steps:

1. **Click the scene panel in the Production Editor pane that contains the color panel to which you want to add your text.**

   VideoWave shows that this color panel is selected by surrounding its rectangle with a non-moving marquee.

2. **Click the Add Text Effect link in the Add Content pane.**

   VideoWave opens the Add Text Effect dialog box that displays the first of many text samples. To narrow the samples to a particular category, click the drop-down button on the right of the drop-down list box at the top of dialog box and then click the category.

3. **Click the text sample in the Add Text Effect dialog box that you want to use with your own text and then click OK.**

   VideoWave opens an Add Text Effect dialog box. By default, the Add to Production option button is selected, meaning that your text effect will add to all the video and still images in the entire video production (very useful when you need something like a copyright to appear on every frame of the movie). However, if you only want the text effect to appear for as long as the black matt panel is displayed, you must follow Step 4.

4. **Click the Insert on Internal Text Track or Selected Panel option button before you click OK.**

   After the Add Text Effect dialog box closes, you will notice that only the color panel is selected in the video production (indicated by the fact that all the other panels in the Production Editor are now grayed out). Also, you will notice that the Object buttons to the right of the Playback controls are now active and the Formatting toolbar appears in the second row at the top of the Preview pane (see Figure 10-10).

   The next step is to replace the stock text (often, Type your text here) in the effect's text box with the text you want to actually appear on the color panel.

5. **Click the Text Editor button on the Formatting toolbar and then edit the stock text in the Text Editor window by replacing it with the text you want to appear on the color panel before you click OK.**

   After replacing the stock text, you can use the other buttons on the Formatting toolbar to enhance the text, including changing the font, font size, and color as well as the bold, italic, and alignment attributes of the text. In addition, you can assign a motion effect or change the one you assigned by clicking the Motion button and then selecting the motion effect from its pop-up menu.

6. **(Optional) Use the buttons on the Formatting toolbar at the top of the Preview panel to change the formatting and style of the text.**

   After entering and formatting the text, you can preview it by clicking the Play button on the playback controls in the Preview pane (this is especially important when your text uses a motion effect). If you are satisfied with text effect, move on to the last step.

7. **Click the Edit Internal Tracks or Entire Production button on the Preview pane toolbar and then save the project (Ctrl+S).**

After adding a text effect to color panel, a small abc icon appears in the lower-left corner of the color panel in the Production Editor, indicating that the panel now has text assigned to it. You can click this icon to open the Settings dialog box where you edit any of the text attributes, formatting, or other settings.

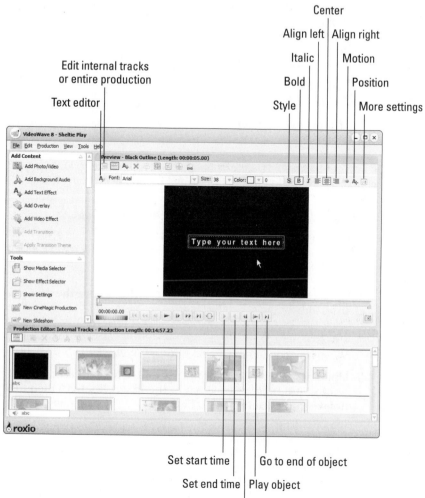

Center

Align left | Align right

Italic | Motion

Bold | Position

Edit internal tracks
or entire production

Text editor

Style | More settings

Figure 10-10:
Adding a
text effect
to a black
matte color
panel.

Set start time | Go to end of object

Set end time | Play object

Go to start of object

You can quickly add text to any panel in the video production by selecting
it in the Production Editor and then clicking the Add Text button on the
Preview pane's toolbar (to the immediate right of the Edit Internal Tracks
or Entire Production button).

If you decide that you want to get rid of the text that you've added to a particular photo or color panel, you can remove the text without removing the
image or color panel by right-clicking its scene panel in the Production Editor
pane and then clicking Remove➪Text Effects on its shortcut menu.

If you decide that you want to delete the color panel from the video production (along with any text that you've added to it), you can just click its scene panel in the Production Editor pane to select it and then press the Delete key. VideoWave immediately displays a VideoWave 8 alert dialog box asking you if you want to delete the transition that follows the panel. If you click Yes in this dialog box, VideoWave deletes the selected panel as well as the transition following it, pulling all the remaining panels in the production one to the left. If you click No, the program deletes the color panel and its text replacing it with an empty panel while at the same time leaving the transition that follows untouched.

If you get a case of "Deleter's angst," you must immediately press Ctrl+Z or choose Edit⇨Undo on the VideoWave menu bar to bring the still image back.

Adding video clips and still images to your movie

The basic technique for adding video clips or still images such as scanned graphics or photos that you've captured to your VideoWave video productions couldn't be simpler:

1. **Click the panel in the Production Editor where the new panel is to be inserted.**

2. **Click the Add Content link in the Add Content pane.**

   VideoWave opens the Insert Photos/Video dialog box.

3. **Open the Smart View, album, or folder that contains the clips or photos and then select them in the Insert Photos/Video dialog box before you click the Open button.**

   VideoWave then displays the Insert Photo/Video dialog box containing the following option buttons:

   - **Insert After Current Panel** (default) to insert the media you selected in the Insert Photos/Video dialog box in a new panel following the one that's selected

   - **Insert Before Current Panel** to insert the media you selected in the Insert Photos/Video dialog box in a new panel in front of the one that's selected

   - **Insert as Overlay** to overlay the media you selected in the Insert Photos/Video dialog box on top of the media in the selected panel (note that the overlayed media then remains visible in all the rest of the panels in the production)

   - **Replace Panel** to replace the media in the selected panel with the media you selected in the Insert Photos/Video dialog box

   - **Insert on Internal Overlay Track of Selected Panel** to overlay the media you selected in the Insert Photos/Video dialog box on top of the media in the selected panel only

4. **Indicate where and how you want the new media inserted by selecting the appropriate option button in the Insert Photo/Video dialog box and then click OK.**

You can also insert a new video clip or photo into a production with the Show Media Selector link in the Tools pane. Click this link and then select the Smart View, album, or folder that contains the video clip or image you want to add. After you have it open in the Media Selector, drag its icon from this dialog box and then just drop it onto the panel in the Production Editor where you want it inserted.

You can also play musical scene panels by rearranging the still images and video clips that you've added to the Production Editor pane. Just click the panel with the image or clip that you want to move and then drag it to and then drop it on the panel where it should go. VideoWave will then insert the image or clip you moved in the panel where you dropped it and adjust the panel position of all the remaining images and clips in the production as needed.

To duplicate an image or clip that you've added to the production, right-click its panel in the Production Editor pane and then click Copy on the panel's shortcut menu. Then, to insert the copied image or clip, right-click the panel in the Production Editor pane in front of which the duplicate image or clip is to go and then click Paste on that panel's shortcut menu. VideoWave then inserts the copied image or clip into a new panel at the place in the production, moving the panel you originally right-clicked and all the panels that come after it down one.

If you want to remove an image or clip from the video production, click its panel in the Production Editor pane and then press the Delete key or you can right-click the panel and click the Delete item on its shortcut menu. VideoWave deletes your photos and video clips without asking for your confirmation. The only way to bring them back to the production if you made a boo-boo is to press Ctrl+Z or choose Edit⇨Undo on the VideoWave menu bar right away.

Use the Tools⇨Find Panel command on the VideoWave to quickly locate and select a particular clip or still image that you've added to your production. When you select this command, VideoWave opens a Find Panel dialog box that sequentially lists the names of all the scene and transition panels in your production along with a short description and the scene or transition's starting and ending time. To go directly to a particular panel or transition in the Production Editor pane, click in the Find Panel dialog box and then click the OK button. VideoWave then closes the Find Panel dialog box and then goes to the selected panel or transition in the Production Editor pane. VideoWave also positions the Storyline Playback Head right in front of the panel so that you can review the scene or transition in the Production Preview pane simply by clicking that pane's Play button.

Trimming your video clips

Some of the video clips that you add to a production may require some trimming to make them just the right length and to ensure that clip starts and ends on just the frames that you want included. To trim a video clip that you've added to your video production, click its panel in the Production Editor and then click the Adjust Duration button (the one with the alarm clock) at the beginning of the toolbar on the second row of the Preview pane.

VideoWave then opens a Video Trimmer dialog box similar to the one shown in Figure 10-11. Here, you can reset either the starting or the ending frame of the video clip or reset both the starting and ending frames. To reset the starting frame, use the playback controls under the center preview area to display the frame where you want to clip to begin playing and then click the Mark button under the thumbnail of the Start frame on the left side of the trimmer. To reset the ending frame, use the playback controls to display the frame where you want to clip to stop playing and then click the Mark button under the thumbnail of the End frame on the right side of the Video.

Figure 10-11:
You can trim the start and/or ending of any video clip in your production in the Video Trimmer dialog box.

To preview the trimmed clip from start to end, click the Go to Start button in the playback controls and then click its Play button. If you're happy with how the clip now plays, click the OK button to close the Video Trimmer dialog box and return to the VideoWave window. If you're not happy with where the clip now starts or ends, drag the starting point (the green triangle pointing right) or the end point (the red triangle pointing left) in the slider under the clip preview to make any necessary adjustments. To reset the clip to its original starting point or ending point, click the Reset button under the Start or End thumbnail.

Keep in mind that you can adjust how long a still image remains on screen in your production by clicking its panel and then adjusting the value (representing seconds) in the Duration text box on the toolbar on the second row of the Preview pane.

Adjusting the quality of your video clips and still images

Not all the video clips and still images that you add to your video production will be of the highest quality. If you need to, you can tweak the overall brightness, contrast, and color balance and tint of any video clip or still image in the Production Editor pane.

To make any of these adjustments to the video clip in your production, select its panel in the Production Editor and then click the More Settings button to open a Settings dialog box containing Brightness, Contrast, Saturation, Red, Green, and Blue sliders that you can adjust before clicking its Close button. As you adjust the values with these sliders, you can immediately see the effect on the first frame of the selected clip in the Preview pane (VideoWave also adjusts the values in the Brightness, Contrast, and Saturation text boxes shown at the top of the Preview pane if you make changes to these sliders in the Settings dialog box).

To adjust the brightness, contrast, or color saturation for a photo, click its panel in the Production Editor and then click the Edit Photo button (the one second from the right on the toolbar on the third row in the Preview pane). VideoWave then opens a Preview window that contains Brightness & Contrast and Saturation buttons (among others including AutoFix, Cropping, and Red Eye). To display the Brightness and Contrast sliders to adjust these values, click the Brightness & Contrast button. To display the Saturation slider to adjust the color richness of the color, you click the Saturation button.

If your photo does not fill the entire panel, black bars will appear around the perimeter or just on the top and bottom or left and right sides. To eliminate these bars, click the button to display the drop-down list to the right of the box that contains text Bars on the toolbar on the third row of the Preview pane. Select Fill from the list. VideoWave 8 then resizes the photo so that it fills the entire panel in the Preview pane as well as final movie (note the bars will remain visible in the panel in the Production Editor pane even after you select the Fill option).

Automatically panning and zooming your still images

VideoWave has this really cool Auto Motion feature that you can apply to the still images such as scanned graphics and digital photos that you add to a new video production. When you apply the Auto Motion feature to a photo, VideoWave gives the illusion of animating it by panning and/or zooming in or out on the image.

To apply this feature to a still image that you've added to the Production Editor pane, right-click its panel and then click the Auto Motion option on its shortcut menu. VideoWave then applies the feature to the image and immediately positions the Storyline Playback Head immediately in front of the still image in the video production. You can then preview actual panning and zooming applied to your still image by then clicking the Play button in Production Preview pane. If you don't happen to like the Auto Motion effect that VideoWave has applied, press Ctrl+Z or choose Edit⇨Undo on the VideoWave menu bar immediately to remove it and return it to its original completely static image.

Adding panning and zooming to still images and video clips

If you like to remain in control of any pan-and-zoom effects that you add to your still images or would like to control the camera motion in a video clip that you've added to video production, you can use VideoWave's Pan & Zoom Editor to do this. Click the panel with the image or video clip you want to pan and zoom and then click Edit⇨Pan & Zoom Editor on its shortcut menu (you can also open this editor for photos by clicking the Pan & Zoom Editor button on the third row of the toolbar in the Preview pane).

VideoWave opens the Pan & Zoom Editor window similar to the one shown in Figure 10-12. In the upper-left corner of this window, you find option buttons that enable you to create pan and zoom effects in three modes:

- **Preset,** which enables you to select a predefined pan and zoom effect (Zoom & Pan, Zoom In, Zoom Out, Pan Only, Horizontal Pan, or Vertical Pan) on the associated drop-down list box to its right

- **Manual,** which enables you to define the amount of zoom and the direction of the pan in the image or video clip by manually adjusting the size and position of a red bounding box at the Start and/or the Finish of the pan-and-zoom effect

- **Advanced,** which enables you to define the amount of zoom and the direction of the pan in a video clip by creating keyframes by manually adjusting the size and position of a red bounding box at keyframes you add to the clip as well as at the Start and/or the Finish of the pan-and-zoom effect

The trick to creating your pan-and-zoom effect in Manual or Advanced mode is the red bounding box. To zoom in on part of an image or frame, drag the slider below its thumbnail to the left. To start a pan from a particular part of an image or frame, drag the bounding box so that it encloses that part.

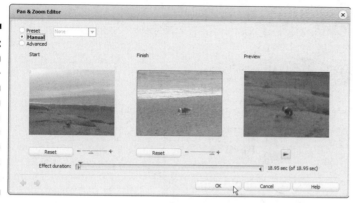

Figure 10-12: You can create pan-and-zoom motion effects for a still image or video clip in the Pan & Zoom Editor.

If you are using Advanced mode to create a pan-and-zoom effect for a video clip, use the Play/Pause or drag the Scrubber until you see a frame where the zoom or pan should change, and then click the Add button to insert a numbered KeyFrame (using the next available number) in the Key Frame list box before you adjust the size and position of the bounding box.

When you finish selecting a Preset effect or adjusting the zoom and pan for an effect you create in Manual or Advanced mode, preview the effect in the Preview window on the right side of the Pan & Zoom Editor window by dragging the Scrubber to the beginning of the effect and then click the Play button. When you have the effect you want, click the OK button to close the Pan & Zoom Editor window.

Adding transitions to the scenes in your movie

VideoWave offers you a wide choice in transitions that can smooth the changeover from one scene to the next in your movie. To add a transition between the scene panels in the Production Editor pane, you follow these steps in the VideoWave window:

1. **Click the panel immediately following the transition (in other words, the panel you transition to) in the Production Editor pane.**

2. **Click the Add Transition link in the Add Content pane.**

   VideoWave opens the Add Transition dialog box that displays thumbnails for the first few rows of its transitions as shown in Figure 10-13. To reduce the display to only the transitions in a particular category, click the drop-down list button to the right of All and click the desired category (Reveals, Pushes & Slides, Page Turns, 3-D, Particles, Distort, or Custom) in the drop-down list box.

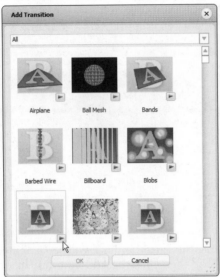

Figure 10-13:
To add a
transition,
click its
thumbnail in
the Add
Transition
dialog box
and then
click OK.

To get an idea of how the transition works, click the tiny Play button in the lower-right corner of its thumbnail. The thumbnail demonstrates the transition from A (in dark blue) to B (in gold) with A representing the current scene in the panel to the immediate left of the transition panel in the Production Editor pane where you set this transition and B representing the very next scene in the panel to the immediate right.

3. **Click the thumbnail of the transition you want to use and then click OK to close the Add Transition dialog box.**

The Add Transition dialog box opens with three option buttons:

- **Add/Replace Transition Before Current Panel** so that the current panel is the one transitioned to with the selected transition

- **Add/Replace Transition After Current Panel** so the current panel is the one transitioned from with the selected transition effect

- **Add/Replace Transition Between All Panels in the Production** to make the selected transition effect the one used between all panels throughout the entire video production

Because you have selected the panel that is to be transitioned to with the new transition effect, you can just click OK to accept the Add/Replace Transition Before Current Panel default.

4. **Click OK to close the Add Transition dialog box and insert the new transition effect in front of the selected panel.**

VideoWave inserts the effect before the selected panel and automatically moves the Playback head so that is positioned immediately in front of the new transition in the Production Editor. To see how the effect works with your media, simply click the Play button in the Preview pane.

Sometimes the transition will play so quickly that your audience doesn't get the full visual effect when the movie goes from one scene to the next. If this is the case, you can lengthen the duration of the transition to slow it down.

5. **(Optional) To adjust the length of the new transition, right-click it in its transition panel, click the Set Transition Duration option on its shortcut menu, and then enter or select a new length (in seconds) in the Duration text box before clicking the Set Transition Duration dialog box's OK button.**

Instead of repeating the previous steps to individually add the same transition over and over again to the rest of the transition panels in your video production, you can apply the first transition that you add manually to all the other transition panels. Right-click the transition panel containing the first transition that you added by hand and then click the Apply Transition to All option that appears on its shortcut menu. VideoWave then displays an alert dialog box asking you to confirm the replacement of all transitions in your production. As soon as you click the Yes button in this dialog box, the program adds the first transition to the all the rest of the transition panels that occur between occupied scene panels.

If you don't really want to use the exact same transition between every scene in the video production, instead of selecting the Apply Transition to All option on the transition panel's shortcut menu, try using the Apply Transition Theme option instead. When you click this option, VideoWave opens the Apply Transition Theme dialog box where you can select among a whole bunch of different transition themes (Dissolves, Fast Dissolves, and Slow Dissolves just to name a few).

When you click one of these transition themes and then click the OK button (and click the Yes button in the alert dialog box asking you to confirm the replacement of all existing transitions in your production), the program applies a progression of related transitions (that is, those in a similar style) to all the rest of the transition panels between occupied scenes in the production.

Adding special effects and overlays to your movie

VideoWave offers a wide variety of special effects (that consist mostly of filters with some cutouts) and overlays (that consist mostly of cutouts and frames) that you can apply to the video clips and still images that you've added to the scene panels of your production in the Production Editor pane.

To choose a particular filtering or cutout effect for your video production, click the Add Video Effect link in the Add Content pane. Videowave opens the Add Video Effect dialog box displaying the thumbnails for the first few rows of all the special effects you can choose from. To narrow the display to particular sub-categories of effects, click the drop-down button to the right of the drop-down list box that currently contains All and then click the subcategory to display (Colorize, Distort, Pixelate, 3-D, or Custom) on this list.

To choose a particular cutout or frame for your video production, click the Add Overlay link in the Add Content pane. VideoWave opens the Add Overlay dialog box displaying the thumbnails for the first few rows of all the overlays you can choose from. To narrow the display to certain subcategories of overlays, click the drop-down button to the right of the drop-down list box that currently contains All and then click the subcategory to display (Banners, Edges, Frames, Textures, All – Widescreen, Edges – Widescreen, Frames – Widescreen, Textures – Widescreen, or Custom) on this list.

You can add a particular effect or overlay to an individual scene panel or to all the panels in the entire production. To add an effect or overlay to an individual scene panel, click the panel in the Production Editor before you click the Add Video Effect or Add Overlay link. Then after selecting the thumbnail of the effect or overlay you want to apply to that panel in the Add Video Effect or Add Overlay dialog box, click the Insert on Internal Effect Track of Selected Panel or the Insert on Internal Overlay Track of Selected Panel option button in the respective dialog boxes that follow. Of course, to apply the selected video effect or overlay to all the panels in the entire production, you would leave the Add to Production option button selected in these dialog boxes before clicking OK.

You can sometimes effectively combine an effect with an overlay to lend a definite mood to your production. For example, to give your movie a really old feel, try combining the Sepia Low or Sepia Medium special effect with the Vintage Photo overlay. Together, your movie seems more like something produced around the turn of the last century (that is, the early 1900s) than something produced with twenty-first century computer software.

Removing special effects and overlays

Sometimes after reviewing the footage with a special effect or overlay that you've added to a scene in the Production Preview pane, you'll decide that you definitely don't want to keep it. To remove an effect from a scene panel, right-click the panel and then click Remove⇨Video Effects on the shortcut menu. To remove an overlay, you follow the same procedure except that you click Remove⇨Overlays on the panel's shortcut menu.

If you've added an effect or overlay to an entire video production and then decide that you need to lose it fast, you need to right-click somewhere in the Production Editor Background (that is, in the space in between the scene and transition panels) and then click the Remove⇨Effects or the Remove⇨ Overlays options on the shortcut menu.

Adding audio clips to your video production

VideoWave makes it easy to add background audio to your video productions. When adding audio, you have a choice between adding a prerecorded audio file and recording your own narration sound track for your video production. You can even add both types of audio tracks to the same video production if you so desire (although you have to be careful that the different audio tracks don't start competing with each other for the poor audience's limited listening attention span).

Keep in mind when adding either or both types of audio tracks to your video production that this audio plays in the background of the movie without in anyway canceling the audio that's been recorded as part of the video clips added to the production. In some cases, this will mean that your background audio tracks will compete with the sound recorded as part of each individual video clip. As a result, you may end up having either to turn down the volume on the background audio tracks or on the audio that's part of each video clip (I give you instructions on how to adjust the volume of each kind of audio clip later in this chapter).

Often, a prerecorded audio file can serve as a background track that sets the mood of your movie. To add a prerecorded audio file to your entire video production, follow these steps:

1. **Click somewhere in the Production Editor window (but not on a panel) to activate it and then click the Add Background Audio to Production button (the one with the eighth note and the plus sign) in the middle of Production Editor pane's toolbar.**

   VideoWave opens the Select Background Audio dialog box where you locate and select the audio file that you want played as the background music or narration for your movie.

   Note that you can only add audio files in the Select Background Audio dialog box for which you have the Digital Management Rights. If you try to add a file whose thumbnail has a small padlock in the lower-right corner, when you click the Open button, VideoWave displays an alert dialog box indicating that you don't have the rights to the audio you selected and fails to add the selected track to your video production.

2. **Select the audio file in the folder that you want to add as the background audio in the Select Background Audio list box and then click the Open button.**

VideoWave closes the Select Background Audio dialog box and a bar representing the length of the audio clip in relation to the total running time of the video appears immediately above the playback controls in the Preview pane and a Speaker icon appears on the tab in the lower-left corner of the Production Editor.

If the audio clip you add to your production is not long enough to accompany all the video and still image, you can add more audio clips by repeating these steps. Just be sure to click the No button in the VideoWave 8 alert box that appears after reopening the Select Background Audio dialog box asking if you want to replace the existing background audio (VideoWave then automatically appends the new clip to the end of the first).

After adding an audio clip to your production, you can use options on the pop-up menu attached to the Volume button (the one with the Speaker with sound waves coming out of it) on the second row of the toolbar in the Preview window to add a fade-in or fade-out effect, temporarily mute, or to adjust the volume by entering a new decibel level in the Volume (dB) text box. If your audio clip is not long enough for the entire production and you don't want to add other audio clips, click the Loop check box (to the immediate right of Volume button in the Preview pane) to have VideoWave repeat the audio file as needed to cover the entire production.

Recording a narration for your video production

To record narration for your video production, click the Add Narration (the one with the old-fashioned microphone) on the Production Editor pane's toolbar after activating this window. VideoWave then opens a Narration window containing its own Preview window (like the one shown in Figure 10-14).

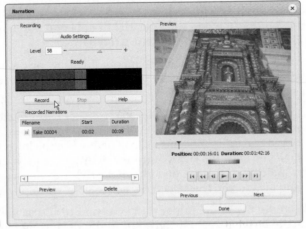

Figure 10-14: Recording a narration track for the video production you're creating.

The great thing about recording the narration track for your video is that you get to watch the video footage in the Production Preview pane as you actually record the accompanying narration. This enables you to describe in words what the audience is seeing as you watch the video footage (which is helpful even if you're reading from a prepared script, which is always recommended).

Before you begin recording your narration, you may need to make the following adjustments:

- Select the device (sound card) and input (which is most often the microphone that's built into your computer or that you've connected to your computer) as well as the directory on your hard disk in which the narration audio files are saved. To do this, click the Audio Settings button and then select the proper Device, Input, and Directory settings in the Select Audio Device dialog box before you click OK.

- Adjust the recording volume by dragging the Level slider in the Narration dialog box (which usually should be somewhere in the center).

- Use the Go to Start, Scrubber button, or Jog Wheel in the playback controls at the bottom of the Preview pane to cue up the frame at which you want the narration to start.

To begin recording, click the Record button and begin speaking directly into the microphone (in a normal tone). As you speak, VideoWave will automatically begin playing the movie from the current frame in the Preview pane. You can then tailor your comments to the actual footage that's being shown (I often remember details when watching the footage that I'm able to capture as part of the narration).

As soon as you finish making your narrative comments, click the Stop button (which becomes active the moment you click Record). As soon as you click the Stop button, VideoWave saves your recorded audio as a WAV file with the filename Take followed by the next available sequential number as in Take 00000.wav for the first narration track that you've saved.

Note that you can record several individual narrations for different scenes in the movie as part of the Narration track. Just cue up the starting frame for the next narration, click the Record button, record your comments for the next segment in the video, and then click the Stop button when you're finished.

To preview your movie with its new narration track, click the name of the narration in the Recorded Narrations list box and then click the Preview button. To remove a narration, click its filename in the Recorded Narrations list box and then click the Delete button.

If you're satisfied with what you now see and hear, click the Done button at the bottom of the Narration dialog box to return to the normal VideoWave window where the Production Editor is in its default Storyline mode.

If you don't like what you hear and would like to edit one or more of your narrations, click the Speaker icon on the tab in the lower-left of the Production Editor. If your production contains background audio as well as narration tracks, you need to click Nar (for Narration) in the pop-up menu that appears below this icon. If you have recorded more than one narration track for the production, you must select the track's filename in the Object Selector dialog box and then click OK. The Audio Editor window then opens with the waveform of your narration track. You can then use this window's controls (which are very similar to those in the Sound Editor covered in Chapter 5) to make edits, including trimming the audio, adding fade-in and fade-out effects, and adjusting the overall volume.

Adding audio clips to individual panels in the video production

Instead of, or in addition to, a background audio file that plays through the entire video, you can add audio files to the individual items (color panels, video clips, and still images). These audio clips play only as long these particular panels play in the video production. These audio clips can contain prerecorded sound effects, narration, or music that you want should just play as part of the panel.

To add an audio clip to a particular panel, click the Show Media Selector link in the Tools pane and then select the audio file to add in the Media Selector dialog box. Drag the thumbnail of this audio file to the Production Editor pane and then drop it on the particular scene panel to which it is to be associated. VideoWave lets you know that you've added an audio file to that panel by displaying a Speaker icon in the lower-left corner of the panel (which you can use to open the file in the Audio Editor window).

The program automatically trims any clip that runs longer than the duration of the panel to which it is affixed (if the audio clip is shorter than the panel's duration, you can loop it so that it repeats until the panel finishes playing — see "Editing audio clips in Timeline mode" later in this chapter for details).

After adding an audio file to a particular pane, you must be sure to remember to click the Edit Internal Tracks or Entire Production button, the second button to the left on the top row of the toolbar in the Preview pane, to re-activate all the panes in the production.

Working in Timeline mode

As the name implies, Timeline mode represents the various elements used in your video production as in different tracks plotted along a timeline. Figure 10-15 shows the VideoWave window after switching from Storyline to Timeline mode by clicking the Timeline button near the beginning of Production Editor pane's toolbar. The Production Editor pane in this figure shows the information that I've added to the entire video production in the Video, Music (background audio), Nar (narration), Fx1 (Effects, in this case, Sepia Medium), and there's also an Ovl (Overlay) and abc (Text) track that isn't visible in this figure).

Figure 10-15:
Editing the
current
video
production
in the
Production
Editor when
it's in
Timeline
mode.

When you switch to Timeline mode, the Production Editor pane presents all the information in your current video production in individual tracks rather than by sequential panels.

Hide and seek Track style

If you haven't added an effect, text, or overlay to the video production and aren't likely to, you can make more room for yourself in the Production Editor pane by hiding the Fx (Effects), Ovl (Overlay), and Text tracks. If you want to be able to edit the audio that's recorded as part of the video clips added to the Video track (referred to as Native), you can display the Native audio track.

Also, if you want to add an audio clip to the video production as a sound effect or have already done so, you need to display the Sfx (Sound Effects) track in order to add the audio clip to it (by dragging its audio file from the Media Selector dialog box and dropping it onto this track in Production Editor pane) and to later be able to edit the audio clip.

To hide certain tracks that you don't need in the Production Editor pane or to display tracks that are now temporarily hidden, right-click in anyone of the tracks in the Production Editor and then click Tracks on the shortcut menu. VideoWave then opens the Show/Hide Tracks dialog box that has check boxes in front of the names of all the video/effect tracks and audio tracks you can view in the Production Editor – Timeline pane (Fx 1, Ovl 1, Text 1 for the Video/Effect tracks and Native, Music, Nar, and Sfx as the Audio tracks). To display a particular track in the Show/Hide Tracks dialog box, click the track's check box until it contains a check mark. To hide a particular track, click its check box until the check mark is cleared.

If you need to insert additional text, overlay, effect tracks to the Timeline view of the Production Editor onto which to add supplementary Text tracks, Overlay tracks, and Effect tracks which can then overlap those in original Text 1, Ovl 1, and Fx 1, click the Add Text, Add Overlay, or Add Effect button in the Show/Hide Tracks dialog box. Each time you click any of these three buttons, VideoWave adds an additional Text, Overlay, or Effect track with the next available number (as in Text 2, Ovl 3, and Fx 4).

Marking time with the Timeline ruler

At the top of the tracks in the Production Editor: Timeline pane, you find the Timeline ruler. This ruler enables you to estimate the relative length of the individual items in the tracks below. You can zoom in and expand the level of detail in the tracks at the place in the Timeline ruler that you click with the Hand mouse pointer and then drag to the right. So too, you can return to your previous level of detail by dragging the ruler to the left.

Keep in mind that the zooming in and out that you do by dragging the Timeline ruler (one of the coolest features of VideoWave in my humble opinion) is more generalized than zooming in and out by clicking the Zoom In and Zoom Out buttons or dragging the Zoom slider in the Timeline toolbar. Use these buttons to zoom in and out on the particular part of the Video track displayed in the Production Editor pane after using the ruler-dragging method to bring that part into view in Production Editor.

The benefits of editing your video production in Timeline mode

At first blush, the benefits of editing your video production in Timeline mode may not be apparent. Actually, there are two main benefits to editing your video production in Timeline mode:

✔ In the tracks in Timeline mode, you can add multiple items, including audio clips, narration, text, special effects and overlays to the entire video production or to a single still image or video clips the production contains.

✔ By comparing information in different tracks In Timeline mode, you can see clearly how the different elements of the video production overlap and relate to one another.

The first benefit point is by far the most important. If you try, for example, to add two different audio files that you want to play one after the other as the background audio for your video production in Storyline mode, VideoWave will ask you if you want to replace the first audio file as soon as you try to add the second one. If, however, you switch to Timeline, you add the second audio file right after the first one in the Background Audio track simply by dragging it into position on this track.

When editing in Timeline mode, you need to be aware that there are two views that you can switch between:

- **Production** (the default) in which the tracks in the Production Editor: Timeline pane show only the elements applied to the entire video production
- **Internal tracks** in which the tracks in the Production Editor: Timeline pane show only the elements applied to the particular still image or video clip in the production that you have selected

To switch from the Production view to the Internal tracks view, you simply locate the still image or video clip in the Video track whose internal tracks you want displayed and then double-click somewhere within that image or clip. The Production Editor: Internal Tracks pane then appears at the bottom of the VideoWave window. This pane contains the tracks for just the still image or video you double-clicked. You can then edit the audio, text, effects, and overlays applied only to this element in the appropriate tracks in this view. When you're finished editing in the localized Internal Tracks view, you can return to the more general Production view by clicking the Edit Internal Tracks or Entire Production button (the one with the filmstrip icon) on Preview pane toolbar.

When editing elements in the tracks of the Production Editor (either in the Production or the Internal tracks view), you can drag the bars representing the different types of media items (audio, effects, text, overlays, and whatnot) to resize or reposition them on its particular track. To resize an item, such as an effect or an overlay, position the mouse pointer at the end of the item in its track and then when the mouse pointer turns into a double-pointed arrow, drag its blue bar to the left (to make it shorter) or to the right (to make it longer).

When editing certain items such audio clips, effects, text, and overlays at the Production view, you can split the items in two at the position of Timeline playback head in the Production Editor by clicking its track and then clicking the Split the Selected Item button on the Timeline toolbar. After splitting an item, you can then resize and drag its now separate parts to different positions on the timeline so that they each affect only a certain part of the video production.

Editing audio clips in Timeline mode

Although you can edit the length and the position (how long and where they play) of the audio clips in your video production by directly manipulating their bars in their respective tracks (Native, Music, Nar, and Sfx) in the Timeline view in the Production Editor, if you want to the trim the audio or modulate its volume or adjusting some other aspect of its sound, you need to open the clip in the Audio Editor.

To do this, locate the audio clip in its track in the Production Editor: Timeline pane and then right-click and then click the Edit option on its shortcut menu. VideoWave then generates a preview of the selected audio clip and opens it in the Audio Editor window similar to the one shown in Figure 10-16.

In the Audio Editor, you can make any of the following edits to the selected audio clip:

- ✔ **Adjust the overall volume of the audio clip** by dragging the Overall Volume (dB) slider to the right (to increase the volume) or the left (to diminish the volume)

- ✔ **Adjust the volume throughout the audio clip** by clicking different places in the waveform envelope to add edit points that you can then drag up above the centerline to increase the volume or down below the centerline to diminish the volume

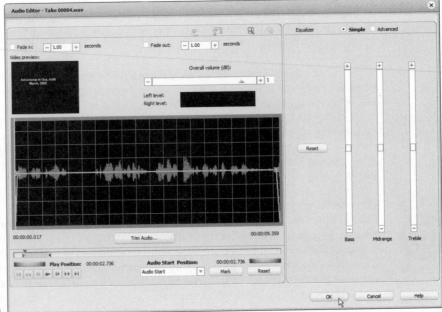

Figure 10-16:
You can edit the sound quality and volume of the audio clip and trim it in the Audio Editor window.

✔ **Fade the volume in at the start and out at the end of the audio clip** by clicking the Fade In and Fade Out check boxes and then enter the fade-in and fade-out times in the associated text boxes (in seconds) or select them by clicking the Plus (+) or Minus (–) buttons.

✔ **Equalize the sound in the audio clip** by dragging the Bass, Midrange, and/or Treble sliders in the Equalizer area to the right (to modulate the sound using a 10-band equalizer, click the Advanced option button at the top of Equalizer area; to select a predefined equalization, click the Open button and click its name in the Media Selector; to save your customized settings, click the Save button and enter a name for the audio settings in the Save dialog box).

✔ **Trim the audio clip** by clicking the Trim Audio button to open the Audio Trimmer. There, you drag the Current Position marker (the yellow vertical bar) to the new start position and click the Mark Start Point button before you drag the Current Position marker to the new end position and click the Mark End Point. You then complete the trimming sequence by clicking OK.

When you finish making some or all of these editing changes to your audio clip, you can preview the modifications by clicking the Play button in the playback controls at the bottom-left of the Audio Editor window. When you're satisfied with the tweaks and edits you've made to your sound clip, click the OK button to close the Audio Editor and put the new audio settings into effect in the VideoWave window.

To remove the audio portion that's been recorded as part of a video clip, right-click its clip in the Native audio track and click Edit on the shortcut menu. Then in the Audio Editor window, drag the Overall Volume (dB) slider all the way to the left so that in the future the video clip plays completely silently in the movie as though it no longer had any audio associated with it.

Outputting the Video Production

When you finish having fun with the hundreds of VideoWave editing features and finally have your video production just the way you want it and all the last-minute changes are saved with the File⇨Save command (in the native VideoWave 8 DMSM file format), you're ready to output your finished production as a movie that you can share it with the rest of the world (Sundance look out!).

VideoWave attempts to make outputting your finished production as easy as possible. All you have to decide during this process is where you want the finished movie shown (on what device) and in what quality (which determines how much compression is used in the final video file and how large the file is).

To output your finished and saved video production, click the Output As button near the end of the Preview pane's toolbar or choose File➪Output As on the VideoWave menu bar. VideoWave displays the Make Movie dialog box shown in Figure 10-17.

Here, you must select the tab for any of the following destinations for your movie:

✔ **Video File** (selected by default) to make a movie that you can play on your computer using a program such as Windows Media Player

✔ **DV Camera** to make a movie that you can output to digital tape on your DV camcorder

✔ **TV/VCR** to make a movie that you can output to a video cassette tape and then show on TV

✔ **E-mail** to make a movie that you can send as an attachment to an e-mail message

Figure 10-17:
Outputting
your
finished
video
production
in the Make
Movie
dialog box.

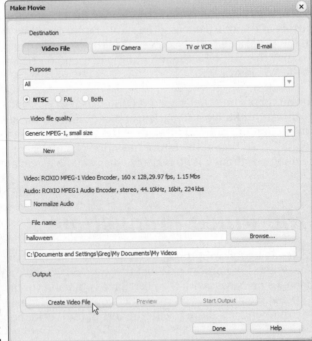

As soon as you click the appropriate tab in the Make Movie dialog box, you are presented with the options for determining the quality of the video. The exact options that this window contains depend on which destination tab you click. In general, you need to specify the quality of the movie that you're making. In selecting the quality of the final video file, you are necessarily selecting the amount of compression to be used and how large the resulting file will be (the higher the quality, the less the compression and the bigger the final video file).

Note that when you select Video File as the destination, you must also select the purpose of the video file in the Purpose drop-down list box (you select the Playback on Another PC option on the drop-down list when your intention is just to play the movie with Windows Media Player). After selecting the purpose of the video, you can specify the amount of compression to use by selecting an option on the Video File Quality drop-down list (such as Generic MPEG-1, Small Size or Generic MPEG-1, or Normal Quality).

Keep in mind when selecting a video format, physical movie size, and frames per second from the Purpose drop-down list that each aspect affects the overall size of the resulting movie file. The larger the physical movie size and the higher the frames per second, the larger the resulting movie file. Large movie file sizes are not only more difficult to share on the Internet but require more processing power for playback on a personal computer.

After specifying the quality of the finished movie, you need to specify the name of the new video file and its location in the File Name and Location text boxes. To select a new location and filename for the video file, click the Browse button to open the Save File As dialog box where you select the folder and enter the filename before clicking the Save button.

After specifying the video settings and filename, click the Create Video File button to open the Render dialog box where VideoWave creates the finished movie file by rendering it frame-by-frame in the video file format you specified. After the program finishes rendering the video file, the Render dialog box closes and you can then click the Preview button in the Make Movie dialog box to preview the finished product. After you finish previewing the movie, click the Done button in the Make Movie dialog box to close the it and return to the VideoWave 8 window.

Burning the Video Production to Disc

Instead of outputting your finished video production to video file, you can burn it to a DVD. To burn your finished and saved video production to a DVD, click the Burn with MyDVD Express button (the one sporting the DVD icon) at the very end of the Preview pane's toolbar or choose File➪Burn with MyDVD Express on the VideoWave menu bar.

As soon as you choose this command, the VideoWave application closes, the MyDVD Express application launches with the video you created in VideoWave already added to the main menu of a new DVD project (see Chapter 11 for details on completing this project in MyDVD and burning it to disc).

Chapter 11

Building and Burning DVDs

MyDVD is the place to go to when you want to build and burn your DVD projects. With MyDVD 8, you can construct projects that play on standalone DVD players (including the latest machines using the newer VCD and SVCD formats) as well as your computer's DVD drive. As with all the other applications in the Roxio Creator 8 suite, MyDVD makes it as easy as possible to build and burn sophisticated DVD discs.

This chapter acquaints you with all the aspects of using MyDVD to create your DVD projects and burn them to disc. It starts by familiarizing you with the different DVD projects supported by MyDVD. The chapter then goes on to introduce you to the MyDVD window and its features (which will be very familiar to those of you who have used the information in Chapter 10 to design and build video productions in the VideoWave application). As part of this introduction, you find out how to use and customize MyDVD's built-in themes, add new DVD titles to your project, as well as how to create a menu system for selecting titles you add to your DVD.

The chapter ends by giving you pointers on how to preview and test out your DVD project before burning it to disc and then giving you the ins and outs of burning your finished project to disc.

Getting Cozy with the MyDVD Window

You can launch MyDVD from the Roxio Creator 8 Home window by clicking the MyDVD link in the Applications Project window opened by clicking Applications on the Home tab of the Project List pane. You can also open this application by clicking the Create DVD link on the DVD & Video tab of the Project List pane or its younger brother, MyDVD Express, by clicking its Quick DVD link.

When you first launch MyDVD, a new, untitled DVD project opens in the MyDVD 8 window (see Figure 11-1). This window contains four panes:

✔ **Menu Tasks** pane with links for adding movies and submenus to your DVD project

✔ **Edit** pane with links for editing movies or chapters within movies

✔ **Project View** pane that depicts the layout of the menu system in your DVD project

✔ **Preview** pane that shows you the current menu or submenu in your DVD project

Preview area

Figure 11-1:
The MyDVD window is the place where you build your new DVD project.

Task pane

Building Your DVD Project

As soon as you launch MyDVD to start a new DVD project, you notice that the program has already created a main menu for you called My Menu. This menu uses a simple menu style whereby thumbnails for the movies and submenus you add are arranged in simple rows beneath the My Menu banner. The background of to the main menu is a movie of rushing water that plays whenever you play the DVD.

Modifying the menu style

The first thing you may want to do in a new DVD project is modify the menu style. MyDVD offers a whole bunch of prefab styles that include the graphics for the menu background, the look of the menu, chapter, and navigation buttons, the fonts used in displaying the main menu and chapter menu names and the button labels, and even the background music that plays whenever the main menu screen is displayed.

To select a menu style for your new DVD project, click the Change Menu Style link in the Edit pane or choose DVD Menu⇨Change Menu Style on the MyDVD menu bar. MyDVD opens the Select Menu Style dialog box containing thumbnails of the various styles available. To preview the type of background graphic, menu, chapter, and navigation buttons, and the font that a particular predefined menu style uses, click its thumbnail in the list on the left side.

If you want the menu style to apply only to the main menu, leave the Current Menu Only option button selected. If you want to apply the new menu style to all the menus in the DVD project, click the Entire Project option button before clicking OK.

Click the More Styles button to go online to the Roxio Web site and download additional menu styles to use in the projects you create with MyDVD 8.

MyDVD enables you to modify the following aspects of any style that you choose for your DVD project:

- **Menu background** by clicking the Change Menu Background link in the Edit pane and then selecting the image, video, or slideshow to use in the Select Media File dialog box

- **Menu audio** by clicking the Change Menu Audio link in the Edit pane and then selecting the audio file to play in the Select Audio File dialog box

> ✔ **Menu title fonts** by clicking the title, selecting its text, and then using the buttons on the Preview toolbar to change the font, font size, color, attribute, and/or alignment
>
> ✔ **Menu item layout** by clicking the Rows drop-down list box and then selecting another layout (such as Columns) on its list

To get an idea of how your changes to the menu background will appear in the final DVD, choose DVD Menu➪Animate Preview on the MyDVD menu bar. MyDVD will then animate any background that uses video or a slideshow as well as play the background music assigned as part of the style.

Modifying the main menu title

After you select the theme you want to use in your new DVD project, you probably want to change the generic title of the main menu from the completely uninspiring **My Menu** to something more descriptive such as **The French Riviera**, **Wedding Bells**, and **Baby's First Year**.

To modify the menu title, click the mouse pointer somewhere in the title text to display its bounding box and marquee, and then drag through the text to select it for editing. To change the font, font size, color or other attributes of the text, use the Font, Size, Color, Style, Bold, and Italic buttons on the second row of the toolbar in the Preview pane.

To reposition the menu title on the main menu screen, position the mouse pointer on one of the borders and then when the pointer changes to a four-headed arrow drag the title to its new place on the screen. To reflow the title text, change the size and shape of its bounding box by positioning the mouse pointer on either of its sizing handles (the tiny squares) and then dragging the double-headed arrow pointer.

Keep in mind that the main menu name is not restricted to a single line (simply press Enter to add a second line). If the text of any of your menu titles extends beyond the edges of the screen, you will have to reposition them or reduce the font size of their text until it all fits on the screen. Keep in mind as well that any text that extends beyond the safe areas on the left or right side of the main menu screen may be cut off when the DVD project is played on some televisions. Click the Show/Hide TV Safe Zone button on the first row of the Preview pane's toolbar to display the safe area and check if any text is in danger of being cut off (indicated by characters in the unsafe, checkerboard area).

Adding movies to your DVD project

After you have the menu style and the menu title the way you want them, you're ready to start adding the movies with the content you want to play to your DVD project. Most of the time, these movies will be in the form of video productions that you've created ahead of time in the Roxio Creator's VideoWave application (see Chapter 10 for details). They can also consist of slideshows that you put together in VideoWave or using the SlideShow Assistant. If you haven't yet created the slideshow you want to include in a DVD project, you can launch the SlideShow Assistant by choosing Movie⬧ Add New Slideshow on the MyDVD menu bar (see Chapter 10 for help on using the Slideshow Assistant).

To add a new movie from an existing VideoWave production, click the Add New Movie link at the top of the Menu Tasks pane and then click the name of the DMSM file (the filename extension given to Roxio Media Production files) in the Select Media File dialog box before you click the Open button.

MyDVD then adds a thumbnail with the first frame of the movie as a menu button with the name of the video production's filename on the main menu screen (see Figure 11-2).

Figure 11-2: Adding an existing VideoWave movie to the main menu of a new DVD project.

Editing movies in MyDVD

You can edit a movie that you add to your DVD project right within MyDVD. Simply click the movie's button to select it and then click the Edit Movie button (the one third from the end on the second row) on the Preview toolbar. MyDVD then redraws its window to include playback controls at the bottom of the Preview pane and a Production Editor pane in Storyline mode at the bottom of the window (see Figure 11-3).

You can then use the Production Editor controls (both in Storyline and Timeline modes) to make all necessary changes to your video. When you are finished editing the movie, click the Back to Menu button in the middle of the Preview pane toolbar to return to the normal MyDVD window.

Renaming, repositioning, and resizing menu buttons

Many times after adding a number of different movies to a menu screen, you find that you need to rename, reposition, and even resize their menu buttons. To rename a menu button, click its title to select it and then drag through its text and edit the name as you would any other text. When you finish editing the menu button's name, click the mouse button somewhere on the screen background outside of its text box.

To reposition a menu button on its menu screen, click the button's thumbnail and then position the mouse pointer somewhere within the thumbnail image. When the pointer changes into a four-headed arrow, drag the button to its desired position.

Figure 11-3:
Editing a movie added to your DVD project in the MyDVD window.

To reposition more than one button at a time, Ctrl+click the buttons and then drag their images to the desired position. If you want MyDVD to automatically align the selected buttons for you, click the Align button on the Preview toolbar.

Many times the menu buttons that you add to a menu screen are larger than you want them to be. To avoid overcrowding on the menu screen and overlapping the text of the button labels, you may want to make the buttons smaller (MyDVD automatically reduces the size of a button's label when you make its button image smaller).

To resize a menu button, click its thumbnail to select it (indicated by the red border around the image with teeny-tiny sizing handles in each corner). Then position the mouse pointer in one of the corners on a sizing handle. When the mouse pointer changes into a double-headed arrow, drag the pointer toward the center of the image to make the button smaller or away from the center to make the button larger.

Assigning a new thumbnail image to a menu button

Many times you will find that you need to change the thumbnail image for a movie that you add to your DVD project (by default, MyDVD uses the first frame in the video or the initial photo in a slideshow as the button's thumbnail). To assign a new image to a button, click the button to select it and then click the More Settings button on the second row of the Preview pane's toolbar (this is the very last button on the right).

MyDVD opens a Settings dialog box containing three tabs: Main, Position, and Style. Click the Style tab and then click the Custom option button in the Thumbnail section (doing this automatically de-selects the Use Link Menu/Movie option button as well as activates the Browse button). Click the Browse button to open the Movie dialog box and then select the image to use as the button's thumbnail.

The Movie dialog box is initially set up to find only video files in the Smart Objects, albums, and folders you select in the Movie dialog box. In order to select a still image as the button thumbnail, you must remember to take the extra step of changing the Files of Type setting to one of the accepted graphics file formats (BMP, MPG, GIF, PNG, or TIFF).

Adding a submenu to the DVD project

Many of your DVD projects, especially those of the DVD project type that you burn to DVD discs, will include too many movies for just the one main menu screen. To add a new submenu to your DVD project, click the Add Submenu link in the Menu Tasks pane after selecting the level to which to add this submenu in the hierarchy on the Menus tab of the Project View pane. MyDVD then adds a new submenu screen using the same background graphic and generic menu name as the main menu screen.

The program also adds Home and Previous navigation buttons (in the style of the theme you selected for the project) that the user can click to either return to the main menu screen or the previous menu level (which is not the same as the main menu when your DVD project contains more than two menu levels).

You can then rename this submenu screen and add new movies to it just as you did in the main menu screen. To jump between the menu screens as you continue to build and modify your DVD project, click the name of the menu in the Project List pane.

You can add as many title menu screens as you need to accommodate all the titles you want to add to your DVD project. Just watch the Estimated Size indicator at the bottom of the MyDVD window as you add your movies to see how close you're coming to filling up the DVD disc.

Adding an Intro Movie to your DVD project

An Intro Movie is one that automatically plays at the beginning of your DVD disc when the user puts the disc into his or her DVD player. When the Intro Movie finishes playing, the main menu screen appears and stays onscreen, from which you can choose the next movie that you want to watch by selecting that movie's menu button.

To add an Intro Movie to your DVD project, click the Add Intro Movie link in the Menu Tasks pane or choose Movie⇨Add Intro Movie on the MyDVD menu bar. MyDVD then opens the Select Media File dialog box where you can select the video production, video clip, or still image that you want to use as the Intro Movie for your DVD project.

After adding an Intro Movie, you then need to click the Intro Movie link on the Menus tab of the Project View pane in order to display it in MyDVD's Preview pane.

For your Intro Movie, you may want to add a color panel or still photo on which you place some introductory text with an overview of the disc's contents or the credits for your production, including yourself, of course, as the director, best boy, key grip, and who knows what else!

Dividing a movie into chapters

Sometimes, you'll want to break up a long video sequence in a movie or provide certain jump points in a title composed of a long sequence of photographic images. You do this by adding chapters to the movie. When you add chapters to a movie, your users can jump back and forth to these jump points by clicking the Previous (|<) and Next (>|) buttons on their DVD player's remote control. When creating chapters for a movie, you also have the option of creating chapter menus whose buttons your users can click to jump back and forth between the movie's chapters.

To mark the chapters in one of the movies in your DVD project, follow these steps:

1. **On the Menus tab of the Project View pane, select the menu that contains the movie you want to divide into chapters and then click its button to select it.**

2. **Click the Edit Chapters link in the Edit pane or choose Movie⟳Edit Chapters on the MyDVD menu bar.**

   MyDVD opens the Edit Chapters dialog box similar to the one shown in Figure 11-4. Here, you can add, change, or delete chapter markers in the current title. When adding chapter markers, you can have MyDVD automatically detect chapters by looking for changes in brightness and color between successive frames and the pauses in the title and add chapter markers at each pause. Or you can add them manually by scanning the frames or photos in the title.

   To use MyDVD's automatic scene detection feature to detect the changes or pauses and add the chapter markers for you, click the Go button. To increase the program's sensitivity in differentiating chapters by changes in the brightness and color of frames, you drag the Sensitivity slider to the right or click the Plus (+) button. To control how long a pause must be before the detection feature will insert a new chapter marker, enter the number of seconds in the Every Seconds text box.

   To add the chapter markers manually, you use Scubber, Jog Wheel or the playback controls (Play, Next Frame, and Fast Forward) found under the title's preview on the left side of the dialog box to find the frame or photo where you want to start a new chapter. When you come upon this frame or photo, you then click the Add Chapter Here button to add a new chapter marker (whose thumbnail with its time code then appears in the list box on the right side of the dialog box).

3. **To have MyDVD detect and add the chapter markers for you, click the Go button. To add the markers yourself, use the playback controls to display the frame (or photo in a slideshow title) where the marker is to occur and then click the Add Chapter Here button.**

   Sometimes MyDVD's Auto Detect feature adds chapter markers that you decide you really don't need to retain. In that case, you can follow Step 4 to remove any unwanted chapter markers.

4. **(Optional) To remove any chapter marker that you don't want to use, click its thumbnail in the list box on the right and then click the Remove button (the one with the red X).**

   When you have indicated which chapter markers you want in your title, you're ready to have MyDVD create them.

5. **Click the OK button to close the Edit Chapters dialog box and add the chapter markers to your project.**

Figure 11-4:
You use the controls in the Edit Chapters dialog box to add, change, or delete chapter markers in the current movie.

TIP

If you added chapter menus to your title, you can check them out when you preview the finished DVD project as described in the next section.

Previewing the finished DVD project

After you've got all the media you need in your DVD project, it's time to preview the final production before you burn it to DVD or CD disc. To preview the DVD project you're working on, you simply click the Preview Project button on the top row of the Preview pane's toolbar.

As soon as you click the Preview button, a preview window similar to the one shown in Figure 11-5 appears. This window contains two panes: the DVD Controls pane on the left, which contains a virtual DVD remote control, and the Preview pane on the right, which contains a preview of your project's main menu screen.

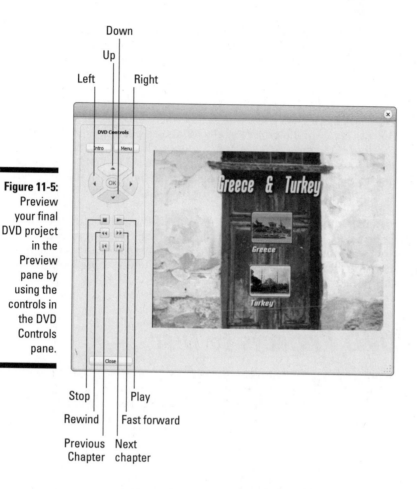

Down

Up

Left   Right

Figure 11-5:
Preview
your final
DVD project
in the
Preview
pane by
using the
controls in
the DVD
Controls
pane.

Stop   Play

Rewind   Fast forward

Previous Next
Chapter   chapter

If your project contains an Intro Movie (see "Adding an Intro Movie to your DVD project" earlier in the chapter for details), the Intro button at the top of the DVD Controls will be available (otherwise it's grayed out) in addition to the Menu button. To preview the Intro Movie in your DVD project, click the Intro button on the virtual DVD remote (remember that the Intro Movie plays automatically on the disc you create from this project as soon as the user puts the disc in the player).

To preview the other movies on the Main menu, click the Left, Right, Up, and Down controls on the virtual remote until the title you want to view is selected (indicated by a highlighted outline around its thumbnail) and then click the OK button on the virtual remote. When the title begins playing, you can then use the other playback controls such as Pause and Fast Forward to preview its contents. If you added chapter markers to your title, you can use the Next Chapter and Previous Chapter buttons to jump to and from different chapters in the title.

When you finish previewing a certain movie, you can return to the main menu screen by clicking the Stop button. If your DVD project contains more than one menu screen, you can advance to the next menu screen by highlighting the Next button (an arrow in the project's selected theme pointing to the right) near the bottom of the main menu screen and then clicking the OK button on the virtual remote. You can then return to the main menu screen by highlighting this new menu screen's Back button (an arrow in the style of the selected theme pointing up or to the left) and clicking the virtual remote's OK button.

When you finish previewing the movies on your DVD project, click the Close button in the upper-right corner of the window to return to the original MyDVD window. From there, you can make any necessary changes that you noted when previewing the titles in the project, or, if everything looks good, you can burn the DVD project to disc.

Burning DVD Projects to Disc

After you preview your DVD project and make any necessary last minute changes to it, you're ready to burn it to disc. The procedure for burning your DVD projects to DVD disc with MyDVD is very much like burning a data disc project (see Chapter 3) or Audio CD or MP3/WMA project (see Chapter 8) with Music Disc Creator.

After saving the finalized DVD project in the program's native DMSD file format by choosing File➪Save or File➪Save As and putting a blank DVD-R disc in your computer's CD/DVD drive, you begin the process by clicking the Burn button at the far right on the Preview pane's toolbar.

MyDVD then opens the Burn Project dialog box shown in Figure 11-6 where all you have to do is click the Burn button.

Regardless of whether you play a newly burned DVD disc in your computer's DVD drive using software such as Windows Media Player, you will definitely want to try playing the new DVD disc in your standalone DVD player using its remote control to test out and select the various titles on the disc's menus. Note that you can also prepare an adhesive label for your DVD disc and inserts for its jewel case using Roxio's Label Creator (as described in Chapter 9). If you don't want to take the risk of applying an adhesive label to the disc (see the end of Chapter 2 for my warning on using adhesive labels on discs), identify the disc by writing its name with a non-solvent based marker on the label (what is commonly called the top) side of the disc.

Figure 11-6:
You select
the settings
for burning
your
finalized
DVD project
to disc in
the Burn
Project
dialog box.

Of course, you never, never write on the bottom, shiny side of the disc
because that's the side the laser reads.

Plug & Burn: From tape to disc in one step

MyDVD's Plug & Burn feature enables you to burn your raw, unedited digital
video directly from your camcorder or your TV or VCR connected to your
computer directly to a DVD disc in your computer's DVD drive. This is a great
feature for transferring video such as lectures or live entertainment events
(when video recording is not prohibited) where editing is not really required
for the DVD disc.

To use the Plug & Burn feature, connect your camera, TV, or VCR to the computer using the appropriate cable and then insert a blank DVD disc in your
computer's DVD drive. Then launch the Roxio Creator 8 Home and follow
these steps:

1. **Click the Plug & Burn link on the DVD & Video tab of the Project List
   pane in the Roxio Creator 8 Home window.**

   MyDVD opens the initial, Set Production Options, Plug & Burn window
   shown in Figure 11-7. This dialog box contains options for selecting the
   menu style, the drive containing the DVD disc, and the disc type (4.7 or
   8.5 GB DVD disc).

2. **(Optional) To select a new menu style, click the Style button and then click the thumbnail of the Style to use in the Select Menu Style dialog box before you click OK. To create a disc without any menus, click the NoMenu option button instead.**

3. **Click the Next button to open the second Plug & Burn window — Capture Video.**

   The Capture Video Plug & Play window (shown in Figure 11-8) is where you select your capture settings (Device, Quality, and Create Chapters) before you actually begin capturing the video.

   By default, Plug & Burn captures your video using the HQ (High Quality) setting that saves the video at 720 x 480 pixels using the Dolby Digital AC-3 compressed audio file format. To modify these settings or the audio recording level or balance, select another Quality option button or click the Custom option button, followed by Settings, and then select the settings you want used in the Capture Quality dialog box before you click OK.

   By default, the program does not add any chapters to your video. To have Plug & Burn create chapters from scene breaks in the video, click the From Scene Breaks option button. To have the program create chapters at set intervals, click the Every check box and then enter the number of seconds in the Seconds text box.

4. **(Optional) Make any necessary changes in the Quality and/or Create Chapters settings.**

   Next you need to enter a new name for your movies in the Movie Name text box.

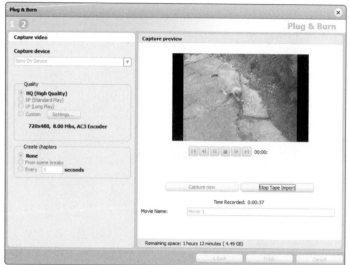

Figure 11-8:
You select
the capture
settings and
start the
capture in
the Capture
video Plug &
Burn
window.

5. **Click the Insertion point in the Movie Name text box and highlight the temporary disc name before you begin typing to replace this text with the name you want to assign to the movie you're about to capture.**

   Plug & Burn gives you a choice between manually recording the video and capturing the entire tape. If you want to capture the video manually, you have to cue up the tape using the playback controls under the preview pane.

6. **If recording a video or cassette tape, find the frame in the tape where you want to start recording (this is the first frame if you want to record the whole tape) and then click the Capture Now or Capture Entire Tape button. If recording from your TV tuner, select the right channel and then click the Capture Now button.**

   As soon as you click the Capture Now button, it becomes a Stop button. If you want to pause the video capture (either to miss a commercial break or find a new place in the tape), click the Stop button. Then, when you want to restart the recording (after the break or when you've cued the tape), click the Capture Now button again (which replaces the Stop button as soon as you click it). Note that each time you click Start after stopping it, MyDVD creates a new movie for the disc.

7. **As soon as you finish recording your video, click the Finish button at the bottom of the Plug & Burn dialog box.**

As soon as you click the Finish button to close the Plug & Burn dialog box, MyDVD displays the Burn Project dialog box, which keeps you informed of the program's progress as it begins burning your captured video to the DVD disc. When the burn process is complete, click the OK button to close the Burn Project dialog box and return to the Roxio Creator 8 Home window.

Part V
The Part of Tens

In this part . . .

Part V, the delightful Part of Tens, is the place to go to get some quick, concise information about the versatile components and features offered in Roxio's Creator 8 Suite. Chapter 12 briefs you on each of the major components in the suite with valuable information on what in the world it's good for. Chapter 13 gives you my take on the ten coolest features (many of them new) offered by Roxio Creator.

Chapter 12

Top Ten (or So) Components of the Roxio Creator 8 Suite

As you soon discover when you start using Roxio Creator 8, it's more like a combo of different mini-programs than a single software program. This chapter looks at each of the top ten modules in the Roxio Creator 8 suite, with an eye toward its basic functions and features. Use this list to get the lowdown on each of the major applications and tools that you use to collect, organize, and create cool projects using all the different forms of digital media: audio, still image, and video.

Disc Copier

Disc Copier is the application to use when you need to duplicate the CD and DVDs that you create and burn with the other Roxio Creator components including Creator Classic and MyDVD. In addition, you can use this nifty program to make backup copies of non-protected commercially produced CDs and DVDs.

The greatest thing about this program is that you don't need to have two CD or DVD drives on your computer in order to make your copies: Disc Copier can make backups using one CD or DVD drive by temporarily copying the disc files from the original CD or DVD disc to your hard disk and then copying these files from the hard disk onto a new CD or DVD disc that you put in the same drive.

You can access this program from the Roxio Creator 8 Home by clicking any of the following links:

✔ **Disc Copier** in the Applications Project window opened by clicking Applications on the Home tab of the Project List pane

✔ **Copy Disc** on the Copy tab or the Data tab of the Project List pane

See Chapters 3 for details on using Disc Copier to make backup copies of your discs.

Backup for All Types of Data

Creator Classic is the place to go when you need to back up the media or data files on your computer. You do this by compiling diverse data or media files into a single project that you then burn to CD or DVD discs. You can even create a Bootable Disc that contains enough of the Windows operating system to boot your computer from your CD/DVD drive rather than your hard disk.

Creator Classic also supports the creation of a Multimedia Disc that not only contains the various types of media files (graphics, audio, and video) but also contains play lists and menus for accessing the media following either the HighMAT or MPV standards.

When you need to back up your data on CD or DVD disc on a regular basis, you can turn to the Roxio Backup program. This application not only enables you to specify the data files to be backed up but also to schedule the times for the backups and have Roxio Creator give you reminders. You can then use Roxio Retrieve to restore data files from data and backup discs created with these applications.

In addition, you can use the CD Extra Disc Creator to create two different kinds of special projects that mix data and audio. You can burn Enhanced CDs that combine data and audio in separate sessions that can be played in any CD player or CD-ROM drive (CD players play only the music tracks in the later sessions, while CD-ROM can read both the data in the first session and the audio files in the later sessions) from Enhanced CD Projects. You can also burn Mixed-Mode CDs that combine data and audio in a single session that can only be played in your computer's CD-ROM or DVD drive with software programs like Windows Media Player from Mixed Mode CD Projects.

From the Roxio Creator 8 Home, you can launch Creator Classic, Roxio Backup, or CD Extra Disc Creator by using the following links:

- ✔ **Creator Classic** in the Applications Project window opened by selecting Applications on the Home tab or on the Data tab of the Project List pane

- ✔ **Roxio Backup** in the Applications Project window opened by selecting Applications on the Home tab of the Project List pane or **File Backup** on the Backup tab to open the Roxio Backup application

- ✔ **CD Extra Disc Creator** in the Applications Project window opened by selecting Applications on the Home tab to launch Roxio CD Extra Disc Creator

- ✔ **Retrieve** in the Utilities column of the Applications Project window opened by selecting Applications on the Home tab to launch Roxio Retrieve

See Chapter 3 for specific information on using Creator Classic, Roxio Backup, and Roxio Retrieve to create and burn data discs and backup projects as well as to restore data from their discs. See Chapter 7 for information on using CD Extra Disc Creator to create Enhanced CD and Mixed-Mode CD projects.

Acquiring Digital Media with Roxio Media Import

Roxio Media Import program enables you to acquire digital media files from both digital and analog sources connected to your computer. You can use Media Import to acquire still images from scanners and digital cameras connected to your computer. You can also use Media Import to acquire digital video directly from your digital camcorder or from an analog device such as your VCR connected to your computer. And if that's not enough for you, you can use Media Import to acquire audio files from audio CDs in your computer's CD-ROM or DVD drive, as live audio using a microphone, or from some other analog playback device such as a record player or audio cassette player connected to your computer. And finally, you can use Media Import to acquire individual movie titles from unencrypted DVD discs (usually the ones you create with MyDVD) that you put in your computer's DVD drive.

To launch Roxio Media Import from the Roxio Creator 8 Home, you can click either of the following links:

- ✔ **Media Import** in the Applications Project window opened by selecting Applications on the Home tab of the Project List pane

- ✔ **Capture Video** on the DVD & Video tab of the Projects pane

To get detailed information on using Roxio Media Import to acquire any of the previously mentioned types of digital media, see Chapter 9.

Audio Recording and Editing

Roxio Creator 8 enables you to record new audio files from a sound card using its Easy Audio Capture as well as to rip tracks from your favorite audio CDs and organize them into your own audio mixes.

In addition, its Sound Editor program enables you to create an audio mix from recorded audio from various digital and analog audio devices connected to your computer and to edit audio files that you've already acquired. In addition, you can use Sound Editor to convert one type of audio file into another (for example, if you have an audio file saved in the uncompressed WAV audio file format that you want to add to an MP3 Disc Project that you're preparing with Creator Classic). You can open it in Sound Editor and then convert it to a compressed MP3 file (after selecting the audio quality and the amount of compression).

When it comes to editing audio files, Sound Editor not only enables you to trim the audio file, add fade-in and fade-out effects at the beginning and end, and adjust the overall volume, but it also enables you to insert or remove silences in a recording, add track breaks, as well as enhance the audio using any of a number of useful and some not so useful but zany and fun special effects.

To launch Easy Audio Capture, Music Disc Creator, or Sound Editor from the Roxio Creator 8 Home, you click the following links:

- ✔ **Easy Audio Capture** under the Utilities column of the Applications Project window opened by selecting Applications on the Home tab or the Audio tab of the Project List pane

- ✔ **Music Disc Creator** in the Applications Project window opened by selecting Applications on the Home tab or **Advanced Projects** on the Audio tab of the Project List pane

- ✔ **Sound Editor** in the Applications Project window opened by selecting Applications on the Home tab of the Projects List pane

For information on creating Audio CDs and DVD Music Discs with Music Disc Creator, see Chapter 7. For information about recording audio with Easy Audio Capture and mixing the audio tracks with Sound Editor, see Chapter 5.

Disc Labeling with Label Creator

Label Creator is a really fun and surprisingly efficient utility for designing and printing labels and jewel case inserts for the CD and DVD discs you create with its Creator Classic, Music Disc Creator, and MyDVD applications. Label Creator makes short work of the design end of the process by offering you a wide variety of disc label and jewel case inserts to choose from. In addition, its Auto-Fill feature enables you to automatically obtain the track, artist, and album information for audio CDs and volume information for data discs.

After designing your disc labels and jewel case inserts, you can use Label Creator to print out labels either on plain paper, specially prepared adhesive disc label, or even directly on your disc, as well as on perforated case insert paper. The utility also makes it easy to make any necessary printing adjustments to get the label and case inserts to print just where you want them on the page.

To launch Label Creator from the Roxio Creator 8 Home, click the Label Creator link in the Applications Project window opened by clicking Applications on the Home tab of the Project List pane. You can also launch this utility from the Progress Information dialog box when burning a CD or DVD disc with Creator Classic by clicking the Create Label button. For complete information on using the Label Creator, see Chapter 8.

Organizing Digital Media with Media Manager

Media Manager is a godsend when it comes to managing all the different files of different media types that you end up using with the projects you create with the various Roxio Creator applications. Among the most useful of its features are its Smart Views and media albums. Smart Views automatically catalogs media files by type that you put into special watched folders on your computer system.

Albums are special files that gather together whatever media files you add to them without requiring you to physically locate the files together in the same file folder on your hard disk. Because albums don't require you to physically relocate the media files they contain, you can make the same media file (such as a company logo or often-used audio track) a part of as many different collections as you want. Whenever you open a particular album in the Media Manager window, all of its files are available to you without your having to pay any attention to where in the world they're actually located on the computer system.

In addition to organizing your media files into Smart Views and albums, Media Manager also makes it easy to find specific media files by tagging them with keywords, textual comments, and sound tags. You can then later use Media Manager's Search feature to quickly and easily find media files that contain the same keyword or commentary text.

You can launch Media Manager from the Roxio Creator 8 Home by clicking either of the following links:

- ✔ **Media Manager** in the Applications Project window opened by clicking Applications on the Home tab
- ✔ **Organize** on the Organize tab of the Project List pane

To get detailed information on using Media Manager's cool features for organizing your media files, see Chapter 4.

Enhancing and Managing Digital Photos

PhotoSuite 8 provides multipurpose editing for your digital photos. In addition to being able to make enhancements that fix flaws such as redeye, over- and under-exposure, and blurriness, you can also do standard editing such as rotating, cropping, and resizing images. PhotoSuite also has tools that enable you to annotate your photos by adding text and to retouch them by painting and drawing on them.

Beyond these very useful but very typical photo-editing features in PhotoSuite itself, Roxio Creator 8 offers some really exciting and unusual ones as well:

- ✔ **Multi Photo Enhance** to fix and enhance a batch of digital photos that all need the same type of editing in one operation
- ✔ **Photo Projects Assistant** to use your photos in projects such as photo collages, greeting cards, gift tags, postcards, and calendars
- ✔ **Panorama Assistant** to create sweeping panoramas from multiple individual photos that pan a landscape and overlap one another

✔ **Print Photos** to make short work of printing more than one photo in groups using different printing templates or even as thumbnails organized into contact sheets

✔ **E-mail Assistant** to quickly and easily e-mail groups of photos to friends and family

To launch PhotoSuite or any of these other photo-related utilities from the Roxio Creator 8 Home, you click the following links:

✔ **PhotoSuite** in the Applications Project window opened by clicking Applications on the Home tab or **Fix & Enhance Photos** on the Photo tab of the Project List pane to launch PhotoSuite 8

✔ **Multi Photo Enhance** in the Utilities column of the Applications Project window opened by clicking Applications on the Home tab of the Project List pane to open the Photos to Enhance dialog box where you can edit multiple photos

✔ **More Projects** on the Photo tab of the Project List pane to launch the Photo Projects Assistant

✔ **Create Panoramas** in the Utilities column of the Applications Project window opened by clicking Applications on the Home tab of the Project List pane to launch the Panorama Assistant

✔ **Print Photos** on the Photo tab of the Project List pane to launch the Print dialog box where you can print multiple photos

✔ **E-mail Photos** on the Photo tab of the Project List pane to launch the E-mail Assistant

For complete information on using PhotoSuite 8 and these other photo-related utilties, see Chapter 6.

Easy Video Editing with VideoWave

VideoWave 8 is one of the most amazing digital editing programs available for personal computers. It combines an easy-to-use interface and a couple of step-by-step assistants with sophisticated video editing features and the option between editing the production in its default Storyline or Timeline mode.

The CineMagic Assistant enables you to quickly and easily assemble video productions using your favorite digital video or photos that you can output to popular movie formats, CD or DVD disc, or to VideoWave 8 for further editing. The SlideShow Assistant enables you to put together slideshows from preferred groups of photos that you can then output in exactly the same way.

VideoWave 8 itself enables you to add background audio or actually narrate your production in real time. The program also offers you a choice among a wide variety of scene transitions along with a good assortment of text, overlay, and filter effects. In addition, VideoWave contains a powerful Pan and Zoom Editor that enables you to pan and zoom around still images (giving them the illusion of motion) and video clips (enabling you to focus on the action within the frames).

When you complete the editing of your video production, VideoWave 8 makes it easy to output your finished movie to whatever format suits your needs, be that showing the movie on your computer with the Windows Media Player, uploading it to the Internet for viewing on the Web, sending it to an external device such as your VCR or digital video camera, or even sending it as an e-mail attachment.

To launch VideoWave 8, CineMagic, or SlideShow Assistant from the Roxio Creator 8 Home, you can click any of the following links:

- **VideoWave** in the Applications Project window opened by clicking Applications on the Home tab or **Edit Video** on the DVD & Video tab of the Project List pane to launch VideoWave 8

- **Auto-edit Video with CineMagic** on the DVD & Video tab of the Project List pane to launch the CineMagic Assistant

- **Create Slideshow** on the Photo tab of the Project List pane to launch SlideShow Assistant

For details on using VideoWave 8, CineMagic Assistant, and SlideShow Assistant, refer to Chapter 10.

Creating and Burning DVD Projects with MyDVD

The MyDVD application enables you to assemble your digital video and still images into DVD projects that you can then burn to CD or DVD disc complete with menus for viewing in standalone DVD players or in your computer's DVD drive. MyDVD makes it easy to assemble your media in finished productions using readymade themes that you can easily customize.

When you're finished assembling, editing, and previewing your DVD project, you can then use the program to burn the finished production to DVD disc. In addition to its powerful tools for assembling DVD projects, MyDVD also includes its Plug & Burn feature, which enables you to burn your video directly from camcorder or video cassette player to DVD disc.

To launch MyDVD or the Plug and Burn utility from the Roxio Creator 8 Home, you can click the following links:

- ✔ **MyDVD** in the Applications Project window opened by clicking Applications on the Home tab or **Create New DVD** on the DVD & Video tab of the Project List pane to launch MyDVD 8

- ✔ **Plug & Burn (DV to DVD)** on the DVD &Video tab of the Project List pane to launch the Plug & Burn utility

For complete details on using MyDVD and Plug & Burn, see Chapter 11.

Copying files on the fly with Drag-to-Disc

Last but certainly not least is Drag- to-Disc, the program that makes it a snap to backup media files of any type on disc. All you have to do to start a backup is put a CD or DVD disc in your computer's CD-ROM or DVD drive, drag the icons for the folder or file to backup from Windows Explorer, and then drop them on the Drag-to-Disc program icon, which you keep on your Windows desktop at all times when using the computer. The Drag-to-Disc program formats the CD or DVD disc if the disc requires it and then proceeds to copy the files. You can continue to copy files to the disc if there's still additional space.

In addition to copying media files to disc on the fly, Drag- to-Disc offers a nifty little ScanDisc utility that can check your disc for errors and attempt to repair discs whose files have become unreadable or otherwise corrupted.

To launch Drag-to-Disc (when its program icon doesn't automatically appear when you start up Windows) from the Roxio Creator 8 Home, click the Drag To Disc link in the Applications Project window opened by clicking Applications on the Home tab of the Project List pane. To get more information on using Drag-to-Disc to back up files, see Chapter 3.

Chapter 13

Ten (or So) Coolest Features in the Roxio Creator 8 Suite

Roxio Creator 8 sports some very remarkable and definitely cool features for working with all types of media. This chapter highlights the ten coolest of the cool with an eye toward how they can help you get your work done in crack time or, at the very least, have yourself a rocking good time! As I note, some of these features are brand spanking new to version 8 of this suite, but whether new or old, they are all just plain great to use.

Home Is Where Access to Every Roxio Creator Component Is

In Roxio Creator 8, the Home module is the be-all and end-all of the various applications, tools, and utilities. This new module gives you instant access to all these Roxio Creator components with its single-click hyperlinks arranged on category tabs (Audio, Backup, Copy, Data, DVD & Video, Organize, Photo, and Tools) in the Project List pane or in the Applications and Utilities columns of the Applications Project window (opened by clicking Applications on the Home tab of the Project List pane).

I guess the best thing about Home is the way that it interconnects Roxio Creator's diverse components. By launching different applications and tools using its links, you're assured that you'll return Home the moment you exit the program or utility that you launched. This gives you the opportunity to then launch the next module that you may need in the editing process. In any case, launching and then returning to the Roxio Creator 8 Home gives you a much better sense of how all its diverse components come together to make almost any type of media editing possible. See Chapter 1 for more on using the Roxio Creator 8 Home module.

Keeping Up with Your Media via Smart Views

Smart Views is the brand new feature in the Roxio Creator 8 suite that automatically keeps tabs on all the different media files on your computer system. The best part about this feature is that you don't have to do anything to make use of it. The program automatically watches the My Documents folder and Desktop for the addition of any media files (graphic, audio, or video) — and you can add to this list.

Roxio then adds the files it identifies as media files to the Smart Views tab in the Media Manager program or the Media Selector dialog box available in programs such as VideoWave and My DVD. Thumbnail images of these media files are then automatically categorized and placed in the All Photos, All Music, or All Videos area of the Smart Views tab, making it super-easy to find and use them in your audio and video productions.

Videos, Slideshows, and Play lists to Go with QuickShow

One of my most favorite features in Roxio Creator 8 is quietly tucked away in the Media Manager module. This is the QuickShow feature that enables you to instantly turn a group of video clips, photos, or audio tracks into impromptu movies, slideshows, or play lists, respectively. All you do to put on any of these instant shows is open the Smart View, album, or folder that contains the media you want to use. Then select the thumbnails of all the same media type (video, still image, or audio files) in the Contents area of the Media Manager window and click the QuickShow link on its toolbar.

Media Manager then arranges the selected media files into a show that Windows displays full screen on your computer. This screen contains a simple playback controller that you can then use to pause the show, advance to its next element, or even close to return to the Media Manager window. QuickShow is not only fun to use but is a great way to put together quick-and-dirty video sequences to create a kind of instant storyboarding. See the sidebar in Chapter 4 for more on this cool feature.

Simple-to-Create Videos and Slideshows

The CineMagic Assistant and SlideShow Assistant are two fun and easy ways to convert your digital video and photos into finished productions in no time at all. With the CineMagic Assistant you can turn the digital photos or video clips of your favorite vacation into a music video set to a music track of your own choice. All you have to do is select the media files and the background music to use in your production and CineMagic does the rest (making all the editing decisions for you).

With the SlideShow Assistant you can quickly turn the digital photos into a slideshow that you can output to a favorite movie format or edit further with VideoWave 8. Like the CineMagic Assistant, the SlideShow Assistant makes all the editing decisions, including what background music to use. See Chapter 10 for details on creating your own video productions with the CineMagic and SlideShow Assistant.

More Complex Video Editing in Timeline Mode

VideoWave 8 supports an editing mode known as Timeline in addition to its more familiar Storyline editing mode. When editing your video productions in Timeline mode, you have more control over your production, including the ability to add multiple elements (such as background audio, narration, text, special effects, and overlays) to either the entire video production or just one of its elements such as a particular video clip or still image that you've added to one of its panels.

In addition, editing in Timeline mode gives you a view of each of the elements in your video production as they relate to the Timeline ruler. This ruler gives you the time code for any point in the production and can be instantly expanded from the current position by simply dragging one of its indicators with the mouse.

Combined with the intuitive Storyline mode, editing in Timeline mode gives you much finer control over video productions where you want to time and overlay different elements with great precision. See Chapter 10 for details on editing your video production in Timeline mode.

Scene Stealing in SmartScan Mode

SmartScan mode in the Media Import program is a dream come true when it comes to capturing digital video from your camcorder. Instead of forcing you to manually scan and then capture each and every scene on your videotape, in SmartScan mode you can have VideoWave do all the work. SmartScan mode will scan your entire videotape for scene breaks. It then presents each scene with its own thumbnail and time code, enabling you to pick and choose the scenes that you actually want captured as video clips on your hard drive.

After selecting the scenes to capture, SmartScan will then automatically locate these scenes in the videotape and copy them to your hard disk without your having to click another button. For more on this timesaving feature, see Chapter 9.

Direct From Tape to Disc with Plug & Burn

The Plug & Burn utility is another one of those wonderful features that you didn't know you missed until you got it and then you wondered how you ever did without it. This little wonder enables you to go directly from videotape to DVD disc without having to bother with the intermediate step of using a DVD editor such as DVD Builder. This is perfect for transferring finished video cassettes to the more durable disc media or for immediately creating DVD discs from digital videotape that doesn't need any type of editing such as recordings of live events (for which you have the right to copy, of course!).

All you need to do to use Plug & Burn to convert videotape into DVD disc is connect the videotape player or camcorder to your computer, put the DVD disc in your computer's DVD drive, and then cue up the place in the tape where you want to start the recording. If you want to record the entire tape to disc, all you have to do is click the Capture Entire Tape button in the Plug & Burn dialog box. For more on using this nifty feature to go from tape to disc in one step, see Chapter 11.

Easy DVD Disc Copies

In addition to making copies of your audio CDs, you can use Roxio Disc Copier to make copies of any unencrypted DVD disc (which, of course, includes all the DVD projects that you burn to DVD disc with DVD Builder). Because Disc Copier visually displays the video and audio contents of your DVD disc, you can easily remove any unwanted content from the copy. If you want to make a duplicate disc, all you have to do to make the copy is switch the original and blank DVD disc when Disc Copier prompts you to do so. Duplicate discs make it possible to keep one set on the business site and another off-site just in case anything goes wrong at the office.

Multi Photo Editing, Printing, and E-mailing

Last but not least among the coolest Roxio Creator 8 features are the utilities — Multi Photo Enhance, Print Photos, and E-mail Photos, respectively — that give you the ability to make editing changes, print, and even e-mail groups of digital photos at one time. (Multi Photo Enhance is available from a link in the Utilities column of the Applications Project window and Print Photos and E-mail Photos from links on the Photo tab of the Project List pane).

Multi Photo Enhance enables you to select a group of photos and then apply the same type of fixes (including exposure, color saturation, sharpness, and red eye), transformations (including rotating, flipping, and resizing), special effects, conversion to another graphics file format, and renaming to them.

Print Photos enables you to print multiple photos on a single sheet using various standard paper sizes and print layouts as well as to print out thumbnails of your photos on contact sheets. E-mail Photos gives you the ability to gather together a group of your favorite photos and then have them resized and added to a blank e-mail message in your e-mail program ready for sending.

Index

SINESS, CAREERS & PERSONAL FINANCE

0-7645-5307-0

0-7645-5331-3 *†

Also available:

- Accounting For Dummies †
  0-7645-5314-3
- Business Plans Kit For Dummies †
  0-7645-5365-8
- Cover Letters For Dummies
  0-7645-5224-4
- Frugal Living For Dummies
  0-7645-5403-4
- Leadership For Dummies
  0-7645-5176-0
- Managing For Dummies
  0-7645-1771-6

- Marketing For Dummies
  0-7645-5600-2
- Personal Finance For Dummies *
  0-7645-2590-5
- Project Management For Dummies '
  0-7645-5283-X
- Resumes For Dummies †
  0-7645-5471-9
- Selling For Dummies
  0-7645-5363-1
- Small Business Kit For Dummies *†
  0-7645-5093-4

ME & BUSINESS COMPUTER BASICS

0-7645-4074-2

0-7645-3758-X

Also available:

- ACT! 6 For Dummies
  0-7645-2645-6
- iLife '04 All-in-One Desk Reference
  For Dummies
  0-7645-7347-0
- iPAQ For Dummies
  0-7645-6769-1
- Mac OS X Panther Timesaving
  Techniques For Dummies
  0-7645-5812-9
- Macs For Dummies
  0-7645-5656-8

- Microsoft Money 2004 For Dummies
  0-7645-4195-1
- Office 2003 All-in-One Desk Reference
  For Dummies
  0-7645-3883-7
- Outlook 2003 For Dummies
  0-7645-3759-8
- PCs For Dummies
  0-7645-4074-2
- TiVo For Dummies
  0-7645-6923-6
- Upgrading and Fixing PCs For Dummies
  0-7645-1665-5
- Windows XP Timesaving Techniques
  For Dummies
  0-7645-3748-2

OD, HOME, GARDEN, HOBBIES, MUSIC & PETS

0-7645-5295-3

0-7645-5232-5

Also available:

- Bass Guitar For Dummies
  0-7645-2487-9
- Diabetes Cookbook For Dummies
  0-7645-5230-9
- Gardening For Dummies *
  0-7645-5130-2
- Guitar For Dummies
  0-7645-5106-X
- Holiday Decorating For Dummies
  0-7645-2570-0
- Home Improvement All-in-One
  For Dummies
  0-7645-5680-0

- Knitting For Dummies
  0-7645-5395-X
- Piano For Dummies
  0-7645-5105-1
- Puppies For Dummies
  0-7645-5255-4
- Scrapbooking For Dummies
  0-7645-7208-3
- Senior Dogs For Dummies
  0-7645-5818-8
- Singing For Dummies
  0-7645-2475-5
- 30-Minute Meals For Dummies
  0-7645-2589-1

ERNET & DIGITAL MEDIA

0-7645-1664-7

0-7645-6924-4

Also available:

- 2005 Online Shopping Directory
  For Dummies
  0-7645-7495-7
- CD & DVD Recording For Dummies
  0-7645-5956-7
- eBay For Dummies
  0-7645-5654-1
- Fighting Spam For Dummies
  0-7645-5965-6
- Genealogy Online For Dummies
  0-7645-5964-8
- Google For Dummies
  0-7645-4420-9

- Home Recording For Musicians
  For Dummies
  0-7645-1634-5
- The Internet For Dummies
  0-7645-4173-0
- iPod & iTunes For Dummies
  0-7645-7772-7
- Preventing Identity Theft For Dummies
  0-7645-7336-5
- Pro Tools All-in-One Desk Reference
  For Dummies
  0-7645-5714-9
- Roxio Easy Media Creator For Dummies
  0-7645-7131-1

arate Canadian edition also available
arate U.K. edition also available

ble wherever books are sold. For more information or to order direct: U.S. customers visit www.dummies.com or call 1-877-762-2974.
stomers visit www.wileyeurope.com or call 0800 243407. Canadian customers visit www.wiley.ca or call 1-800-567-4797.

 WILEY

SPORTS, FITNESS, PARENTING, RELIGION & SPIRITUALITY

0-7645-5146-9

0-7645-5418-2

Also available:

- Adoption For Dummies
  0-7645-5488-3
- Basketball For Dummies
  0-7645-5248-1
- The Bible For Dummies
  0-7645-5296-1
- Buddhism For Dummies
  0-7645-5359-3
- Catholicism For Dummies
  0-7645-5391-7
- Hockey For Dummies
  0-7645-5228-7

- Judaism For Dummies
  0-7645-5299-6
- Martial Arts For Dummies
  0-7645-5358-5
- Pilates For Dummies
  0-7645-5397-6
- Religion For Dummies
  0-7645-5264-3
- Teaching Kids to Read For Dummie
  0-7645-4043-2
- Weight Training For Dummies
  0-7645-5168-X
- Yoga For Dummies
  0-7645-5117-5

TRAVEL

0-7645-5438-7

0-7645-5453-0

Also available:

- Alaska For Dummies
  0-7645-1761-9
- Arizona For Dummies
  0-7645-6938-4
- Cancún and the Yucatán For Dummies
  0-7645-2437-2
- Cruise Vacations For Dummies
  0-7645-6941-4
- Europe For Dummies
  0-7645-5456-5
- Ireland For Dummies
  0-7645-5455-7

- Las Vegas For Dummies
  0-7645-5448-4
- London For Dummies
  0-7645-4277-X
- New York City For Dummies
  0-7645-6945-7
- Paris For Dummies
  0-7645-5494-8
- RV Vacations For Dummies
  0-7645-5443-3
- Walt Disney World & Orlando For Dumm
  0-7645-6943-0

GRAPHICS, DESIGN & WEB DEVELOPMENT

0-7645-4345-8

0-7645-5589-8

Also available:

- Adobe Acrobat 6 PDF For Dummies
  0-7645-3760-1
- Building a Web Site For Dummies
  0-7645-7144-3
- Dreamweaver MX 2004 For Dummies
  0-7645-4342-3
- FrontPage 2003 For Dummies
  0-7645-3882-9
- HTML 4 For Dummies
  0-7645-1995-6
- Illustrator cs For Dummies
  0-7645-4084-X

- Macromedia Flash MX 2004 For Dumm
  0-7645-4358-X
- Photoshop 7 All-in-One Desk
  Reference For Dummies
  0-7645-1667-1
- Photoshop cs Timesaving Techniqu
  For Dummies
  0-7645-6782-9
- PHP 5 For Dummies
  0-7645-4166-8
- PowerPoint 2003 For Dummies
  0-7645-3908-6
- QuarkXPress 6 For Dummies
  0-7645-2593-X

NETWORKING, SECURITY, PROGRAMMING & DATABASES

0-7645-6852-3

0-7645-5784-X

Also available:

- A+ Certification For Dummies
  0-7645-4187-0
- Access 2003 All-in-One Desk
  Reference For Dummies
  0-7645-3988-4
- Beginning Programming For Dummies
  0-7645-4997-9
- C For Dummies
  0-7645-7068-4
- Firewalls For Dummies
  0-7645-4048-3
- Home Networking For Dummies
  0-7645-42796

- Network Security For Dummies
  0-7645-1679-5
- Networking For Dummies
  0-7645-1677-9
- TCP/IP For Dummies
  0-7645-1760-0
- VBA For Dummies
  0-7645-3989-2
- Wireless All In-One Desk Reference
  For Dummies
  0-7645-7496-5
- Wireless Home Networking For Dumm
  0-7645-3910-8

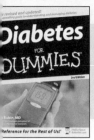

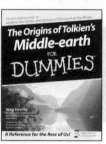

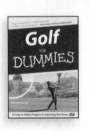